D1453841

DATE DUE

			PRINTED IN U.S.A.

Feeling Lonesome

Feeling Lonesome

The Philosophy and Psychology of Loneliness

Ben Lazare Mijuskovic

PRAEGER™

An Imprint of ABC-CLIO, LLC

Santa Barbara, California • Denver, Colorado

Copyright © 2015 by Ben Lazare Mijuskovic

Library of Congress Cataloging-in-Publication Data

Mijuskovic, Ben Lazare.
Feeling lonesome : the philosophy and psychology of loneliness / Ben Lazare Mijuskovic.
    pages cm
   ISBN 978-1-4408-4028-9 (hardcopy : alk. paper) — ISBN 978-1-4408-4029-6
(ebook) 1. Loneliness—Philosophy. 2. Loneliness—Psychological aspects. 3. Consciousness.
I. Title.
B105.L65M537   2015
128—dc23   2015008847

ISBN: 978-1-4408-4028-9
EISBN: 978-1-4408-4029-6

19 18 17 16 15   1 2 3 4 5

This book is also available on the World Wide Web as an eBook.
Visit www.abc-clio.com for details.

Praeger
An Imprint of ABC-CLIO, LLC

ABC-CLIO, LLC
130 Cremona Drive, P.O. Box 1911
Santa Barbara, California 93116-1911

This book is printed on acid-free paper ∞

Manufactured in the United States of America

To Ruth: My constant companion for fifty years—
when I am with her, I am never lonely.

"Each man is like a nautilus, who lives in a house of his own making, and carries it around on his back."
—Brand Blanshard, *The Nature of Thought*

Contents

Introduction

Every human being who attains 16 years of age becomes her or his own philosopher and psychologist. Each and every one of us early on formulates general rules about (1) what exists, the difference between what is real and what seems, and how stones and thoughts are different from each other (metaphysics, ontology); (2) what can be known and what cannot, whether rational arguments are more persuasive than experience, or whether anything can be known at all; indeed, perhaps all is appearance and reality is unknowable (epistemology); (3) whether the standard of goodness is absolute and the same for everyone or whether it is relative and subjective and varies from culture to culture and person to person (ethics); and (4) what motivates human beings, how, and why (psychology). During the course of this study, I shall commit myself to a set of ultimate "first principles," basic assumptions, or unquestioned premises in the areas I have just outlined that can be challenged readily by others of a contrary persuasion. These defining principles fall between a number of metaphysical choices: (1a) materialism, which posits that all reality is reducible to matter plus motion; (1b) idealism, which fundamentally assumes that all existence is mental, mind-dependent, or spiritual, for without minds nothing could exist or be known; and (1c) dualism, which holds there are irreducible differences between physical objects and space as opposed to minds and thoughts and therefore both material and mental entities exist, although they seem to share nothing in common.

In addition, epistemological principles offer the following options: (2a) empiricism claims that *all* our knowledge is derived from prior sensations and experience, whereas (2b) rationalism holds that there are *some* "pure" concepts and truths that are known independently of sensation; and, mean-while, in opposition to the two previous assumptions (2c) skepticism main-tains that there are no truths at all and nothing can be known with certainty.

I alert the reader to the foregoing options because the commitment I have chosen supports a qualified version of dualism as well as a form of rationalism, which includes the notion of synthetic but *a priori* relations or more technically formulated, synthetic judgments *a priori*. By synthetic I mean a combination of two or more distinct but related concepts, and by *a priori* I intend that these concepts are intrinsically, that is, universally and necessarily connected. But I am fully aware that there are other choices in terms of both metaphysical and epistemic principles that might apply or appear more convincing to others. After pondering for many years the reality and the role of loneliness in human life, I have elected to make my case as best I can in what follows.

Questions surrounding what is reality, how we gain knowledge, and the relation of matter to mind are already manifestly present in Plato's Divided Line passage in the *Republic* (Plato, 1966, pp. 509d–511e), but they become profoundly disturbing by the time we reach Descartes's *Meditations on First Philosophy* (Descartes, 1955). The difficulty first becomes acute and eventu-ally chronic because Descartes so radically distinguishes matter as extended and inert from minds as immaterial and active. For if this is truly the case, several troubling questions naturally arise. How can a mental substance *know* that an independent, material world exists beyond and apart from the self; how can nonphysical thoughts *interact* with physical objects; how can immaterial concepts copy, represent, or correspond to physical objects if they share no property in common; and, finally, how can the self have any knowledge or contact with other selves or minds if each mind is confined to its own sensations, feelings, thoughts, perceptions, or repre-sentations? If Descartes is right, absolute solipsism and loneliness inevitably follow.

After Descartes, two philosophers, Spinoza (1955) and Schopenhauer (1966), hold that there is only one substance but that it exhibits a "double aspect." It displays both a mental and a physical attribute or nature; the first follows psychological laws and the second, physical laws. But in terms of loneliness, both thinkers are monists: There is only one universal sub-stance, and consequently, the "self" is ultimately not real; it's merely a mode of an all-encompassing infinite and eternal reality. But without a real self, loneliness is a contradiction in terms.

Very recently, Brian Greene, in *The Elegant Universe*, offers a very dif-ferent answer and expresses his confidence that "string theory," a form of materialism, consisting of a set of ten (or more) one-dimensional strings, can explain it all.

For the first time in the history of physics, we therefore have a framework with the capacity to explain every fundamental feature upon which the universe is constructed. For this reason, string theory is sometimes described as possibly being the "theory of everything" (T.O.E.) or the "ultimate" or "final" theory. These grandiose descriptive terms are meant to signify the deepest possible theory of physics—a theory that underlies all others—and that in principle absolutely everything, from the big bang to daydreams, can be described in terms of underlying microscopic physical processes involving the fundamental constituents of matter. (Greene, 2000, pp. 16–17)

My own preference for a "theory of everything" is rather grounded in something David Hume argues following Malebranche (Doxsee, 1916, pp. 692–710). If causes and effects are distinct concepts; and what is distinct is separable; and what is conceivable without contradiction is possible; then it follows that anything is *empirically* imaginable; a pebble could extinguish the sun; biting into an apple could turn it into a puff of smoke; or, under certain material conditions, an immaterial thought could emanate or spontaneously erupt from a physical base. As Hume proposes, "reason, as distinguish'd from experience, can never make us conclude, that a cause is absolutely requisite to every beginning of existence" (*Treatise*, I, XIV, *Of the idea of necessary connection*); and further, that "Anything may produce anything. Creation, annihilation, motion, reason, volition; all these may arise from one another, from any other object we can imagine" (I, XV, *Rules by which to judge causes and effects* [Hume, 1973]). Consequently, my conviction is that there are contingent "creations" in the universe and, under certain circumstances, material conditions not only may but actually do produce immaterial thoughts, as I argue in *Contingent Immaterialism* (Mijuskovic, 1984). Generally speaking, thinkers who posit the nonphysical nature of thought and mind are concerned to conclude with the soul's immortality. But this is not a necessary conclusion, and it is certainly not mine; one can assert the former without drawing the latter inference and implication.

More recently, Noam Chomsky, in citing my discussion, in *The Achilles of Rationalist Arguments* (1974), regarding Hume and Locke's suggestion that God could have created "thinking matter," states: "Having no intelligible concept of 'matter' (body and so on), we cannot dismiss the possibility of living or thinking matter, particularly after Newton undermined common-sense understanding" thus making it abundantly clear that these issues continue to be perpetual and remain as alive and vital today as they have always been in the past.

In Hume's judgment, Newton's great achievement was that while he "seemed to draw the veil from some of the mysteries of nature, he showed at the same time the imperfections of the [materialist] mechanical philosophy and thereby restored Nature's ultimate secrets to that obscurity, in which they ever did and will remain." (Chomsky, 2009, p. 169)

As living matter has evolved from its inanimate sources to produce sentient beings, just so *mental* predicates of thought may have arisen from an inanimate ground as well. The empirical conceivability of matter producing or evolving into life is analogous to the empirical possibility of matter producing or evolving into consciousness. This is a theme that will repeatedly occupy us throughout this study.

The present work explores not only the nature of loneliness but also its ultimate origins and whether in its beginning, as well as in its end, it is grounded in the mechanisms of the brain or instead centered in the creations of the mind. So like our sixteen-year-old philosopher and psychologist, we shall have quite a bit to say about the choices of opposing first principles that animate and advocate for both the brain and the mind. In the end, however, each reader must decide which principle and paradigm affords the most plausible explanation *or* the deepest insight into human existence and loneliness.

REFERENCES

Chomsky, N. (2009). The mysteries of nature: how deeply hidden. *The Journal of Philosophy,* CVI:4.

Descartes, R. (1955). *Philosophical Works of Descartes.* New York: Dover.

Doxsee, C. W. (1916). Hume's relation to Malebranche. *The Philosophical Review,* 25:5.

Greene, B. (2000). *The Elegant Universe.* New York: Random House.

Hume, D. (1973). *A Treatise of Human Nature.* Oxford, UK: Clarendon Press.

Mijuskovic, B. (1974). *The Achilles of Rationalist Arguments: The Simplicity, Unity, and Identity of Thought and Soul from the Cambridge Platonists to Kant.* The Hague: Martinus Nijhoff.

Mijuskovic, B. (1984). *Contingent Immaterialism: Meaning, Freedom, Time and Mind.* Amsterdam: Gruner.

Plato. (1966). *The Collected Dialogues of Plato.* Hamilton, E. & Cairns, E. (Eds.). New York: Pantheon, *Republic,* VI.

Schopenhauer, A. (1966). *The World as Will and Representation.* New York: Dover.

Spinoza, B. (1955). *The Ethics.* New York: Dover.

Chapter 1

Historical and Conceptual Overview

The basic assumption of this study is that the cluster of phenomena that we commonly describe as instances of loneliness cannot be addressed and penetrated unless a preliminary investigation is initially secured in terms of how certain philosophical and psychological theories of human consciousness interact with each other in accounting for human loneliness and its disquieting sense of isolation, alienation, and estrangement. The primary task of this study is the final ascertainment of just such a comprehensive theory, methodology, and paradigm sufficient to account for the feeling, meaning, and dynamic of loneliness. Accordingly, the present work seeks to fuse (1) a traditional theory of self-consciousness or reflexivity—promoted by Plato, Aristotle, Plotinus, St. Augustine, Descartes, Leibniz, Kant, Fichte, Husserl, and many others—with (2) the much later paradigm, although of equal importance, of intentionality, transcendence, or freedom—first suggested by Descartes and subsequently advocated by Fichte (again), Brentano, Husserl (again), and Sartre—and then to synthesize both within a cognitive as well as a motivational theory of *a priori* (i.e., universal and necessary) loneliness (Mijuskovic, 1988, pp. 39–50). Against this position, the combined tenets of materialism, empiricism, and behaviorism are arrayed, which collectively argue that loneliness is temporary and sporadic. Man alone, from the very inception of his awareness that there are other conscious beings, struggles to connect, to supplicate, to influence, or to master the other self in order to lessen his own sense of frightening loneliness.

Most current researchers studying loneliness contend that it is *caused* by external and physical conditions—environmental, cultural, situational, and even chemical imbalances in the brain—and hence transient and avoidable. By contrast, I argue that loneliness is innate; that it is *constituted* by the intrinsic activities and structures of both self-consciousness and intentionality and therefore permanent and unavoidable. Scientific, causal explanations operate externally in the world and allegedly would continue to do so independently of the existence of human consciousness. By contrast, constitutive acts emanate from the internal resources of the mind and proceed to structure a world beyond ourselves. That being the case, without the activities of human consciousness, causal events would disappear from the fabric of reality without minds to actively structure them. In effect, the controversy pits Science against Humanism, materialism against idealism (Mijuskovic, 1976, pp. 292–306; 1984).

Accordingly, in previous publications, I have argued in support of a universal principle of loneliness, insisting *that* all human existence, without exception, is innately lonely; *that* the fear of loneliness permeates and colors all aspects of life; and *that* once the biological needs for air, water, food, and sleep are met, the psychological drive to escape loneliness is the most insistent motivator in all mankind and certainly more powerful than the desire for sexual fulfillment or gratification. And I have sought to show *why* this is the case by appealing to a theory of a genuine self, in turn grounded in a Janus-faced dynamic of an active consciousness, which is both able to look within as well as without as emanating from the self. Consciousness on this view is (a) reflexive, that is, self-conscious as well as (b) creatively thrust "beyond itself," intentional, transcendent, meaning-intending in the classic phenomenological sense of the term. The first mental activity of the infant mind strives to *unify* its own sensations, feelings, and thoughts as directly "belonging to its self" and as *actively* unified by the self. Consciousness is thus constituted as a mental entity (a self) as well as an activity, which progressively views its self as separate from surrounding objects and as it further develops in terms of loneliness distinct from other selves as well. Awareness also exhibits a principle of intentionality, a power of transcendence, the freedom to explode *beyond* the relative confines of reflexion, which allows the self to escape from its prison of solipsism. These two activities of the mind, though mutually constitutive, display distinct powers (Mijuskovic, 1977a, pp. 113–132, 1977b, pp. 202–216, 1977c, pp. 19–32).

In the last chapter, I will also propose several beneficial measures by offering some therapeutic principles to aid us in dealing with our separate sense of isolation.

Loneliness: An Intrapsychic or Interpersonal Phenomenon? Before continuing, however, I need to make a vital distinction concerning loneliness as an ultimate principle dwelling within human consciousness. My contention is that in order to understand loneliness, we must *first* initially approach it intrapsychically as opposed to interpersonally; psychologically as opposed to sociologically. It is one thing to claim (1) *that* man is a social or political animal, one among many other animals that are "social," which, according to Aristotle, even includes certain insects, such as bees (*Politics*, I, 2, 1253a, 25–31). Or, similarly, to assume, as sociologists do, that considerations focusing on the relations among the family, group, community, and *polis* members come *first* and are determinant in the formation of individual consciousness and only *later* does loneliness follow. But it's quite another matter to insist, as I do, (2) *that* loneliness is original and primary because it is constituted by the activities and structures of self-consciousness and intentionality and therefore universal and inescapable, while, by contrast, social relationships are derivative and secondary. My view is not only that man is the loneliest of *all* animals precisely because of the depth and intensity of human reflexivity but that *first* loneliness is *felt* and only subsequently *conceptually* recognized as a problem to be overcome and transcended by social interaction. For only *after* experiencing a sense of isolation do issues concerning intimacy, friendship, and all the other strategies of "socialization" follow as "solutions" to the original problem, which is always dependent on the awareness of loneliness. The desire to be with and among others is only grasped within the context of possible answers to human existence *after* one has initially felt, acknowledged, and understood the pervasive sense of isolation that haunts the human soul. This means that loneliness is the *preexisting* concern, the presupposition, to invoke a Kantian concept, and socialization subsequently follows as the pursued remedy. It also means that in order to understand human existence deeply, one must first address *why* and *how* loneliness emerges and develops within the human psyche, its meaning, and its dynamic. And that can only come *after* considering the strengths and weaknesses between the two doctrines of reflexivity and intentionality, on the one hand, *versus* causal mechanisms and behaviorism on the other hand.

Whatever loneliness is, it implies separation. The three primary sources of cataclysmic and traumatic separation in humans consist initially in the infant's ejection from the womb during the violence of birth (object–object separation); second, the realization of separation of the subject/self from the external world (subject–object separation); and third, the subject's separation from the mother (subject–subject separation).

Initial confirmation for the primacy of loneliness in terms of *individual* human development, in opposition to theories of a *social* grounding, can be shown by the fact that very young infants can achieve self-consciousness *before* they are aware of the mother as a distinct consciousness or separate self. Ego identity and narcissistic self-centeredness *precede* the realization of the need for socialization and intimacy. Thus, for instance, Harry Harlow's infant rhesus monkeys, reared in complete isolation from other primates, are able to survive *physically* apart from any awareness of separation from their mothers. They are self-conscious and recognize their distinctness, their separation from the material objects that surround them, since they are restricted in their primary functions to interacting with lifeless sculpted constructions made of wire, terrycloth, and button eyes serving as surrogate "mothers." Thus, their interaction within their severely limited environment is conducted solely in the context of inanimate objects. The point is that self-consciousness can exist independently of a social environment. That means that the dynamic of separation–isolation is instituted and prevalent *before* socialization has had a chance to occur. It also follows that when the distress of loneliness is extreme, the self perceives the universe through the lenses of consciousness as a lifeless, impersonal, and uncaring world.

Following that, it is true, as the work of Anna Freud, Dorothy Burlingham, Rene Spitz, and John Bowlby have amply demonstrated, after the child forms a bonding relation to the mother, the child will dramatically regress if the mother's care is withdrawn. Thus, at this third developmental level of consciousness of affective and cognitive separation, when the infant realizes pronounced withdrawals of care and attention provided by a responding and nurturing other, the child will release its interest in an interactive social world and retreat inwardly, deeply within its self, by pulling back toward the womb. We can conclude therefore that *initially* the infant is self-aware of objects *before* it is conscious of the other self (the mother) and only subsequently of its separation from its caretaker (Mijuskovic, 1990, 1991, pp. 39–48). As we shall show, both Kant and Freud will argue the same, namely, that self-consciousness is *first* based in a dual relation holding between an animate self and inanimate objects. It's only at a later stage of development, when the more sophisticated and complex dyadic relation of self-mother (subject–subject separation) takes place, that the child develops a sense of social loneliness by realizing his separation from a responding *self-consciousness*—as opposed to the separation from lifeless objects. As Margaret Mahler reports, not until five to ten months of age is the infant able to distinguish its self from a separate world of objects (Mahler et al., 1975, p. 213). Thus, only later does the child recognize another level of deeper separation, this time from the mother and/or other selves. The importance of this distinction is that in order to understand loneliness, we must trace its development through all phases of separation because the early patterns imprinted within the human psyche will serve as prototypes for subsequent senses of separation. According to Mahler et al., it is only in the third stage that

the child recognizes for the first time his separateness from his mother. This is an achievement of [cognitive] representational intelligence that makes possible the internal capacity to differentiate self representation. This brings in its wake (in normal development) the gradual realization on the part of the child that he is relatively small and helpless and has to cope with overwhelming odds as a relatively weak and lonely (because separate) individual. (Mahler et al., 1975, p. 213)

We may conclude then that after the trauma of birth and the infant's physical separation from the womb, two other crises of painful disruptions/separations follow: The self becomes self-aware of its distinction from a sphere of inanimate objects and only later from the mother as a distinct other self. Both crises involve major developmental adjustments and future implications in terms of loneliness.

The fear of loneliness grounded in perceived neglect, rejection, abandonment, or betrayal is innate and lasts throughout our lives—from infancy until we expire. No human being would ever wish to be immortal at the price of existing as the only conscious creature in an otherwise completely lifeless universe. In emphasizing this critical affective and cognitive principle, I am reminded of Kant's retelling of "Carazan's Dream" from the *Bremen Magazine*. The following passage represents the most extreme metaphysical argument—a "clinching proof"—depicting the fear of cosmic loneliness and the threat of eternal isolation that the human spirit can possibly conceive.

The more his riches had grown, the more did this miserly man bar his heart to compassion and the love of others. Meanwhile, as the love of mankind grew cold in him, the diligence of his prayers and religious devotion increased. After this confession, he goes on to recount: One evening, as I did my sums by my lamp and calculated the profits of my business, I was overcome by sleep. In this condition, I saw the angel of death come upon me like a whirlwind, and he struck me, before I could plead against his terrible blow. I was petrified as I became aware that my fate had been cast for eternity, and that to all the good I had done nothing could be added, and from all the evil I had done, nothing could be subtracted. I was led before the throne of he who dwells in the third heaven. The brilliance that flamed before me spoke to me thus: Carazan, your divine service is rejected. You have closed your heart to the love of humankind and held on to your treasure with an iron hand. You have lived only for yourself, and hence in the future you shall also live alone and secluded from all communion with the entirety of creation for all eternity. In this moment, I was ripped away by an invincible force and driven through the shining edifice of creation. I quickly left innumerable worlds behind me. As I approached the most extreme limits of nature, I noticed that the shadows of the boundless void sank into the abyss before me. A fearful realm of eternal solitude and darkness! Unspeakable dread overcame me at this sight. I gradually lost the last stars from view and finally the last glimmer of light was extinguished in the most extreme darkness. The mortal terror of despair increased with every moment, just as every moment my distance from the inhabitable world increased. I reflected with unbearable anguish in my heart that ten thousand years were to carry me further beyond the boundaries of everything created. I would still see forward into the immeasurable abyss of darkness without help or hope of returning—In this bewilderment I stretched my hands out to actual objects with such vehemence that I was awakened. And now I have been instructed to esteem human beings for even the least of them, whom in the pride of my good fortune I had turned away from my door, would have been far more welcome to me in that terrifying desert than all the treasure of Golconda. (Kant, 2011, pp. 16–17)

As Carazan's description of his despair and dread testifies, the ultimate terror of absolute and perpetual loneliness demonstrates that the primary psychological and motivational drive in mankind is first to avoid isolation and second to secure divine, human, or sentient contact at any cost. The drive to escape loneliness animates all our passions, thoughts, and actions; all we feel, think, say, and do. The highest goal and protection against loneliness is intimacy, the ability to fill the emptiness of loneliness through an emotional fusion with another sentient, thinking being. I have quoted this passage from Kant at length because I believe it conveys both the essential fear of loneliness, which inhabits the human psyche, while at the same time it provides a promise of its resolution. Thus, at the heart of Carazan's nightmare is the unspoken implication that no human being would ever choose to be immortal at the price of being the only self-conscious existence within the cosmic dimensions of infinite space and eternal time. That would be an unbearable metaphysical *and* psychological loneliness! In those frightening circumstances, the mind would simply self-destruct.

First Principles. Aristotle defines philosophy as the search for first principles, basic assumptions, underived premises (Aristotle, 1941). First principles are always critically important because the construction of the ensuing system is designed to follow as consistently as possible from the assumed basic premise(s). However, it's vital to notice that *ultimately* all first principles are a matter of the heart and not the head (Pascal, *Pensees,* # 423); the result of our passional natures (James, "The Will to Believe"); or, in the last analysis, a final choice simply made by personal interest or inclination between *either* idealism *or* materialism but not both (Kierkegaard).

Neither of these two systems [of idealism and materialism] can directly refute its opposite, for their quarrel is about the first principle, which admits of no derivation from anything beyond it; in each of the two, if only its first principle is granted, refutes that of the other; each denies everything in its opposite, and they have no point at all in common from which they could arrive at mutual understanding and unity. . . . Now the presentation of the independence of the self, and that of the thing, can surely coexist [as in dualism], but not the independence of both. Only one of them can be the first, the initiatory, the independent one: the second, by virtue of being second, necessarily becomes dependent on the first, upon which it is to be conjoined. Now which of the two should be taken as primary? Reason provides no principle of choice; for we deal here not with the addition of a link in the chain of reasoning, which is all that rational grounds extend to, but with the [volitional] beginning of the whole chain, which, as an absolutely primary act [of the will], depends solely upon the freedom of thought. Hence the choice is governed by caprice, and since even a capricious decision must have some source, it is governed by *inclination* and *interest*. The ultimate basis of the difference between idealists and dogmatists [or materialists] is thus the difference of their interests. (Fichte, 1970, pp. 12, 15–16; emphasis in the original)

It's also crucial to notice that first principles, as Fichte indicates, cannot be combined; they are mutually exclusive: One is either pregnant or not pregnant; one cannot be a "little bit" pregnant.

In what follows, I intend to investigate, compare, and contrast two sets of opposing first principles and their generated paradigms that are directly relevant to the Philosophy and Psychology of Loneliness. Accordingly, I propose to demonstrate that there exists a universal and necessary, that is, *a priori* relation between metaphysical dualism and an epistemic subjective idealist theory of consciousness, which I wholeheartedly support, and the inevitability of human loneliness.

Although there are four notable paradigms of awareness that dominate Western thought, I shall leave aside consideration of William James's 1904 essay, "Does Consciousness Exist?" (James 1962, pp. I, 207–221) and Bertrand Russell's lengthy treatise, "The Philosophy of Logical Atomism" (1966), both of which argue in behalf of neutral monism, as well as Sartre's neutered version of the intentionality principle in the *Transcendence of the Ego* (Sartre 1970) because of their joint rejections of (1) a viable concept of the self; and (2) self-consciousness. Consequently, we are left with two strong candidates of competing philosophical and psychological *systems*: (a) materialism, empiricism, phenomenalism, nominalism, behavioral therapy, evidence-based practices, and science on the one hand *versus* (b) idealism, rationalism, phenomenology, existentialism, conceptualism, insight-oriented therapy, and humanism on the other hand. It further follows that the therapeutic interventions designed to address loneliness as the most significant crisis facing each of us individually—apart possibly from death—will ultimately depend on which of the two conflicting principles and systems of the brain or mind we will decide to endorse.

Materialism versus Idealism. Now that we have started in earnest and before continuing any further, it's obviously important to provide some more adequate working definitions for our discussion. Roughly, in terms of metaphysics, *materialism* is the thesis that *all* that exists is reducible to matter *plus* motion (gravity/energy). It assumes that the sun, the moon, and stones would still exist apart from the presence of any sentient creatures; it is causal and mechanistic in intent. The brain is like a computer, and it is programmed by external physical motions, by stimuli that cause behavioral responses and reactions (Democritus, Hobbes, Skinner). Psychological behaviorism is a natural and logical outcome of materialism. Science itself is materialistic in its intent and procedures. It assumes the existence of a domain of things, of objects independently of human consciousness.

By contrast, following G. E. Moore's definition, *idealism* is the thesis that *all* that exists is, in the last analysis, mental, mind-dependent, or spiritual; that the *concepts* of matter, space, time, and "physical objects" are only meaningful as creations of the human mind (Leibniz, Kant, Hegel).

Dualism is the thesis that there are two irreducible substances, matter and mind(s) or extension and thoughts; and hence two sorts of radically separate realities. More specifically, there are (c) inert, spatially extended objects, *passive* sensations, stimulus-response mechanisms, and brains on the one hand (Democritus, Hobbes) as opposed to (d) *active* thoughts, concepts, rational inferences, and minds on the other hand (Plato, Descartes, Kant).

Empiricism versus Rationalism. In an epistemological context, *empiricism* is the premise that *all* our ideas are derived from precedent sensations and therefore *passively* generated from without by external causes; or, alternatively, there is *no* idea in the mind which is not first given in experience. The mind is like a *tabula rasa,* a blank tablet upon which experience "writes" (Aristotle, Locke). The key notion of causality is attributed to the *imagination,* to habit, and to custom—but not reason—which results in the "principle of the "association of ideas." The ideas of cause and effect are contingently related when sensations are experienced together through contiguity and resemblance, thus resulting in a sense of "constant conjunction," a psychological *feeling* of anticipation, of "necessity" and succession; a *belief* that certain events will be followed by similar events in the future (Hume). A further meta-principle in empiricism is the assumption of the "uniformity of nature," that the future will repeat and resemble the past (Mill). (Hume, however, had already shown, before Mill, that the inductive principle of the uniformity of nature has no basis in either reason or experience.) *Phenomenalism,* a species of empiricism, is the premise that the external world, other selves, and even the self are "constructions" of discrete mental impressions, sensations, sense data, or *qualia* (Hume again). The mind is thus restricted to subjective perceptions and ideas. Further, nominalism argues that only particulars exist and thus our knowledge can be reduced to a fortuitous composition of simple sensations.

In opposition, *rationalism* is the opposing premise that there are *some* ideas, often technically termed "pure" or nonsensory concepts, as well as structural laws, which are *actively* generated from within the mind, from its own internal resources, and thus presupposed independently of sensation and experience. These concepts include relations, categories, and connecting links that are created or produced by the activities of the mind, as, for example, substance-attribute and cause-effect, which function as unifying principles of connection that are universal (true in any conceivable universe) and necessary (the opposite assertion implying a contradiction); in short, they are *a priori* (Descartes, Leibniz, and Kant). Or, as Leibniz quips, there is nothing in the mind which is not first given in experience, *except the mind itself. Phenomenology* rests on the premise that consciousness is actively intentional; it is consciousness *of* or *about* something *other* than itself; something beyond or transcendent to the self; it is meaning-intending; it "points toward" or "targets" objects, emotions, moods, laws, values, and so on, as *meanings* constituted by acts of intentional consciousness (Brentano, Husserl, and Sartre). *Conceptualism* holds that both particulars and universals exist, the first in external reality and the second in the mind. *Existentialism* is the conviction that the human condition should be described and expressed in terms of ultimate concerns, such as the individual's sense of loneliness, meaninglessness, freedom, and death (Kierkegaard, Nietzsche, Heidegger (?), and Sartre).

The battle over the ultimate origin and force of loneliness is arrayed between these two lines of engagement: materialism, empiricism, and behaviorism on the one side and idealism/dualism, rationalism and insight on the other side.

The Metaphysical Issue of "Whether Senseless Matter Can Think?" The controversy between the priority of the brain over the mind, or the reverse, forms one of the most important philosophical issues in the history of Western thought. It consists in the "Battle between the Giants and the Gods" prefigured in Plato's *Sophist* (Plato, 1966b, pp. 245e–246e). It is grounded in the conflict between materialism and empiricism *versus* idealism and rationalism, both of which ultimately underlie their respective disagreement concerning first principles and their ensuing radically opposed systems in regard to the issue concerning reality, consciousness, knowledge, and, for our purposes, most importantly loneliness. It pits Democritus against Plato; Epicurus against Plotinus; Skeptics and Atheists against Augustine and Aquinas; Valla against Ficino; Hobbes against Descartes; Locke against Leibniz; Marx against Hegel; Mill against Bradley; Gilbert Ryle and D.M. Armstrong against H.D. Lewis and Richard Swinburne; and so on. The crux of the continuing disagreement between materialists and empiricists against idealists/dualists and rationalists is centered on a single question: *"whether senseless matter can think?"* It is helpful to keep this issue in mind throughout the course of this study because it not only makes *a* difference, it makes *all* the difference.

Because this controversy has a special application to man's sense of loneliness and isolation, in what follows I intend to volley back and forth by alternating between key advocates for both of these two antithetical positions while criticizing the behavioral agenda, and at the same time attempting to make the strongest case possible in behalf of the humanist approach to loneliness.

More specifically, we may ask how does all this relate to our discussion of loneliness and whether its occurrences are transient or permanent? And what are the implications for possible therapeutic approaches and strategies in addressing issues of human loneliness?

Because behaviorism is a form of materialism, it ultimately reduces the "mind" to the brain, the central nervous system, and finally to physiology. And although it invokes terms such as "sensation," "thought," "consciousness," and "mind," in the last analysis they all reductively point to physical substances, to aggregations of cells situated in the skull, which, when triggered by sensory stimuli from outside and external to the brain elicit behavioral responses. Our brains react to external, material stimuli through our five senses, thus causing physical behaviors, which, in turn, can be monitored and recorded by a machine, an electroencephalograph. As William James said, "We do not cry because we are sad; we are sad because we cry." In effect, it eliminates the mind by substituting in its place the brain as a passive recipient, which remains inactive by its very nature unless jostled by external physical forces. Hence, the term "patient" implying passivity is usually used by clinicians and behaviorists sympathetic to the model instead of the term "subject," which rather implies an active agent. Behaviorism stresses physical factors as well as stimulus-response mechanisms; it emphasizes *quantitative* features as opposed to *qualitative* ones; observable and measurable physiological and chemical reactions; it favors both physical and psychological determinism over freedom; and control and predictability over choice and creativity. But even so, although an electro-encephalograph can tell us *that* a person is thinking, it cannot tell us *what* they are thinking. But most importantly, materialism, empiricism, and behaviorism all deny any *significant* reality to a "stable" self. The only possible recourse in terms of a criterion of "personal identity" or "selfhood" for behaviorism is to refer to the individual's stable DNA molecular structure as the criterion of "identity," since already in the eighteenth century anatomists were well aware that all the cells in the body undergo a complete transformation within seven years time and therefore personal identity could not be established on the basis of bodily identity alone. Behaviorism, together with its attendant doctrines, is the position I shall challenge as an inadequate *explanation* for human loneliness. Accordingly, I shall argue that materialism, empiricism, and behaviorism are unable to account for the reality of the self and the mental *activities* of reflexion and intentionality.

Improved Behavior or Insight? What Is the Goal and Criterion of Successful Treatment? Therapeutically, the two viewpoints also differ in the following regard: Behaviorism favors formal written "contracts" between the therapist and the patient designed to be specific, measurable, attainable, realistic, and time limited (SMART). The contracts are frequently used, not unexpectedly because of their fundamental material grounding in the brain, in conjunction with psychiatric medications. Thus, behavioral and cognitive therapies favor empirical, evidence-based practices, which focus on the *present* in promoting psychological relief. Further, behaviorism believes that all disorders are caused by operant conditioning and/or chemical imbalances in the brain. Indeed, contemporary physiological science is currently promoting a doctrine of "neuroplasticity," which subscribes to the thesis that (mental?) emotions actually *cause* a physical restructuring of the brain as the scientific wave of the future. This view, for example, has been advocated very recently in John McGraw's comprehensive Volume I of his study on loneliness (p. 21). Of course, illicit street drugs do the same. (McGraw's claim, however, doesn't resolve the question of whether these emotions are physical or mental.) But if loneliness is reducible to operant conditioning, then conceivably one could self-administer an electric shock each time he felt or thought about being lonely and then it would magically extinguish the emotion and no one would ever feel or be lonely again.

By contrast, insight treatments are grounded in reviving and reliving the past and exploring the unconscious, hidden, and long-forgotten feelings and meanings embedded within the self. By a process of excavating and uncovering the irrational and dysfunctional connections within the mind, it seeks to liberate the self. Insight therapy posits the *active* nature of the mind; it promotes self-conscious or reflexive mental *activity* as well as acts of intentionality, transcendence, freedom, spontaneity, and the creative aspects of consciousness. And, just as importantly, it defends the existence of a stable self, a real self. By a "real self," I simply mean that the ego, at the very least, displays *some* cognizable temporal duration and continuity within consciousness. Further, it will turn out that the filament of the unconscious is actually continuous throughout life and therefore constitutes a contributing condition serving as a criterion for ongoing personal identity (Mijuskovic, 2010, pp. 105–132).

Loneliness and the History of Philosophy and Ideas. My training is in the History of Philosophy and more specifically in the discipline that goes by the title of the History of Ideas, which traces "unit" concepts, premises, or arguments by applying an interdisciplinary method throughout various historical periods as defined by Arthur Oncken Lovejoy (1964). I have strong sympathies with these two disciplines, as will be apparent throughout the present text. But I should caution the reader that in the process of tracing the conceptual history of loneliness, the emphasis is always on its theoretical flowing stream of principles, concepts, and arguments rather than on any particular swimmer who plunges into its waters either briefly or permanently.

Over time, however, I developed a special interest in theories of consciousness, and in this context the present study is an effort to connect a specific historical and contemporary view of consciousness with the reality and power of loneliness.

Many years ago, I became involved in ferreting out the multiple implications embedded in a unique Platonic premise that has been repeatedly invoked in behalf of four distinguishable conclusions throughout the History of Philosophy: (a) the immortality of the soul; (b) the unity of consciousness; (c) personal identity; and (d) epistemological or transcendental idealism. The principle (or assumption) connects two interrelated mental aspects: (1) the mind is an immaterial *substance; a self;* and (2) thinking is an *activity* of consciousness. In Plato's dialogue, *Phaedo,* he enlists the premise in his second argument for the individual immortality of the rational soul by contending that whatever is *both* immaterial *and* active cannot be destroyed because it has no parts; it is "simple." And since mortal destruction is defined as the decomposition of a compound, it follows that the soul "escapes" when the body disintegrates, and hence death is avoided (Plato, 1966b, pp. 78b–81a). Citing my discussion of the *Phaedo* in *The Achilles of Rationalist Arguments* (1974), Raymond Martin and John Barresi connect the immortality argument and the substantial nature of the self with early conceptions of personal identity (Martin & Barresi, 2006, pp. 6, 13–16, 35). Following Plato, Plotinus will connect it to inferences concerning the unity of consciousness. And in the seventeenth century Descartes will initiate its employment in arguments entailing epistemological and eventually transcendental idealism. The term "transcendental" refers throughout this study to the *a priori* conditions which underlie the possibility of human cognition; for without these conditions being fulfilled, consciousness could not exist; indeed, awareness would not be possible. For example, without *some* structural notion of the relation of causes to effects; or without *some* internal account for time-consciousness, human thought would be an inexplicable mystery (Kant). Objects would appear and disappear at random, and time sequences would be nonexistent or at best completely random, unexpected, and utterly disorganized.

Five years later, in *Contingent Immaterialism*, I argued for three additional uses for the Achilles or Simplicity Argument, which will be shown to provide strong supportive roles in the Philosophy and Psychology of Loneliness. They consist in: (e) the immaterial nature of meanings and relations (Mijuskovic, 1976, pp. 292–306; 1984); (f) the freedom or transcendence of self-consciousness (Mijuskovic, 1978b; 1984); and (g) immanent or personal time-consciousness (in opposition to time as interpreted by classical Aristotelian physics and later Newtonian mechanics as the external movement of objects through empty space (Mijuskovic, 1978a, pp. 276–286; 1984). All seven uses depend on (a) an immaterialist and (b) active theory of the mind and finally lead to a paradigm of enforced solitude. With the exception of its employment in proofs for personal immortality, the remaining half dozen inferences all assume significant roles in the dynamics of loneliness. But whether one is convinced of only one or all seven applications of the Achilles Argument, it follows that even if one agrees with a single use, it opens the possibility of viewing loneliness through idealist and rationalist lenses.

The Inadequacy of Behavioral, Cognitive, and Psychoanalytic Methodologies and Treatments. In the following, I intend to reject three current theories of therapy in regard to loneliness: behavioral treatment because it is stuck in the brain; cognitive treatment because it is stuck in the present; and psychoanalytic treatment because it is stuck in "scientific" determinism.

Lest the reader consider these metaphysical and epistemological issues as irrelevant or unduly esoteric digressions, allow me to point out that

Freud's psychoanalytic theory, for example, started from a materialist neurological base but later depended heavily on rather humanistic metaphors involving Greek myths in order to "explain" sexual urges and internal conflicts as grounded within an unchanging conception of human nature. Although Freud depends on insight through a "free associative" process focused on uncovering the repressed sources of anxiety to enlighten individuals about their internal conflicts, to my knowledge he never explicitly undertakes to account for *self-consciousness* itself, thereby taking it for granted and thus leaving his notion of insight rather unclear. And how exactly does the Oedipal conflict relate to neurons? He seems to have one foot in biology and the other in the mind. Beyond that, he says very little about loneliness—though a great deal about erotic and unrequited love and the loss of the "love object." However, there is a notable passage in which he cites a little boy's anxiety in his dark bedroom yearning to be reassured by his aunt's voice of her continued presence close by confirming that he is not alone (Freud, 1920, pp. 340–355). In *Mourning and Melancholy*, Freud, to be sure, discusses the distress and sense of loss in losing a "love object" when death intervenes but it's primarily from a therapeutic point of replacing it.

REFERENCES

Aristotle. (1941). *Physics,* Book I, 184a, 9–12.

Descartes, R. (1955). *Philosophical Works of Descartes.* New York: Dover.

Fichte, J. W. (1970). *Science of Knowledge.* New York: Appleton-Century-Crofts.

Freud, S. (1920). Part Three: General Theory of Neuroses: XXV. Fear and Anxiety. In *A General Introduction to Psychoanalysis.* New York: Boni and Liveright.

Hume, D. (1973). *A Treatise of Human Nature.* Oxford, UK: Clarendon Press.

James, W. (1962). Does consciousness exist? In *Twentieth Century Philosophy.* W. Barrett & W. Aiken (Eds.). New York: Random House.

Kant, I. (2011). *Observations on the Feeling of the Beautiful and Sublime and Other Writings.* Frierson, P., & Guyer, P. (Eds.). Cambridge: Cambridge University Press.

Lovejoy, A. O. (1964). *The Great Chain of Being.* New York: Harper & Row.

Mahler, M, Pine, F., & Bergman, A. (1975). *The Psychological Birth of the Human Infant.* New York: Basic Books.

Martin, R., & Barresi, J. (2006). *The Rise and Fall of the Soul and Self: An Intellectual History of Personal Identity.* New York: Columbia University Press.

Mijuskovic, B. (1974). *The Achilles of Rationalist Arguments: The Simplicity, Unity, and Identity of Thought and Soul from the Cambridge Platonists to Kant.* The Hague: Martinus Nijhoff.

Mijuskovic, B. (1976). The simplicity argument *versus* a materialist theory of mind. *Philosophy Today,* 20:4.

Mijuskovic, B. (1977a). Loneliness: an interdisciplinary approach, *Psychiatry: Journal for the Study of Interpersonal Processes,* 40:2; reprinted in Hartog, J., Audy, J., & Cohen, Y. (Eds.). (1980). New York: International Universities Press.

Mijuskovic, B. (1977b). Loneliness and the reflexivity of consciousness, *Psychocultural Review,* 1:2.

Mijuskovic, B. (1977c). Loneliness and a theory of consciousness. *Review of Existential Psychiatry and Psychology,* X:1.

Mijuskovic, B. (1978a). Loneliness and time-consciousness. *Philosophy Today,* 22:4.

Mijuskovic, B. (1978b).The simplicity argument and the freedom of consciousness: Hegel and Bergson. *Idealistic Studies,* VIII:1.

Mijuskovic, B. (1984). *Contingent Immaterialism: Meaning, Freedom, Time and Mind.* Amsterdam: Gruner.

Mijuskovic, B. (1988). The self-contained patient: reflexivity and intentionality, *The Psychotherapy Patient,* 3:4; reprinted in Stern, M. (Ed.). (1989). *Psychotherapy and the Self-Contained Patient.* New York: Haworth Press.

Mijuskovic, B. (1990). Loneliness and intimacy. *Journal of Couples Therapy,*1:3/4; reprinted in Brothers, B. (Ed.). (1991). *Autonomous Intimacy: Intimate Autonomy.* New York: Haworth Press.

Mijuskovic, B. (2010). Kant's reflections on the unity of consciousness, time-consciousness, and the unconscious. *Kritike,* 4:2.

Mijuskovic, B. (2012). *Loneliness in Philosophy, Psychology, and Literature.* Blooming, IN: iUniverse.

Plato. (1966a). *Collected Dialogues of Plato.* Hamilton, E. & Cairns, E. (Eds.). New York: Pantheon. *Sophist.*

Plato. (1966b). *Phaedo.*

Russell, B. (1966). The philosophy of logical atomism. In *Logic and Knowledge.* London: George Allen & Unwin.

Sartre, J.-P. (1970). *The Transcendence of the Ego: An Existentialist Theory of Consciousness.* New York: Noonday Press.

Chapter 2

Philosophical Roots:
Self-Consciousness/Reflexivity

In the next two chapters, I contend *that* loneliness is innate to human awareness; *that* it derives and is embedded within the activities and structures of self-consciousness and therefore universal; *that* it has always persisted and can be found in civilization's earliest writings, *The Epic of Gilgamesh, The Iliad* and *The Odyssey* of Homer, the Old Testament, the dialogues of Plato, the treatises of Aristotle, and on into our contemporary movements of Husserlian phenomenology and Sartrean existentialism. This theme is reinforced by UCLA researchers Letitia Anne Peplau and Daniel Perlman who, in discussing "the early work on loneliness and where have we been," state the following:

The experience of loneliness may well be as old as the human race. Mijuskovic (1979) recently criticized those who suggest that loneliness is a recent product of modern society, arguing instead that "Man has always and everywhere suffered from feelings of acute loneliness" (p. 9). Certainly a concern about isolation and loneliness can be found in ancient writings. For example, the Book of Genesis emphasizes the pain of solitude, noting that after God created Adam he observed, "It is not good that man should be alone: I will make him a helpmate." Although the history of loneliness itself is long, the psychological study of loneliness is very young. (Peplau and Perlman, 1982, p. 6)

The majority of current researchers, however, instead often attribute it to the malaise of more recent times beginning with Marx's dialectic of

economic alienation during the industrial revolution, the rise of the bour-
geoisie, the plight of the proletariat, and capitalism in general. It is certainly
true that Marx's concept of alienation has powerful implications in regard
to loneliness. The exploitation of the worker in the nineteenth century, as
portrayed by Marx and Engels, paints man as alienated from nature, his
product (he does not own it), his fellow man (by competition), and even his
self (he is forced to produce against his nature). Indeed, Marx proposes
that man should produce according to the "laws of beauty" (Mijuskovic,
1974a, pp. 157–167). But even when that is granted, we will discover instead
that loneliness reaches as far back as the philosophical debates about the
nature of man and the status of consciousness and knowledge, which began
in antiquity and continues in our present time.

**Self-Consciousness and Loneliness from Greek Thought to the Renais-
sance.** The difference between materialism and idealism in regard to consciousness is readily shown since early Greek philosophy and its perspective
on human cognition. Recall that metaphysical materialism reduces everything to matter *plus* motion. Thus, Democritus, the Pre-Socratic thinker,
in accounting for sensation, postulates the atoms as extended, material,
solid, but indivisible particles moving throughout empty space, which, as
they strike human sense organs *cause* physical sensations. A basic difficulty
with the term *sensation,* however, is that it can be quite misleading, since
intrinsically atoms themselves are *not* sensations. Rather, sensations, as
occurrences in human awareness, as modes of cognition, are *indirectly*
caused by the collision of physical particles moving through sensory conduits and terminating in the brain. I say *indirectly* because we don't experience atoms; rather, we experience sensations, which means that something
has *qualitatively* changed during the conversion of a physical event into a
mental one. For example, atoms are "in themselves" colorless, and yet we
see colors. In any case, without external stimulation, brain states would
remain dormant. Think of a patient in a coma. A key difficulty with the
term *sensation* arises, as we shall see, from the issue of whether sensations
are physical, mental, or both. Nevertheless, it follows that brains are passive,
inert, and dormant until jostled by external stimuli triggering a *re*-active
response and behaviors.

From the beginning, however, the core of the controversy centers on
the question of "whether senseless matter can think." In opposition to
Democritus's metaphysical materialism, Plato provides a much different
view of thought. First, he assumes the soul or mind is immaterial, unextended or "simple," without separable parts. Second, thinking is active; the
mind "moves"; it processes thoughts. Third, thinking implies reflexive
unity and self-containment; it is *self*-conscious. In materialism the brain is

re-active, whereas in both idealism and dualism the mind is active. Here is Plato (1961c) on the soul.

> **Socr:** And do you accept my description of the [active] process of thinking?
> **Theaet:** How do you describe it?
> **Socr:** As a discourse that the mind [actively] carries on with itself about any subject it is considering . . . I have a notion that when the mind is thinking, it is strictly talking to itself, asking questions and answering them, and saying Yes or No. (*Theaetetus,* p. 189e)

Again Plato (1961a):

> **Str[anger]:** And next, what of thinking? Is it not clear that all these things occur in our minds both as false and as true?
> **Theaet:** How so?
> **Str:** Well, thinking [*dianoia*] and discourse [*logos*] are the same thing, except what we call thinking is, precisely the inward dialogue carried on by the mind with its self without spoken words. (*Sophist,* p. 263d)

The underlying assumption is that *unless* the mind is *both* immaterial *and* active, reflexion is not possible. The above quotation underscores four implications: (1) the mind is an immaterial substance; a self; (2) thinking is an activity of the mind; (3) thought is the essential attribute of the soul; and (4) thoughts are a self-contained unity; thought thinks itself, so to speak.

The foregoing is Plato's (1961b, 188e, 203–204a) cognitive theory of awareness, but his motivational view on the importance of loneliness in relation to human existence most notably surfaces in the *Symposium* where he attributes to Aristophanes a speech eulogizing sexual attraction as engrained in human nature and based in our innate emotional desire for each other. The myth describes the original condition of the human race as consisting of powerful, round, roly-poly creatures with four legs, four arms, two opposing faces, and two sexual organs: male–male, female–male, and female–female. Because of their incorrigible and mischievous behavior, Zeus finally in exasperation split them in half in order to lessen their power and to control them:

Now when the work of bisection was complete it left each half with a desperate desire for the other, and they ran together and flung their arms around each other's necks and asked for nothing better than to be rolled into one. So much so, that they began to die of hunger and general inertia. . . . So you see, gentlemen, how far back we can trace our innate love for one another and how this love is always trying to reintegrate our former nature to make it into one and bridge the gulf between one human being and another. (*Symposium*, 188e)

Freud, in *Beyond the Pleasure Principle,* treats this story at length in order to account for our original biological drive and erotic desire for reunification with our former selves (Freud, 1961, pp. 51–52). For Freud, the myth addresses the origin of human sexuality. My view is that it is better understood as a plea to recognize the demands of human loneliness. Similarly, Jung refers to Prometheus, half-man and half-god, "chained to the lonely cliffs of the Caucasus" as a symbol of loneliness. The Greek myth of Deucalion and Pyrrha who, when they were left all alone after the destruction of the human race by a global flood, are pitied by Zeus because of their loneliness and given the means to re-populate mankind (Mijuskovic, 2012). So it's quite misleading to suggest that loneliness is simply caused by some contemporary cultural malady. As we shall see, loneliness is impregnated within human nature and prevails throughout human history.

In Plato, another helpful way to understand loneliness is by insight into its conceptual components. The final speech in the *Symposium* dialogue eulogizing love is given by Socrates, who credits the priestess, Diotima, for his insight into the true nature of the relation between love and loneliness when she recounts the myth of how love was born and came into the world. On Aphrodite's birthday, a banquet was held (much in the manner of the banquet gathering in the *Symposium*), and the god, Poros, symbolizing fullness and resourcefulness, became so drunk that he fell asleep. Meanwhile, the impoverished maid, Penia, symbolizing penury and need, and lacking in everything, desired to have a child and lay next to him. The issue from that union was Eros, the god of Love. But, contrary to popular opinion, he shares the attribute of want, insufficiency, and emptiness with his mother. At the same time, he also exhibits the resourcefulness and successful fulfillment of his father in his search for unity with a beloved ideal. So love is a mixture of want and plenitude as it struggles to overcome its emptiness and achieve fullness, to secure something to fill the void of the soul with intrinsic value and completeness (*Symposium*, 203a–204a). And thus it is that whenever we are lonely, we feel a longing, an emptiness that needs to be filled with love and intimacy.

Next, Aristotle (1941a, *Metaphysics*, 1075a), while expanding on the insular Platonic paradigm of a unified awareness, describes the self-enclosed state of philosophical solitude and in the process discloses a definite hermitic quality to human thought, to self-consciousness. According to Aristotle, the highest form of virtue is intellectual (*theoria*) as opposed to the moral virtues, which depend on practical choices and empirical implementations (*praxis*). Contemplation consists of truths already achieved and actively held by the mind. In the following passage, the observant reader will perceive the first explicit formulation of the rationalist definition of self-consciousness, of *active* reflexivity as a perfect unity of the thinking self with its self as its own conceptual "object." This is precisely the paradigm Descartes will invoke as his reflexive principle in the *cogito*, which will in turn entail a monadic, solipsistic image of the self.

Since, then, thought and the object of thought are not different in the case of things that have not matter, the divine thought and its object will be the same, i.e. the thinking will be one with the object of its thought. A further question is left—whether the object of the divine thought is composite: for if it were, thought would change in passing from part to part of the whole. We answer that everything which has not matter is indivisible [because of its essential simplicity] as human thought, or rather the thought of composite beings is in a certain period of time . . . so throughout eternity is the thought which has itself for an object. (*Metaphysics*, 1075a)

Once more, the reflexive activity of thinking is such that self-consciousness is constituted by the ability to capture itself as the *conceptual* "object" of its own thought. In the case of the Unmoved Mover (or God), as well as during privileged periods of contemplation in man, it is an essential *quality* of the processes of rational thinking that *both* the act *and* the content are able to unify, to coalesce, to fuse with each other because of their shared dual immaterial nature. Hence, thinking is conceived as grounded in the immaterial nature of the mind and so is the "object" of its thought *as a concept*. Reflexion is a revolving circle, with the top rotating with the bottom so that one half is the self and the other half is the object, and both are co-dependent on each other through the center of the sphere. This essential insular, self-contained feature directly points to an enclosed and lonely ego.

As the metaphor theoretically develops, this functional activity and process of an internal relation and unification become the defining characteristics of *rational* thought, dependent on and identical with the attribute of self-consciousness. Reflexivity is thereby conceived as cognitively "moving" from one thought to the next in *a priori* fashion in both (1) a logical, sequential, inferential *order* from antecedent(premise) > consequent (conclusion) in the syllogism as well as (2) an inferential temporal *order* from cause > effect, that is, in the universal principle of causality, namely, that every effect must have a cause. And thus "reason" becomes the basic definition or essence of man according to Plato and Aristotle: "Man is a rational animal."

Aristotle's own view of the negative effects of loneliness on the human psyche is clearly expressed within a social context as opposed to an individual dynamic, interpersonally rather than intrapsychically. In short, I would define his view as sociological. As opposed to Democritus who views man as an individual, Aristotle sees man as essentially defined by the family and the *polis*.

The proof that the State is primary to the individual is that the individual, when isolated, is not self-sufficing; and, therefore he is part in relation to a whole. But he who has no need because he is sufficient to himself, is either a beast or a god. (*Politics*, I, 2, 1253a, 25–29)

A man who does not need or desire the companionship of others is not a human being.

Later, this rich Platonic stream of thought, grounded in the simplicity or immateriality principle, strongly influences the Neo-Platonic philosopher, Plotinus, who systematically expands and deepens its use along the lines of the first three dimensions to which we have already alluded in Chapter 1. Besides employing the Platonic premise to demonstrate (1) the immortality of the soul, since what is immaterial and without parts must be simple, indivisible, and therefore cannot be destroyed, and (2) besides invoking the Aristotelian model showing the interior unity of the self with its own object, (3) Plotinus also demonstrates that what is simple and active must be a unity binding various concepts and thoughts within one and the same consciousness. Thus, he points to the essential factor in establishing personal identity, since what is continuous and unified as the "center" of awareness must persist throughout all of its connected temporal "moments," thereby establishing a unique personal (or moral) identity and continuity. Once more, the argument is placed in an antimaterialistic context.

It is easy to show that if the soul were a corporeal entity there could be no sense-perception, no mental act, no knowledge. . . . There can be no perception without a unitary percipient [or self] whose identity enables it to grasp an object in its entirety [and unity] . . . a face is known not by a special sense for separate features, nose, eyes, etc. but by one [common mental] sense [*sensus communis*] observing all in one act. When sight and hearing gather their varying information, there must be some central unity to which they both report. How could there be any statement of difference unless all sense-impressions appear before a common identity able to take the sum of all? This there must be, as there is a [dimensionless] centre to a circle; the sense impressions converging from every point of occurrence will be as lines striking from a circumference to what will be a true centre of perception as being a veritable unity. If this centre were to break into separate points—so that the sense-impressions fell upon two ends of a line—then, either it must reknit itself to unity and identity, perhaps at the mid-point of the line, *or all else remains unrelated, every end receiving the reports of its particular field exactly as you and I have our distinct sense-experiences.* Suppose the sense-object be such a unity as a face; all the points of observation must be brought together in one visual total, as is obvious since there could be no panorama of great expanse unless the detail were compressed to the capacity of the pupils. Much more must this be true when the sense-objects impinge on the centre of consciousness in the guise of indivisible [immaterial] thoughts. Either the object is unified—or supposing it to have quantity and extension—the centre of consciousness must coincide with it point by point of their co-expansion so that any given pointing of the faculty will perceive solely what coincides with it in the object; and thus nothing in us could perceive anything as a whole. This cannot be. (Plotinus, 1969, p. IV, 7, 6; emphasis added)

The italicized phrase may be the original source of Kant's Second Paralogism, *Of Simplicity,* the Achilles argument. In addition to emphasizing the unity, identity, and continuity of self-consciousness, Plotinus also emphasizes that in order for the mind to be able *to differentiate; to compare;* or *to contrast* the sensation of red *from* blue; or the faculty of sight *from* the faculty of sound and find them *different,* the perceiver must engage in a mental *activity* that goes beyond mere sensations. Sensations are what they are; they are simply given passively to the perceiver and quickly disappear. (Many lower forms of life have sensations but are incapable of "moving" mediately or inferentially.) But the *acts* of differentiating, of comparing, and of contrasting require that the powers of the mind go beyond and transcend the momentary, transient, and ephemeral sensations. These acts are *constituted* as relations, as a mental soldering, which results in binding, unifying functions. Similarly, again, the apprehension of unity and identity, as dependent on functional acts are characteristics peculiar to active minds; they are not sensations. There are no sensations of "difference," "comparison," "contrast," "unity," "identity," as there is a sensation of *this* particular blue color or *this* particular loud noise, and so on.

Plotinus's commitment to loneliness is punctuated in the very last sentence of *The Enneads* when he concludes by describing the soul's lonely spiritual journey through life as a yearning toward eternal salvation, as a union with the One (Reality), as "the passing of the solitary to the Solitary," as "the flight of the alone to the Alone," thus relating it to our theme of loneliness through the prism of mysticism. No longer tethered to the body, the simple, immaterial soul flies free and unhindered seeking an immersive unity with the Absolute, with the One (ibid., VI, 9, 11).

What is important in Plato's definition of thinking as a unified self-containment; in Aristotle's proposition that in self-consciousness the self becomes its own conceptual object, thus forming a self-enclosed unity;

and in Plotinus's argument that the reflexive mind "knits," unifies, binds all its sensations and concepts together in a thoroughgoing unity centered in the identity of the person is that they all agree in defining the reflexive nature of self-consciousness as *actively circular.* As we shall see, when we discuss the materialist, empiricist, and phenomenalist theory of "reflection," it will point instead to a *passive observation* of externally caused sensations; it will consist of a *passive linearity.* As such, it is very different from the paradigm of reflexivity in idealism and rationalism because in the latter the structure of consciousness is generated from *within,* whereas, by contrast, in materialism, empiricism, and behaviorism it is caused by external factors from *without.*

Self-Consciousness and Time-Consciousness. At this historical juncture, it's worth interrupting our discussion in order to fast-forward to the Middle Ages and discuss an important passage from St. Augustine, who was heavily influenced by Plotinus and Neo-Platonism, regarding a critical issue about the relation of the self to the consciousness of time. More specifically, it concerns the role of self-consciousness in the context of a "personal time" that will continue to occupy us as it becomes increasingly relevant in connection to loneliness. Accordingly, in the *Confessions,* St. Augustine offers an interesting insight while discussing the "enigma" of the consciousness of time in regard to the self. He introduces his discussion in a section titled "Bodily Motions as Time" by objecting: "I have once heard a wise man say that time is simply the movement of the sun and the moon and the stars. I did not agree" (St. Augustine, 1960). He then proceeds to provide an example of someone reciting a psalm and draws an important connection between subjective time-consciousness—as opposed to objective time—and the unity of consciousness. The passage is titled "Mental Synthesis":

But how is the future diminished or exhausted, since the future does not exist: or how does the past grow since it no longer is? Only because in the mind, which does all this there are three acts. For the mind expects, attends, and remembers: what it expects passes, by way of what it attends to, into what it remembers. Would anyone deny that the future is as not yet existent? But in the mind there is already an expectation of the future. Would anyone deny that the past no longer exists? Yet still there is in the mind a memory of the past. *Would anyone deny that the present time lacks extension since it is but a point that passes on?* Yet the attention endures and by it that which is to be passes on its way to being no more. Thus it is not the future that is long for the future does not exist: a long future is merely a long expectation of the future; nor is the past long since the past does not exist; a long past is merely a long memory of the past. (ibid., II, xxviii)

St. Augustine's point is that the mind actively binds, connects, relates, or synthesizes all three moments as one continuous flow within the *same* self. The image of time interpreted as essentially consisting in the measure of physical motion through space would make time dependent on space and hence unreal in itself. But St. Augustine rejects the metaphor of time as a spatially extended line consisting of instantaneous points of movement continuing from the past to the present and then proceeding on to the future as composed of discrete and separate units. Time is *not* the measure of the motion of bodies traveling through space. Rather, as St. Augustine intimates, time is a product of the mind's activity and continuous with it. In effect, the awareness of subjective time and mental activity become inseparable. Accordingly, in a single stroke, he establishes an essential relation between self-conscious activity, unity, continuity, subjective temporal awareness, and the permanence of the self. Interestingly enough, Husserl begins his book, *The Phenomenology of Internal Time-Consciousness*, by discussing Chapters 13–18, Book IX, of St. Augustine's *Confessions*, a connection that will gain in importance as we proceed. As this study progresses, we shall have a number of occasions to say a great deal more regarding the difference between a subjective, lonely time that is intimately created and occurs solely within individual consciousness, as opposed to an objective time that is shared in common with others and has no direct implications in terms of human isolation.

Medieval Man, Religion, and Loneliness. Within the context of religious faith, loneliness presents a different dynamic during the Middle Ages. Essentially, when we are psychologically forlorn, we strive to connect with another self or group that we aspire to join. But the desired union can change, disappoint, or elude us because the "targets" of our attempts at a connection is fluid or we ourselves are inconstant. With an absolute and transcendent Being, presumably that is not possible; it will be eternally present and essentially unchanging. Once we are certain that it exists, then the problem becomes grounded in our ability and success or our inability and failure to be worthy of union with that Eternal Being. The order of business is to conform to Its standard of worthiness, obedience, or acknowledgment demanded by that Being. The adjustment and responsibility are uncompromisingly on our side. Devotion is unilateral; the Being in question has no responsibility or obligation on its part toward us. In effect, it's an asymmetrical relation. We have the assurance that in Its Self, it is unchanging. This is not to say that it makes the intended relation easier or more difficult but simply that it is different. Thus, man is assured that if his supplication is successful, he will never be alone. There is no problem of personal identity; the soul is secure; it's grounded in an act of faith that it was created by God. But the dynamic of overcoming loneliness in relation to God becomes the crisis. Accordingly, man's sense of anxiety during the Age of Faith is muted in the sense that the crisis is not so much the loneliness of man but instead the requirements of obedience qualifying the soul's candidacy for eternal unification with the Godhead. Thus, during the extended period of the Middle Ages, Jews, Christians, and Muslims simply assume as an article of faith that God's omnipotent Power or Will creates *ex nihilo* not only the entire universe but indeed each individual soul "out of nothing" and henceforth God will preserve each soul for eternity. Medieval man thus takes for granted the soul's continuous identity as a direct gift from God. Once created, the soul is immortal unless God elects to annihilate it, that is, return it to its original state of nonbeing. Man as a species is set apart and privileged from the rest of sentient creation as a "rational" animal endowed with free will. It is because of his rational nature that man is said to be created in the image of God. And it is these twin attributes of self-consciousness and the inferential power of reasoning that become the defining property of humanity entitling man to immortality.

The Skeptics, by contrast, unimpressed by the above declarations, point out that certain animals, such as foxes and dogs, are able to perform inferential reasoning in the form of syllogisms as well as men, and in order to make their point they offer the example of a hound chasing a rabbit. Having lost sight of the hare and having arrived at a fork diverging in two different directions, the pursuing animal sniffs the first path and not sensing its quarry, it turns the other way and chases its prey foregoing to scent a second time, thus accomplishing a disjunctive syllogism: either A or B; not A; therefore B. My own speculation on the matter is that many higher order animals are fully capable of self-consciousness and inferential reasoning and consequently are as susceptible to loneliness as well as humans. A dog knows the difference between being with his master or mistress and being left alone. I leave it to the theologians, however, if man's best friend is to be admitted to Heaven or sentenced to Hell as well.

In any event, in terms of loneliness, Medieval Man clings to the consolation that an existing God assures him of the soul's continuous identity as well as its eternal existence once created. God is a Being Who is intimately aware of man's transgressions as well as his every thought, intention, and action. But there is a price to pay for this longing for eternal companionship, since the worst punishment a sinful soul can experience is to be estranged from God's caring acknowledgment and grace and condemned to incommunicable agony in the ninth and lowest sphere of Hell (Dante's *Inferno*). Much later, in the early nineteenth century, Hegel describes the synthetic *a priori* category of religious estrangement in the section titled the "Unhappy Consciousness" (first Jewish and later Catholic) as a dialectical progression in terms of the lonely soul's yearning for eternal salvation and union with God (Hegel, 1977, pp. 207–216). Later, in midcentury, Kierkegaard, whose religious writings are singularly predicated on the subjective nature of self-consciousness, poignantly undertakes to contextualize the existential category of *angst* as man's sense of despair and dread in terms of his sense of an impending separation from God in a dramatic literary portrait of finite man before an infinite and unreachable God. "Deep within every human being there still lives the anxiety over the possibility of being alone in the world, forgotten by God, overlooked among the millions and millions in this enormous household of the earth." (Recall Carazan's nightmare.) *Fear and Trembling* centers on Abraham's paradox of faith against a background of misunderstanding God's commandment to sacrifice his only son, Isaac. Whereas St. Augustine announces, "I believe so that I may understand," first faith, then knowledge; faith is *beyond, above, transcendent* to reason, by contrast, Kierkegaard announces a more radical and absolute doctrine of fideism by declaring, "I believe because it is absurd," faith is *against* reason, *contradictory* to reason; faith is a leap into a fathomless abyss; a commitment to an impossibility, as in the case of Abraham who believes that Isaac will *both* be saved *and* sacrificed. For Kierkegaard, it is the paradox of faith struggling with uncertainty that defines religious estrangement and its overcoming, its transcendence that identifies the existential state of the True Knight of Faith.

Often, religious loneliness in the West, especially in Protestant thought, assumes an unbridgeable gulf between imperfect man and a transcendent God while at the same time stressing the duty of trying to reach, to understand, to communicate with a voluntaristic God whose Will is inscrutable, beyond any possible human knowledge, for example, Calvinism's commitment to a Deity Who has predestined souls to Heaven or to Hell in advance. Durkheim, in *Suicide,* maintains that Protestantism exhibits a much higher rate of suicide because Protestants lack the security of social support accorded by the Jewish religion or the assurance of a sense of belonging within the hierarchically structured order of the Catholic Church (Chapter Two, "Egoistic Suicide"). Dostoyevsky, in "The Grand Inquisitor "section of the *Brothers Karamazov,* censures Catholicism for its permissiveness in removing man's existential freedom through the absolution of the confessional and giving him happiness and a false sense of security. In any event, whatever the relationship between man and God may be in these theistic religions, terrifying, supportive, or both, the fact is that it provides a powerful feeling of intimacy, a promise of a personal relationship with God, as well as the assurance in the existence of a Being that always knows that one exists. It offers the promise of an eternal acknowledgment and companionship. This not only serves as one of the most powerful defenses against the loneliness of man, but it also obviously secures a strong motive for religious commitment.

By contrast, Ludwig Feuerbach, in *The Essence of Christianity,* considers that Man first psychologically projects his qualities of knowledge, power, and goodness into an alien Being, into an independent Substance, only later to dialectically return those identical predicates to himself by realizing that it is Man who is the true Substance and omniscience, omnipotence, and omnibenevolence are in reality his own predicates.

Self-Consciousness, Perception, and the Rise of Skepticism. In AD 529, the Christian Roman emperor, Justinian, expels the pagan schools of philosophy from the Empire and their philosophical works migrate to the Arabic world where they are translated and preserved. In 1327, the writings of the Hellenic and Hellenistic Greek and Roman philosophers begin reentering the culture of the West through Moorish Spain and a major metaphysical and epistemological turn occurs challenging the Christian system, especially through the translated treatises of Aristotle into Latin from their Arabic sources, where they were retained after their expulsion by the Catholic Church. At first, Aristotle's pagan writings are placed on the Index of forbidden readings until St. Thomas Aquinas, the Great Synthesizer, presumably demonstrates the compatibility of Greek reason with Christian faith. In 1562, during the late period of the Italian Renaissance, the works of Sextus Empiricus are rediscovered, introducing a wealth of ancient Greek and Roman arguments supporting both dogmatic and pyrrhonian skepticism and attacking (a) reason as well as (b) sensation by criticizing both criteria as incorrigibly inconclusive because they either lead to an infinite regress or to circularity but never to any truths or certainties. The search for truth and certainty thus becomes increasingly challenged by ancient Greek and Roman skepticism, and soon philosophy, religion, and science are all in danger of being relegated to subjective appearances in the mind (Popkin, 1964). (Indeed, ever since then both the modern and our contemporary ages have been infected by epistemological, religious, ethical, and political skepticism.) According to Hegel, in his *Lectures on the History of Philosophy,* by legend Pyrrho of Elis had to be protected from the paths of horses by his friends because he wasn't sure if the horses existed (Hegel, 1968, p. II, III, 336, 363). These skeptical musings soon find welcome expression in Michel de Montaigne's *Apology for Raymond Sebond* when he reduces the external world and other selves to mental appearances within the isolated lonely ego. ("Life is a dream; when we sleep we are awake; and we wake we are asleep"). Thus, matters radically change in terms of epistemological considerations, and a pronounced shift begins to form toward subjective idealism, the insularity of the self, and the consequent separation of the self from a social world of other selves. Notice how in the passage below, which depends on the fourth version of the Achilles Argument (see Chapter 1), epistemic considerations engender a skepticism concerning our knowledge of the external world, and more importantly for our purposes it also anticipates the separation and alienation of the self from other selves as following directly from the mind's self-enclosed nature. Beyond all this, our knowledge and access to an external reality become prevented by "the veil of perception," with ideas operating as mediating filters interposed between the self and external objects, other selves, and inevitably other minds. A favorite ploy of the Skeptics is to emphasize the relative and subjective quality of sensations and their restriction to the individual mind. The following passage is excerpted from Montaigne's "Apology for Raymond Sebond."

Our [mental] conception is not itself [directly] applied to foreign [physical] objects but is conceived through the mediation of the senses; and the senses do not comprehend the foreign object but only their own impressions. And thus the conception and semblance we form is not the object, but only of the impression made on sense; which impression and the object are different [i.e., distinct and separate] things. Wherefore whoever judges by appearances judges by something other than the object. And as for saying that the impressions of the senses convey to the soul the quality of the foreign objects by resemblance, how can the soul and understanding make sense of this resemblance having of itself no [direct] communication with foreign objects? Just as a man who does not know Socrates, seeing his portrait, cannot say that it resembles him. (Montaigne, 1968, p. II, 12)

Hence, if each of us is restricted to our own ideas, as the representational theory of perception proposes, if ideas are nothing but mere *re*-presentations of inaccessible and thus unknowable things-in-themselves, if ideas are mere appearances in the mind and their presence is restricted therein, then, in principle we cannot judge how well our ideas can ever reach anything beyond ourselves. Further, we recall Descartes's paradox: How can a mental concept resemble or correspond to a physical object if they share no common attribute or property? If ideas are like pictures existing *only* in my mind, then I cannot *in principle* compare my picture with something that is not a picture, any more than I can compare a color with a sound. If that is the case, then not only does the relation of the self to the physical universe become questionable but certainly any possible access to other *minds* is inconceivable. If it is truly the case that the mind and its ideas or perceptions only serve as enveloping mediums cognitively confining us within ourselves, that the mind's ideas interpose between the self and the external world of objects and other selves, thus distorting that which we desire to know, then it inescapably follows that we have no direct contact with or access to other selves, to their feelings and intimate thoughts, and hence certainly no ingress into other minds, which are every bit as enclosed and isolated as our own. Inevitably, loneliness intervenes. In sum, if we are solely restricted to the sphere of our own minds and yet we desperately *believe* there are other minds beyond our own, it creates a powerful longing to know these other selves.

Once more, the oil that unceasingly fuels and enflames the underlying metaphysical controversy between materialism and empiricism against idealism and rationalism remains centered on the question of "whether senseless matter can think." For the critical question is *always* (1) whether consciousness is (completely) reducible to materialistic, mechanistic, and *quantitative* explanations; *or* (2) whether there is something *qualitatively* unique about mental phenomena that is irreducible to the physical, something that impregnates the mind with the ability of thought to be active but at the same time restricts it, inhibits it from a complete and/or even provisional access to the thoughts of others. These issues are directly relevant to questions concerning the reality of the self, the existence of other minds, and by implication the inherent and innate limitations of our separate lonelinesses.

Accordingly, the critical question persists: which of the dueling first principles—materialism *or* idealism—best accounts for loneliness, and *how* does each theory propose to provide us with a solution or remedy for loneliness? A number of scholars of modern philosophy have acknowledged my contributions to the conceptual history of these critical discussions between materialism and idealism as they touch on the unity of consciousness, personal identity, and the transcendental conditions for the possibility of human self-awareness and therefore their implications in terms of loneliness.

A work that touches on the same issues as are discussed here is Ben Lazare Mijuskovic's *The Achilles of Rationalist Arguments: The Simplicity, Unity and Identity of Thought and Soul from the Cambridge Platonists to Kant* (1974, 157–167). Mijuskovic recognizes the central role played by Cudworth's formulation of doctrines in the eighteenth-century arguments about the soul, the person, and the nature of thought. (Yolton, 1983, p. xiii)

Again,

In the following discussion of the relationship between immaterial substances and personal identity, I am indebted to two studies: Ben Lazare Mijuskovic's *The Achilles of Rationalist Arguments* and John Yolton's *Thinking Matter*. Mijuskovic shows how the argument about immaterial substances and the grounding of personal identity developed independently in England prior to Descartes as a reaction to the perceived threat of the rise of Epicurean and newer forms of materialism. Mijuskovic details the intense sensitivity of orthodox thinkers to the threat of materialism posed to immaterial substance and documents their defenses against the threat. (Todd, 1995, p. 304)

Citing the *Achilles,* Professor Heinamaa observes:

In and after the seventeenth century, consciousness figured in a central role in at least four fairly distinct themes: personal identity; immortality of the soul; epistemic certainty; and the transcendental condition of experience, as in Ben Mijuskovic's discussion in *The Achilles of Rationalist Arguments* (1974, pp. 157–167), which touches on all four thematics. (Heinamaa et al., 2007, p. 7)

I mention the above acknowledgments because it's crucial for these theoretical issues to remain involved since I am convinced it can be shown they assume an important role in the formation and the dynamics of loneliness. It's not merely their repetitious or curious historical presence that matters but rather their *conceptual and theoretical* force and value that is important, for they have much to say and to do with major philosophical and psychological problems directly related to loneliness: What is consciousness; what are the powers of the mind; is the mind reducible to the brain; does the mind even exist; if it exists, is it creatively active or is the brain merely programmed like a computer; is there a stable self or only biological and physiological changes; what is time, and how does it relate to the mind; is there a "lonely" time; what are the limits in knowing other minds; where do meanings and relations come from; how do I know my sensations are mine and not yours; are our minds free and creative, or are we conditioned and determined; and, most importantly, do we *have* to be lonely?

So vanity aside, I mention these acknowledgments as welcome confirmation of the simplicity proof's multiple uses against the doctrines of materialism, empiricism, and behaviorism and more specifically in the context of our search for the epistemological and psychological origins of human loneliness. These seventeenth- and eighteenth-century discussions about the self, the mind, the nature of thought, personal identity, epistemic certainty, and the transcendental conditions necessary for the possibility of experience constitute the very foundation and framework of why we are—or are not—innately lonely. And unless we know why, we certainly cannot learn what we can or should do about it; or how to protect ourselves as best we can.

Accordingly, during this same period of time we are discussing, the fourth invocation of the Simplicity Argument continues to gain momentum, enclosing us ever further through the tenets of an epistemic skepticism that is the hallmark of the modern age as it proceeds into our own contemporary times. It progressively isolates the Cartesian soul from any possible contact not only with a sphere of independent objects, but more importantly it prevents the self from any *direct* contact with a realm of distinct other selves and therefore other minds by concluding in the ego's complete ontological and epistemic isolation. Consequently, when Descartes proposes to "slay the skeptical dragon," it is the intuitive certainty of the *cogito,* of self-consciousness, with its criteria of clarity (immediacy) and distinctness (definability) that he enlists in distinguishing mind from matter, soul from body, self from others, and truth from falsity, which, despite his best intentions, inextricably commits him to a theory of an enclosed, solipsistic self in the *Meditations.* Indeed, without a beneficent theistic God (Meditation V), not only Descartes but subsequently Malebranche, Leibniz, and Berkeley each remain self-imprisoned within their own mental spheres as well.

The view that consciousness (or, in general the mind) and its physical basis (or, in general the body) seem so essentially different from one another that they must have distinct existences is based on a deep-rooted idea in the history of philosophy. This idea and its variants were constitutive of arguments for the metaphysical independence of mind and body throughout early modern philosophy of the seventeenth and eighteenth centuries, perhaps most notably exemplified in the work of Descartes [and Ralph Cudworth, the Cambridge Platonist]. The essential and complete nature of the mind, generally speaking, seems to consist solely in thinking, and, as such, it must be unextended, simple (with no parts), and essentially different from the body, and therefore immaterial. This was Descartes's idea in a nutshell, ultimately drawing a strong ontological conclusion (regarding the distinctness of mind and body) from a starting point constituted by epistemic considerations (regarding the distinctness of their appearances). As Ben Mijuskovic (1974, pp. 157–167) observes, in this type of argumentation, "the sword that cuts the Gordian knot is the principle that what is conceptually distinct is ontologically separable and therefore independent" (p. 123). Mijuskovic, in locating this form of reasoning in its historical context, also notes the presence of the converse of its inference: "If one begins with the notion, implicit or explicit, that thoughts or minds are simple, unextended, indivisible, then it seems to be an inevitable step before thinkers connect the principle of an unextended, immaterial soul with the impossibility of any knowledge of an extended, material, external world and consequently of the relation between them" (p. 121). That is, this time an epistemological conclusion regarding an epistemic gap (between mind and body) is reached from a starting point constituted by ontological considerations (regarding the distinctness of their natures)." (Black et al., 2007, pp. 10–11)

But the critical point remains, namely, that if we are unable to veridically access outer objects directly, how much less possible is it to penetrate other minds? And if we are restricted to inferential guesses about what other minds are feeling or thinking, or even whether they exist, doesn't this prospect doom us to an insoluble solipsistic situation in regard to loneliness?

REFERENCES

Aristotle. (1941a). *The Basic Works of Aristotle.* McKeon, R. P. (Ed.) New York: Random House, *Metaphysics,* 1075a.

Aristotle. (1941b). *Politics,* I, 2, 1253.

Black, N., Flanagan, O., & Guzeldere, G. (2007). *The Nature of Consciousness.* Cambridge, MA: MIT Press.

Descartes, R. (1955). *Philosophical Works of Descartes.* New York: Dover.

Freud, S. (1961). *Beyond the Pleasure Principle.* New York: W. W. Norton.

Hegel, G. W. F. (1968). *Hegel's Lectures on the History of Philosophy.* London: Routledge and Kegan Paul.

Hegel, G. W. F. (1977). *The Phenomenology of Spirit.* Oxford, UK: Oxford University Press, Sections.

Heinamaa, S., Lahteenmaki, A., & Remes, P. (2007). *From Perception to Reflection.* New York: Springer.

Mijuskovic, B. (1974). Marx and Engels on materialism and idealism. *Journal of Thought,* 9:3.

Mijuskovic, B. (2012). *Loneliness in Philosophy, Psychology, and Literature.* Bloomington, IN: iUniverse.

Montaigne, M. (1968). *The Complete Essays of Montaigne.* Frame, D. (Ed.). Stanford, CA: Stanford University Press.

Peplau, L., & Perlman, D. (1982). *A Source Book of Current Theory, Research and Therapy.* New York: John Wiley & Sons.

Plato. (1966a). *Collected Dialogues of Plato.* Hamilton, E. & Cairns, E. (Eds.) New York: Pantheon. *Sophist.*

Plato. (1966b). *Symposium. Collected Dialogues of Plato.* Hamilton, E. & Cairns, E. (Eds.) New York: Pantheon. *Sophist.*

Plato. (1966c). *Theaetetus. Collected Dialogues of Plato.* Hamilton, E. & Cairns, E. (Eds.) New York: Pantheon. *Sophist.*

Plotinus. (1969). *The Enneads.* Oxford, UK: Oxford University Press.

Popkin, R. H. (1964). *The History of Scepticism: From Erasmus to Descartes.* New York: Harper & Row.

St. Augustine. (1960). *The Confessions of St. Augustine.* New York: Doubleday, II, xxiii.

Todd, D. (1995). *Imagining Monsters: Miscreations of the Self in Eighteenth Century England.* Chicago: University of Chicago Press.

Yolton, J. (1983). *Thinking Matter: Materialism in Eighteenth Century Britain.* Minneapolis: University of Minnesota Press.

Chapter 3

Philosophical Roots: Intentionality/Transcendence

The following chapter is admittedly a difficult read, but it forms the crux of my objections and responses to behaviorism. To repeat, in order to understand and achieve insight into loneliness, we must retrace its roots from the beginning, from the soil from which it springs.

I wish now to focus on the companion activity of consciousness, namely, its intentional aspects as constituting, along with self-consciousness, not only human awareness but obviously by extension loneliness as well. At the same time, I need to draw a critical distinction between the conception of *an active reflexion* as opposed to a *passive reflection,* which latter is an observation on an introspection of (mental) contents that are not the self, not self-referential as proposed by the doctrines of materialism, empiricism, and phenomenalism. As it will turn out, sensations (Locke) or impressions (Hume) will be unattached to a self.

The Epistemological Age. Descartes is credited with ushering in the epistemological age in Western philosophy with his revolutionary egocentric turn. The metaphysical issues are no longer what defines or constitutes a substance; proofs for the existence of God; the immortality of the human soul; or the freedom of the will. Instead, the questions now become what can we know? What is the criterion of knowledge? What are the limits of knowledge? Can anything at all be known with certainty? Descartes's mission is to answer Montaigne and the Skeptics, and like St. Augustine he will turn within the self for certainty. If so, then, in terms of formulating a doctrine of loneliness, indeed, the critical question becomes how far does our knowledge of *other* selves and more specifically other minds extend? And what is the ontological and epistemic relation of my mind to those of other minds?

Readers of this study will doubtless wonder why so much of the concern is committed and devoted to the following seventeenth- to nineteenth-century philosophers but that is because epistemic questions centering on consciousness—as opposed to metaphysical reality—increasingly become the primary concern of thinkers during those periods and consequently the sensations and feelings and meanings that permeate and surround loneliness will have to be addressed and investigated within that context. In addition, once Descartes and Locke, on opposing sides of the controversy, concentrate their respective focuses on the self, consciousness, perception, and personal identity as *the* major epistemological issues, there is no way that loneliness can be isolated and ignored as a mere peripheral concern. Issues regarding the self, consciousness, and loneliness are inseparably intertwined.

In what follows, I intend to volley back and forth between the views of idealists/dualists and rationalists on the one side and materialists and empiricists on the other side in order to highlight the controversy about the true source, force, and quality of loneliness. The one side affirms the reality of the self and reflexion, while the other side denies them and asserts a model of the brain = "mind" as a *tabula rasa*. Thus, the controversy boils down to two opposing first principles: the spontaneity of thought creating mental structures *versus* the brain as a blank slate upon which experience "writes."

Let us try to envision how all this may have come about. Descartes, along with Malebranche, belonged to the Augustinian congregation of the Oratory, and he was undoubtedly aware of St. Augustine's argument in *Contra Academicos* against the Skeptics that to think is to exist. In Meditation I, Descartes hyperbolically doubts everything: his senses, the existence of the external world as well as the faculty of reason and even mathematical certainty (Descartes, 1955). But in Meditation II, he turns deeper within himself and asserts the *cogito:* "I think = I am." He claims he has discovered the criterion for all truth, for any candidate that aspires to be a true proposition, a standard that is both clear and distinct as well as universal and necessary. In what follows, the critical distinction is between (a) intuitive certainty and the self-evidential nature of the cogito *versus* (b) inferential uncertainty and skeptical doubt about the existence of the external world and other selves. According to Descartes, "I think" presents the self-evident certainty that at least one absolutely solitary substance—

apart from the existence of God—exists. Following Aristotle, he defines a substance as that which can exist separately and independently from any other substance. Further, he contends that the mind is *actively* self-conscious; it is able to reflexively think about its self; its knowledge is intuitive, immediate, and direct; thought can curl back on itself, so to speak. As we have previously seen, the self as a subject has itself as the *concept* of an "object" directly present to its self. This is commonly known as the "principle of reflexivity" and its historical source, once again, is Aristotle's Unmoved Mover. This is idealism's and rationalism's starting point, and it is explicitly denied by all materialists and empiricists. The metaphor is of a circle, of an *active circularity*. Further, the knowledge of one's existence as a thinking self is both clear (immediate) and distinct (conceptually definable apart from any other substance). Hence although a physical pain is clear, that is, immediate, it is not distinct, not conceptually definable or determinable. Further, the assertion that I am a self-conscious substance is *universally, always* true in any conceivable universe not only for my self but also for everyone else when they think; and it is *necessarily* true, since if I were to doubt or deny it, I would contradict myself. To think it is necessary to exist, and I cannot exist without thinking. Even to doubt is to think. According to Descartes, this quartet of criteria, of clarity, distinctness, universality, and necessity, can be applied to any proposition seeking to be accepted as true. The *cogito* is an *a priori,* innate truth.

The Intentionality of Consciousness. But there is also something very different and vitally important going on as well in Meditation II when Descartes offers his celebrated wax experiment. We recall that he places a piece of wax in a (closed) heated oven and all its properties, qualities, or predicates of color, smell, touch, and shape change. The wax represents the problem of the existence of the external world. How does he *know* it's the same piece of wax? How does he *know* it's the same world each time he thinks about it or awakens from sleep? The fact is he *doesn't* know it. Nevertheless, he mediately, indirectly, discursively, but dubitably *infers* or *judges* it to be the *same* piece of wax (and world). He can't know it; instead, he actively *thetically posits* it as existing beyond and independently of himself. In effect, *he intends it!* Next, he sees hats and coats traversing by his window. The figures symbolize the problem of other selves *and other minds*. And once again he *infers*—as opposed to intuits—that the appearances are not robots or automatons but rather men animated by minds like his own. But again he can't know they are men who think as he does. In both of these acts of consciousness, the metaphor is of an arrow directed outwardly, of an *active linearity*. It follows that the same mind exhibits two powers or functions; two synthetic *a priori* internally related but distinguishable acts, which enable the mind to "look within," reflexively, as well as to "look without," intentionally (Mijuskovic, 1971a, pp. 65–81; 1966, III, 312–329). When I am deliberating a decision, I am *actively* searching within my self, trying to come to a decision or resolve an internal problem (Plato's internal self-dialogue). But when I am actively absorbed in viewing a dramatic sporting event or enjoying a painting in a significant sense "I" am not even there. In several important respects, this model already anticipates the later phenomenological principle of intentionality, most notably formulated by Franz Brentano and Edmund Husserl, that consciousness is an active awareness *of* something other than its self—it is *about* a "transcendent" object, a meaning, or a value *beyond* the self. Brentano states that he learned the principle of intentionality from Medieval Philosophy and along with the immaterial nature of consciousness the two attributes constitute human consciousness. Husserl will follow him in these two assumptions. The ability of intentionality to thrust itself forward and beyond its self through empathy may eventually provide us with the power to escape our solipsistic loneliness.

But I am also able afterward to reflexively remember that I was completely immersed in a prior act of intentionality; of being "lost" in the object or event. This second act of consciousness is reflexive. In the first act I am focusing on something beyond my self; in the second act I am returning to my self; in effect, my consciousness has "boomeranged." These are two separate activities or operations initiated by the *same* mind. I can imagine living entities that possess only the first tendency of internalized self-enclosure; and I can also conceive of other creatures exhibiting only the second tendency of propulsion. But in terms of human consciousness, both the activities of reflexion and intentionality prevail in the *same* subject.

If we compare Descartes's model of intentionality with that of the behaviorist's stimulus-response paradigm, we will see that they are universes apart. Whereas in Descartes's *Meditations* (and later Husserl's phenomenological *Ideas*) the "intentional" arrow is *active*, it points from the inside outwardly; it targets *meanings as transcendent* to the self. By contrast, in behaviorism, the arrow instead points from the outside inwardly, and the brain's response is *passive*, re-active. It's the difference between watching a puppy and being hit by a stone. On the behavioral model, consider a bright light from a flashlight = external existence directed toward one's eyes. As the rays strike the eyes, they blink; they are *re-active*. By contrast, Meditation II describes the mind's intentional *activity* as directional, pointing toward the "external world"—the wax, the hats and coats—whether they materially exist or not; the ray of the flashlight is the mind's activity outwardly directed *beyond* the self—the flashlight as it illuminates objects, meanings, emotions, moods, values, etc. It follows that each of us has a "privileged access" to our own minds through reflexion—only I can *know* I'm in pain; you can only *infer* it. However, our "accessibility" to the external world and other minds, as guaranteed by the principle of intentionality, though filtered through the medium of consciousness, nevertheless provides us with a "bridge" in our efforts to reach the other self. The mind, therefore, displays both (1) the ability to withdraw and recede "within," reflexively, as well as (2) the capacity to radiate and expand "without," intentionally; to display *both* inner-directed *and* outer-directed acts of consciousness. But when the mind retreats defensively within itself, when it is injured or embarrassed or unacknowledged and it remains inside, it becomes self-aware of its isolation. If it unduly or chronically prolongs its stay within and remains trapped inside and yet *desires* or *longs* to be "outside," "out and about," amongst other selves—*consciously or unconsciously*—but unable to connect in mutually satisfying relationships, then it has fulfilled the conditions required for loneliness. Think of an invalid shut up in a room. He knows he is incapacitated and yet he longs to be outside. Consequently, the Cartesian twin principles of reflexion and intentionality, both functioning as *acts* of consciousness, constitute a critical paradigm enabling us to understand and deal with our loneliness. Together they highlight both the problem and the solution, both the imprisonment and the escape.

The Primacy of Empirical Perception. Locke serves as a pivotal turning point in terms of the limitations and confusions inherent in the materialist, empiricist, and behaviorist tendencies of thought in Western philosophy and psychology. Locke represents the opposing tradition against Cartesianism with his ambivalent materialism and hesitant empiricism. Metaphysically, Locke is an uncertain dualist. He is committed to theorizing that there are two substances consisting of material objects and immaterial thoughts, but when it comes to explicitly defining them further as substances, he says they are an "I know not what" and he satisfies himself by describing them, respectively, as the "unknown supporters" of physical entities, on the one hand, and mental qualities, on the other.

Locke regards the mind as a substance which is immaterial. He accepts the usual dualism, "the two parts of nature," active immaterial substance and passive material substance. At the same time, he is . . . most uneasy in his mind about the concept of substance itself, both material and immaterial. It is a fundamental principle with [Locke] that the universe cannot be explained in terms of either matter alone or mind alone. The one cannot be reduced to the other. Of the two, perhaps mind is the more indispensable, for mind is the active productive principle. Matter produces nothing. In particular to think of it as producing thought, Locke agrees with Cudworth [the British Platonist] is to think an absurdity. (Aaron, 1955, pp. 142–145)

How do the two substances interact and relate to each other? We remember that according to materialism, all that exists is matter *plus* motion. Both are simply presupposed. It's a form of extreme reductivism, which serves as a method of analyzing and separating material objects, physical events, and bodily behaviors into parts, the same artifice of decomposition that permeates the empirical sciences and the behaviorism of today. Further, according to empiricism, all our ideas are derived from precedent sensations (or, later, Hume's impressions). The critical error committed by Locke's materialism and empiricism is already present in the Montaigne passage quoted in the previous chapter, and it is fully evident when Locke, in *An Essay Concerning Human Understanding,* (a) defines ideas as "*immediate* modes of consciousness"; but (b) assumes they are *caused* by the movement of *material* particles moving through space: (a) "Whatsoever the mind perceives in itself or is the *immediate object of perception,* thought, or understanding, that I call *idea*" (1959; pp. II, viii, 8–11; emphasis added); and (b), "The next thing to be considered is how *bodies* produce [i.e. cause] *ideas* in us; and that is manifestly by [physical] *impulse,* the only way which we can conceive bodies to operate in us" (II, viii, 11; emphasis in the original). But if ideas are mental and bodies are physical, then the obvious problem of dualism engulfs us once again and because (a) *mental* ideas and perceptions and (b) *physical* particles are absolutely distinct, separate, and share no common property between them, no interaction can possibly occur nor can we claim to *know* what causes what.

But Locke's restriction that all we can know is determined by the medium of our mental perceptions serving as filters or "veils," which prevent us from seeing things as they really are, has momentous consequences. It means that our only conceivable contacts with the material world, other selves, and certainly other minds, are indirect and therefore ultimately uncertain. Loneliness follows as a corollary to skepticism about our knowledge of other selves or any access to other minds.

In terms of how we acquire knowledge, Locke rejects Descartes's theory of innate ideas and *a priori* concepts. According to Locke, all our ideas are caused by the motion of physical particles moving through space and striking our sense organs, thus resulting in singular sensations, which he collectively terms "perceptions." Thus, *all* our ideas are acquired through experience. Ideas are either (1) qualitatively simple, for example, blue, round, soft, sweet; or (2) compound/complex, for example, a blue square, a solid ball, a soft pillow, or a sweet candy. "External" experiences produce ideas of sensation, whereas "internal" experiences provide the content for our ideas of reflection, such as "thinking, willing, doubting," which he offers as examples. However, it's important to note that *all* our experiences are *originally* caused by ideas of sensation; they always come first, and ideas of reflection are derivative, secondary, and thus dependent on the former. As mental perceptions, they are intended to "represent" or "correspond to" external objects or events (Mackie, 1976, pp. 37–38). Locke also distinguishes objective or primary ideas/qualities, as for example, solidity, motion, or spatial properties of things as existing independently of the mind in opposition to subjective or secondary ideas/qualities, as for instance mental colors, sounds, smells, and tastes as existing only in the mind. But because both are perceptions, Berkeley soon reduces them to a mental subsistence alone. For example, we cannot be aware of extension without color; but since color is a secondary, mental quality, it follows that it is subjective and ergo it is completely mind-dependent. Along with Berkeley and Hume, the other two classical empiricists, only *particular/singular* sensations or ideas exist and objects and events are compositions of simple sensations (nominalism). Once more the mind is like a "blank tablet" upon which experience "writes." This is the overruling metaphor for understanding consciousness, and it is identical to the behavioral model, which substitutes the brain for the metaphor of the white tablet. Thus, for instance, if I remember suffering an injury yesterday, it's because I "reflect" on my previous sensation of pain; I introspectively "observe" my former sensation. I *remember* the sting of a *particular, specific* painful sensation = experience. Thus, Locke's *reflection* is very different from the rationalist concept of *reflexion* or self-consciousness, which latter unifies, synthesizes, binds a *conceptual* connection between subject–object in a *reciprocal* relation, in an indissoluble unity, and consequently assures us of the existence of a stable self *as* the unifier. *The unifier is not merely an activity but an activity attributable to a self.* Consequently, it's critical not to confuse the principle of "rational" reflexion with that of "empirical" reflection. Self-consciousness in the idealist-rationalist tradition signifies the subject's "self-knowing of its self" and by extension its unification of its own concepts or thoughts within its self; it's similar to the reflexive pronoun in French, *moi-meme,* me-myself. I know that I know. Subject and object are a unity. By contrast, Locke's reflection always means *observing* some specific sensation, object, or event that is different from a self while somehow occurring within a sphere of general consciousness (presumably mine). The implication is that there is no self. The sensations, impressions, or ideas are separate and "detachable" from my self. Thus, consciousness passively "mirrors" or reflects a previous experience. For Locke, imagination and memory, in the vocabulary of Hobbes, are simply "decaying sensations." Although Locke alludes to thinking as reflection, he intends it to mean that consciousness is reexperiencing or passively observing *previous* sensations. That's a necessary implication of the *tabula rasa* metaphor. For example, if there is a memory of being hungry yesterday—if there is a consciousness of sensations of hunger—it's because there is an internal observation of an unpleasant intestinal discomfort. And when Locke tries to allow for "acts of reflection" and he asserts that we are able to "compare" different ideas with each other, a judicious reading discloses that if *all ideas* are *originally* simple, immediate, and passive sensations, then the term "compare" has no significance. There is no sensation of "comparison." Comparison is a relation, a mediate mode of consciousness, an *act* of the mind (Kant). In what follows, we shall see that the self disappears in Locke. All that is left are unattached sensations.

In Plato's dialogue, *Theaetetus,* he suggests that if we assume the mind is like "a good thick tablet of wax," similar to Locke's blank tablet, then it's difficult to account for error or for making mistakes, since the wax merely absorbs and imprints the sensations like a signet ring copies or imprints physical impressions (*Theaetetus,*191c–194c; see Descartes Meditation III). How can the wax—or Locke's tablet—"choose" between different sensations? Sensations are by definition immediate and cannot "move" beyond themselves; they appear instantaneously and disappear forever. Unless the mind is endowed with active powers of some sort, it does not have the capacity or ability to choose one set of sensations over another set.

From Locke's epistemic restriction that *all* we can know is determined by the medium of perception serving as a filter or "veil," it follows that we cannot know reality "in itself"; we do not know things as they really are. We cannot have direct, immediate access to the material world, other selves, or other minds. He has effectively enclosed us within a limited, insular sphere of awareness, which can only lead to skepticism and loneliness. Second, Locke's identification of consciousness with a passive and receptive *tabula rasa* runs on all fours with the materialist, empiricist, behaviorist, and scientific paradigm of the brain. But again the restriction that the brain is only able to "record" the incoming sensory data means it has no capacity for *self*-awareness. Further, the brain as a physical organ is not a self. It is merely an assemblage of cellular parts. It is this consideration that allows us to realize why so many contemporary scientists and physiologists are mesmerized by all sorts of theoretical situations involving brain transplants. It is like Theseus' ship that has all its planks removed. Is it the "same" vessel? Is there any criterion of self identity in such materialistic contexts or situations?

Locke on Personal Identity. To his great credit, Locke is the first philosopher to seriously search for the (empirical) criteria for personal, that is, for ethical and forensic selfhood. He believes, that unless we can establish that the self before us is the same person who committed a past act and whom we now hold responsible in the present, we cannot hold that person accountable. Locke's criterion essentially turns out to be a reflection on the *continuity of consciousness* as established by the memory of past actions and thoughts. And where there are gaps or discontinuities, the problem arises whether it's the *same* self.

For since consciousness always accompanies thinking, and it is that that makes everyone to be what he calls *self*, and thereby distinguishes himself from all other thinking things: in this alone consists *personal identity*, i.e. the sameness of a rational being. And as far as this consciousness can be extended backwards to any past action or thought, so far reaches the identity of that *person;* it is the same *self* now it was then, and it is by the same self with this present one that now reflects on it, that that action was made. (II, xxvii, 9)

But again, the reflection can only be of separate sensations, not a self. In terms of memory, however, Locke is also vulnerable to Leibniz's criticism that there are unconscious thoughts of which we have no memory, but they still "belong" to ourselves. In addition, because Locke insists that in deep, dreamless sleep and swoons, we completely cease to think, he makes it a point to stress that there is no guarantee that we are the same person when we awake. This consideration compels him to feel obligated to consider cases of the transmigration of souls—reincarnations—and transposed identities as, for example, the case of a prince waking up with his past memory but now in the body of a cobbler. Is he then the prince or the cobbler?

God and "Thinking Matter." In the beginning of this study, I alerted the reader that a guiding theme throughout the text is concerned with the issue "whether senseless matter can think." In fact, Locke explodes a religious bombshell in his controversy with Bishop Edward Stillingfleet when he suggests the possibility that God could have created "thinking matter," that He could have endowed matter with the power of thought. The importance of this theological issue initially revolves around the question of immortality, with the Platonic-Neo-Platonic-Cartesian tradition arguing that a necessary condition for immortality is the immateriality of the soul. Locke himself, however, believes otherwise, and he is accused of subscribing to the so-called mortalist heresy, a movement supported by a group of thinkers, including Thomas Hobbes, Isaac Newton, George Withers,

Richard Overton, and John Milton, contending that man is "naturally" mortal but that his *body* will be resurrected on the Day of Judgment by God. For without a body, Locke maintains, one cannot experience pleasures and pains or rewards and punishments in the afterlife (Mijuskovic, 1974a, 1975, pp. 305–315). But apart from the immortality issue, Locke's grounding metaphor of the *tabula rasa* as the final explanation for consciousness seems to have induced him to speculatively reconsider his initial commitment to dualism and consider instead a thoroughgoing materialism. In which case, the substantial nature of the self would be seriously compromised for the very reasons I have presented above. In this context, Locke's paradigm shift would include him in the camp of proto-behaviorism similar to Thomas Hobbes.

Incidentally, as a parenthetical comment, it is the Locke-Stillingfleet controversy over the possibility of "senseless matter thinking" in *The Achilles of Rationalist Arguments* that Professor Chomsky is referring to in his citation in the Introduction to the present text. And as he suggests, these issues are as critical today as they were in the seventeenth century.

The controversy between materialism and idealism over the issue of loneliness revolves around the critical question of whether matter alone can "account" for human consciousness. This continues to be *the* vital issue tying philosophy and psychology together, and it needs to be seriously addressed, if not resolved, before any meaningful dialogue about loneliness can go forward. Bottom line, the question is: Can we operate meaningfully only with passive sensations and the passive "association of ideas" (empiricism); or do we need active relations linking concepts together as well as unifying principles for the self? And if we need relations, where do they come from?

Humans and Language. Whereas the idealist-rationalist tradition in Western thought defines man in terms of his ability to reason, to think within innate structures and *a priori* relations, by contrast the classical materialists, Hobbes, for example, and traditional empiricists, Locke, Berkeley, and Hume, for instance, collectively explore the possibility that the defining essence of human nature is the use of language; it's this special attribute that presumably distinguishes us from the lower animals. That is why Locke offers an extended discussion in his section of *personal identity* by relating a strange and curious report gleaned from a narrative by Prince Maurice, who interviewed a parrot in the Brazilian jungle, which, by reputation, possessed the ability to carry on rational conversations. Prince Maurice was constrained to employ interpreters, a Brazilian and a Frenchman, since the bird only spoke Brazilian and the Prince only spoke French. The result was that indeed the parrot was able to converse reasonably and answer the Prince's questions—where he was from, his occupation in tending to the chickens by clucking at them, and so on. Still Locke complains that being a man implies a certain bodily structure, and so he dismisses the attribution of humanity to the hapless bird.

The emphasis on language—as opposed to reason—it is to be noted, is completely in line with materialism, empiricism, and behaviorism. According to their collective viewpoints, language is an acquired skill; it is not innate; it is a learned behavior; it is grounded in public and social experiences. We shall return to the issue of the relation between consciousness, language, and loneliness in Chapter 6. But for the time being, I beg the reader to bear it in mind because the role of language will gain in importance as we proceed. Originally, it hearkens back to the Epicureans who were materialists and viewed language as a conventional product facilitating practical uses.

Locke and the History of Ideas. In the beginning of this study, I mentioned the discipline of the History of Ideas. The following commentary would qualify as such an enterprise. It initially grounds the theme of idealism in early religions and the philosophic thought of ancient times, both Oriental and Occidental, but then it quickly moves into the modern period. More specifically, the thesis it defends is that especially through Locke, but also Berkeley, Hume, Kant, and Fichte, idealism is based in a single premise, namely, that all we can know derives from our individual subjective states of consciousness, whether we refer to these modes of thought as ideas, perceptions, representations, or phenomena.

Perception and Skepticism. The overriding question is: Are we self-enclosed within our own minds; are we able to access other minds, to "know" an other's feelings and thoughts; or are we ultimately alone? In a strange, remarkable book, Thomas Ebenezer Webb authors a work titled *The Veil of Isis: A Series of Essays on Idealism,* originally published in Dublin in 1885. The title derives from a quotation in Plutarch: "And the shrine of Athena [goddess of wisdom] at Sais (whom they also call Isis) bears this inscription, 'I am all that hath been, and is, and shall be; and my veil no mortal has hitherto raised'" (Webb, 1885, pp. 10–11). The meaning of this cryptic motto is that as humans we initially acknowledge the existence of the material world, but we are obliviously unaware that its questionable ontological and epistemic status rests on our individual subjective perceptions, our *immediate* ideas, as defined by Locke. But our perceptions are inadequate to the task at hand of unmasking or removing the veil from reality, the "veil of Isis"; they prevent us from accessing Isis herself. By the same token, the material world only exists through the veil of our own perceptions as well, which doubly operates to deceive us from realizing that it is the mind that serves as the instrument of accessing existents beyond our consciousness including other selves. But if we recall Montaigne's admonition, if all we can be aware of are our own ideas as pictures, how can we know that our images or pictures are faithful copies, that they truly represent a domain independently of those perceptions and representations? If I have never seen Socrates, how do I know the portrait you show me is a good likeness? We remember that our ideas, as immediate modes of consciousness, prevent us from realizing that the only "realities" we "know" are our own ideas serving as mere *re-presentational* appearances. What lays beyond them, no man can be certain. Further,

it is not to be denied that the idealism of Berkeley had its starting point in Locke. Locke taught that the soul is conscious only of its ideas; and that these bounds were ample enough for the capacious mind of man to expatiate in, though it takes its flight further than the stars, and cannot be confined to the limits of the world—though it extends its thoughts beyond the utmost expansion of matter, and makes incursions into the incomprehensible inane. (ibid., pp. 10–11)

This passage is a clear allusion to Hume's last three paragraphs in Part II, Section VI, *"Of the idea of existence, and external existence"* in the *Treatise,* which states:

A like reasoning will account for the idea of *external existence.* We may observe, that 'tis universally allow'd by philosophers and, pretty obvious of itself, that nothing is ever present to the mind but its perceptions or impressions and ideas, and that external objects only become known to us only by those perceptions they occasion. To hate, to love, to think, to feel, to see; all this is nothing but to perceive. Now since nothing is ever present to the mind but perceptions, and since all ideas are deriv'd from something antecedently present to the mind; it follows, that 'tis impossible for us as to consider or form an idea of something specifically different from ideas and impressions. Let us fix our attention out of ourselves as much as possible: Let us chace our imagination to the heavens, or to the utmost limits of the universe; we never really advance a step beyond ourselves, nor can we conceive of any kind of existence, but those perceptions which have appear'd in that narrow compass. This is the universe of the imagination, nor have we any idea but what is there produc'd.

But this is not only the empiricist manifesto, but it is identical at the same time as the manifesto of loneliness. It announces the inescapable loneliness of man in no uncertain voice.

Through Hume's characterization of our human limitations, Webb makes it clear that our conception of an external material existence is not only grounded but confined to the perceptions in our minds. The universe cannot "exist" independently of the individual mind; and, in pursuit of his thesis, Webb discusses a series of thinkers on both sides of the controversy, both materialists and idealists. In effect, then, from his premise—each of us is restricted to his or her own ideas, perceptions—it follows that various forms of subjective idealism *all* derive from Locke's insistence that all we can be aware of are our own states of consciousness regardless of whether we call them perceptions, ideas, conceptions, representations, or phenomena. They are one and all *appearances*. Thus, when Locke defines ideas as immediate modes of consciousness, he has effectively enclosed each of us within the confines of our own thoughts. As Berkeley went on to declare: "To be is to be perceived" and further asks, "What can be like an idea but another idea?" And as Webb points out, the "weak point in any idealist system is that it leads to solipsism" (p. 42). As he proceeds, he inquires, in sympathy with Hume, "why may we not regard the Soul as sufficient for all the appearances of nature" (ibid., p. 54). Webb also anticipates a theme that will occupy us in Chapter 7, which deals with the distinction between the unconscious and the subconscious.

One of the most important philosophical distinctions [is] that between [consciousness] and spontaneity and volition. It is well known that far below the surface of consciousness and will, in the depths of our mental being, there are agencies at work which manifest their presence by the effects which they produce. Our instincts, our tendencies, our appetites, our affections and desires, our very capacities of receiving sensation from without, if indeed our sensations are to be regarded as determined from without are instances of this [spontaneity of the will]. (ibid., p. 55)

Put differently in terms of consciousness, we are aware of our perceptions *but not of their ultimate and real causes.*

Interestingly, Webb's contentions foreshadow by some 130 years my discussion in Chapter V of *The Achilles of Rationalist Arguments*, "The Simplicity Argument and Its Role in the History of Idealism."

While Webb places the source of the controversy in the context of the battle between materialists and idealists, Plato's Giants and Gods, Hegel before him connects Locke's definition of perception within the context of ancient skepticism—from Protagoras and the Hellenistic skeptics—to the current fashionable skepticism of the modern era, which he lays at the hands of Locke's subjective idealism. It is the great empiricist whom Hegel holds accountable for the pervasive movement of modern skepticism. Thus, in the section titled "Idealism and Scepticism," Hegel discusses the British empiricist philosophers and critically remarks:

This movement of Being-for-self [as restricted only to perceptions] is now an essential [philosophic system or] moment of thought, while hitherto it was outside it; and thus grasping itself as a movement in itself, thought is self-consciousness—at first indeed formal, as individual self-consciousness. Such a form it has in scepticism, but this distinction marks it off from the older [historical pyrrhonian and dogmatic] scepticism, that now the certainty of [internal] reality is made the starting point. With the ancients, on the contrary, skepticism is the return into individual consciousness in such a way that to it consciousness is not the truth, in other words that skepticism does not give expression to the results arrived at, and attains no positive significance. But since in the modern world this absolute substantiality, this unity of implicitude and self-consciousness is fundamental—that is, this faith in reality generally—scepticism has here the form of idealism, i.e. of expressing self-consciousness or certainty of the self as all reality and truth. The crudest form of this [subjective] idealism is when self-consciousness as individual [as in Locke, Berkeley, and Hume] or formal [as in Kant] does not proceed further than to say: All objects are our conceptions. We find this subjective idealism [starting in Locke] in Berkeley and another form of the same in Hume. (Hegel, 1968, III, p. 363)

Again:

The standpoint of the [skeptical dogmatic] Academics is that they express the truth as a subjective conviction of self-consciousness; and this tallies with the subjective idealism of modern times. The truth in so far as it is only a subjective conviction, has hence been called by the New Academy, the *probable*. (ibid, II, p. 311)

This is an obvious reference to Hume's contention that *all* empirical judgments only hold a "probability" value at best and we can have no guarantee that the future will resemble the past.

Original skepticism begins with the Sophists, contemporaries of Socrates and Plato, and with Protagoras's epistemic principle that "[individual] man is the measure of all things; of what is that it is; and of what is not that it is not." Locke's restriction to one's own perceptions results in the identical conclusion that each of us (assuming it's proper to refer to "us") is inevitably alone, cut off from accessing the external world, or reaching other selves and other minds. This philosophic sense of exclusionary isolation serves as the ultimate root for our irredeemable feelings and meanings of loneliness.

Although Freud studiously tries to avoid becoming entangled in metaphysical and epistemological speculations—which is impossible at his level of sophistication—nevertheless, he can be found expressing the following opinion, which thoroughly resonates with the skeptical summaries formulated above by Webb and Hegel in line with the subjective nature of consciousness.

So we endeavor to increase the efficiency of our sense organs as far as possible by artificial aids; but it is to be expected that such efforts will fail to affect the ultimate result. Reality will always remain 'unknowable'. . . . What we "know" is only a reproduction or reflection in the internal world of our thoughts of what is actually present in the external world. (Freud, 1949, p. 105)

The importance of this entire controversy we have been delineating rests on two radically opposed principles: *either* what we experience is grounded in physical sensations, their consequent bodily responses, and their accompanying social interactions (materialism); *or* it is based in active thoughts, synthetic *a priori* relations, and self-consciousness and intentionality (idealism/dualism). I submit that the second option more readily accounts for insight and understanding into the phenomenon of loneliness. Simply put, if all I can "know" are my own ideas and perceptions, how can I ever vanquish loneliness? How can I reach the other conscious being with any sense of certainty?

Sensations as Qualitative and Objects as Quantitative. According to Locke, each *qualitative* sensation is absolutely separate from every other, and therefore there is no conceivable *necessary* principle of connection holding the separate sensations together in *one and the same* unitary consciousness. As Hume later correctly demonstrates, experience alone is always contingent and unable to provide universal and necessary principles of connection, of relation. Metaphorically, Locke's "mind"—ultimately composed of brain cells—can be analogized to a box full of loose marbles (the sensations), with the brain serving as the box. Consequently, the disparate sensations alone cannot establish a unity between each other or establish any continuity because there is nothing *necessarily* securing, binding, or unifying the single marbles to each other. And since the box itself is inactive, it is unable to perform the *act* of unification. Any such aggregation of sensations could only be grouped by chance and could easily disperse at random. There would be no unity of consciousness.

When the "self" reflects on its "internal" ideas, it can only experience simple sensations of blue, loud, sweet; all we can experience are memories and reflections—not *reflexions*—of pain, of pleasure, of hunger, and the like. Presumably, various sets of brain cells as linear conduits are all attached to each of the five senses through nerve endings, and all five terminate in the brain. But we recall Plotinus's objection: What agency or faculty actively "reknits" them into a unity? Plus, again, there is no sensation of "self." The blank tablet can only receive, record, and "stamp" the separate sensations, but in its capacity *as a tablet* it cannot stamp itself. On Locke's account of cognition, our *idea* of a white ball is composed of two separate sensations: white *plus* round. But there is no way to account for their relation. They simply sit there "on top of each other." Missing is the concept of an active, relational process and more specifically the relation of *superimposition*. But once more, sensations are not relations. There is no sensation of "superimposition."

Finally, it may be helpful to jump ahead and interject a later controversy between William Whewell, a Kantian, and John Stuart Mill, an empiricist. Mill claimed that the elliptical orbits of the planets are readily determinable by simply tracing the particular nocturnal paths of these "wandering" heavenly bodies in the sky (Tycho Brahe's observations). But astronomers had been charting the nightly pinpricks of light for millennia before Kepler finally suggested the concept of the ellipse (Snyder, 1994, pp. 785–807). Sensations are mute; they cannot speak for themselves; they need a mind animated by a conceptual and theoretical voice to invest them with meaning. The fact is that an accidental collection, a fortuitous assemblage, or a simple listing of sensations is *not* a meaning. A meaning is something that the mind creates out of the passive *mental* contents of sensations. It is the mind that actively sorts out the relevant from the irrelevant in the chaos of sensory consciousness. It is the mind that conceives and settles upon a specific order out of an infinite number of possibilities (Peirce, 1957, p. 145). Similarly, humans had observed for thousands of years the falling of objects to the ground, the ebb and rise of the tides, and the meandering movements of the planets' trajectories, and yet no one had ever made the connection between all three phenomena as unified through the law of gravity until Newton. Meanings and relations are not only different but much "more" than mere sensations. Sensations alone are not even facts. In all these considerations, empiricism and behaviorism fall profoundly short with their reliance on portraying the "mind" as a *tabula rasa* and perceptions as collections of simple physical sensations imprinting the brain.

As we move forward, we will discover that both (a) sensations and feelings are *qualitatively* unique and vary from person to person in contrast to (b) *quantitatively* extended entities, such as physical objects, bodily reactions, and human behaviors, which are objectively measurable and therefore intersubjectively determinable. The former existences are subjective, personal, intimate, unshareable, and cannot be compared or contrasted between perceivers. This is where loneliness lives. We are each of us separated from others by our feelings and thoughts. Feelings of loneliness are *essentially* nonmeasurable, whereas quantitative features are considered to be objective, impersonal, common, shareable, and scientifically determinable. The latter is where behaviorism resides. If this is correct, then it follows that we exist qualitatively alone but quantitatively together with others. Science strives to be objective and hence communicable in principle. But although we each occupy the same universe of clocks and calendars, streets and cities with other selves, nevertheless each mind experiences qualitative differences, if for no other reason than our sensations and feelings are unique to each self and we all have different biographies and temperaments. It follows that *my* loneliness is very different from yours and yours from mine. Your cancer and mine may be medically given the same category or stage of severity but your feelings, meanings, and thoughts about the disease will not be qualitatively the same as mine, if for no other reason than we differ uniquely in terms of personal background, life events, heredity, environment, relationships, values, and the like.

Leibniz, Monadic Consciousness, and Time-Consciousness. Poised against Locke, Leibniz, who calls himself "the first idealist," exploits the Simplicity Argument's use in all of the first four demonstrations we broached in Chapter 1: immortality; the unity of consciousness; personal identity; and transcendental idealism, while at the same time criticizing the mounting challenge of modern Epicurean materialism, which was quickly and systematically establishing itself as a major influence in the scientific world of the seventeenth and eighteenth centuries through Hobbes, Gassendi, Newton, and Locke. In addition, Leibniz emphasizes the theme of time-consciousness in relation to the self. The issue of time-consciousness inevitably involves a theory of loneliness because when we experience isolation we feel we are separated temporally from the feelings and thoughts of others, that *my* time is qualitatively different from yours as well as from everyone else's. In what follows we shall distinguish an objective time consisting of birthdays and train schedules from a subjective time of loneliness.

In the history of philosophy and science, the concepts of space and time are highly problematic and at the same time foundationally critical. Plato, in his cosmological myth, alludes to space as "the nurse of all becoming" and to time as "the moving image of eternity" (*Timaeus,* 37d). The Demiurge, an artisan god, after fashioning the material world according to the ideal patterns and archetypes of the Forms then puts it into motion and thus creates time. Aristotle defines time as the measure of the movement of objects in and through space (*Physics,* IV, 219a–219b). Later, Descartes maintains that God creates and re-creates, that is, conserves and preserves the entire universe as well as every individual soul at each instant of time. According to Descartes, without God's continual, instantaneous interventions nothing would move or even exist; indeed, the universe would cease and disappear. In any case, the ontological status of space and time is a major problem for philosophers and scientists alike, and yet science naively presupposes their actual stability if not their *conceptual* stability.

But because of the importance of the scientific revolution taking place during the seventeenth- and eighteenth-centuries, philosophers and scientists alike were at great pains to establish the ontological and epistemological status of space and time. If space and time are independent existences or substances existing apart from human consciousness, then their involvement with human loneliness would be irrelevant. But it's only when we get to Leibniz that a deepening relevance begins to appear and the suggestion takes breath that possibly subjective time is very different from scientific time; that perhaps there is a self-enclosed lonely time, which is radically different from the objective time we share together publicly. Leibniz accordingly anticipates a doctrine of internal time-consciousness as an active creation by the mind occurring solely within consciousness, within the solipsistic monad.

Leibniz and Newton engaged in a very important and famous controversy in regard to the ontological and epistemological status of space and time. Newton declined to argue directly with Leibniz because he believed Leibniz had plagiarized his discovery of the infinitesimal calculus during a visit with him. Consequently, Samuel Clarke defended Newton's *absolutist* views in his behalf. *The Clarke-Leibniz Correspondence* was studied later by both Hume and Kant. In the argument between Leibniz and Newton, interestingly enough, Leibniz, a rationalist, and Hume, an empiricist, are on the same side in interpreting space and time as *relative,* as the result of *perceptual* changes and their consequent arrangement and ordering *within* the mind. Newton, in opposition, claimed that space and time are *absolute* and *eternal* containers and that they would exist even if space was empty of objects and time was devoid of events. In effect, for Newton, space and time exist independently of human minds. (Actually, Newton went so far as to describe space and time as God's sense organs so that literally the Deity was present everywhere and always. Newton may have been influenced in this view by Henry More, the Cambridge Platonist, who rather paradoxically argued that immaterial minds or souls were nevertheless spatially extended. Just so, the mind of God, Newton held, although immaterial was present throughout the universe.) In response, Leibniz, and later Hume, insisted that space and time are dependent on an ordering of our mental perceptions *by the mind* and could not exist independently of human minds (Mijuskovic, 1977, pp. 387–395).

The Clarke and Leibniz debate heavily influenced Kant. The significance of this influence will be that Kant was prompted to split the difference between Newton and Leibniz and accommodate Newton by positing the pure passive intuitional forms of space and time as "absolute" *within* the human mind in the Aesthetic so that all human beings intuited the *same* space and time; *but* he also acknowledged Leibniz's insight in the first edition Deduction that an active, creative production of time-consciousness is synthesized, unified *a priori* through a relational binding of past-present-future together in the *same* consciousness. But time-consciousness is synthesized differently in each mind because there is an *empirical* element that varies from individual to individual (Wolff, 1963). In terms of a theory of loneliness, the significance of this controversy is grounded in the issue of whether time is absolute or relative. But if it is intimately subjective and relative to the individual, if time-consciousness is uniquely immanent and varies from person to person, it will entail a solitary and lonely time.

According to Kant, then, in the Transcendental Aesthetic there is a passive, intuitional form of time, which is universally shared by all human beings but perhaps not by other rational extra-terrestrial creatures in the universe. But the second account of time-awareness hinted by Leibniz and amplified by Kant, depends on individually-structured mental activities involving the *re*-productive empirical imagination, which would *vary* from person to person as it is self-engaged in constitutive acts creating temporal relations. Thus, it heralds the possibility of a lonely, individual time, since time-consciousness would then be constituted by subjective, sensory reproductions in memory. This would make time-consciousness very different in each individual and even different in the same individual at different times. This may be why Kant elected to replace the first edition Deduction, grounded in immanent time-consciousness, with the second edition Deduction as based in the unity of consciousness. We shall return to Kant's discussion of time-consciousness in a moment.

In any case, in the opening passages of his seminal work, *The Monadology*, Leibniz unfolds his major metaphysical and epistemological presuppositions. Drawing on the initial 1–21 sections, we find in paraphrased summation the following defining principles/assumptions.

1: The monad exists as a simple, spatially unextended, unified thinking substance. It is "without parts" and self-constituted; it is an indivisible "spiritual atom" and serves as the fundamental constituent of all existence. Human monads are endowed with apperception, i.e. self-consciousness and hence reason.

4 and 6: Because the monad is immaterial, once it is created by God, it is indestructible and hence immortal. Only God can annihilate it. Monads are constituted as unified souls, minds, selves, or egos.

7: The monad consists of an insular center of restricted activity confined to the self; it is "windowless"; it is unable to reach out beyond its self or interact with other substances. Everything that occurs within the self is thus absolutely self-contained.

However by a "pre-established harmony," God co-ordinates the *appearances* of interaction between the monads. Each monad is only conscious of the universe from its own particular point of view. It reflexively knows itself but only "mirrors" others without any direct contact with an external reality.

8–11: Each monad is conscious within its self of *qualitative temporal changes between varying perceptions* and hence of a subjective time-sequence, which is unique to the monad. The changes are continuous.

13–14: Because of its simple i.e. immaterial nature or essence, it is able to unify various perceptions within its self and recognize these as intrinsically belonging to its self—it is *constituted* as a "multiplicity in unity," a "unity of self-consciousness," as well as a *continuous* personal identity. As *temporal* changes occur within its self, it realizes its uniqueness and its ontological isolation.

16: "We have in our selves experience of a multiplicity in a simple substance, whenever we find that the least thought of which we are conscious involves variety in its object. Thus all those who admit that the soul is a simple substance should admit this [internal perceptual] multiplicity in the Monad."

In order to guard against those who argue that thinking can be the product of material conditions, that senseless matter can think, as Locke suggests, Leibniz offers an arresting analogy by likening the brain to a giant factory or a mill.

17: "Moreover, it must be confessed that *perception* and that which depends upon it are *inexplicable on mechanical grounds,* that is to say, by means of figures [extensions] and motions. And supposing there were a machine, so constructed as to think, feel and have perception, it might be conceived as increased in size, while keeping the same proportions so that one might go into it as a mill. That being so, we should, on examining its interior, find only [material] parts which work upon one another, and never anything by which to explain perception. Thus it is in a simple [unified] substance, and not in a compound or a machine, that perception must be sought for." (emphasis in the original; Leibniz, 1968, pp. 217–228)

Materialism and mechanism always imply physical parts external to each other. Thus, it can never be said that matter "thinks" because if the parts are separable from each other, they can never account for the necessary and universal *unity* which is the very definition of reflexivity. Additionally, Leibniz claims that by analogizing the brain to a factory, entering inside, and viewing all the moving parts, nowhere will we discover consciousness, its activities, or its principle of unity. All we will ever observe are the mechanical features and the moving operations; but the activity of the mind is nowhere to be seen. Many things physically move in the universe, but it doesn't follow that they think. Again, matter is not continuous; it is divisible; but thought is indivisible and continuous according to Leibniz.

Lastly:

21: There are continuous unconscious thoughts below the threshold of awareness.

Consequently, Leibniz posits a continuous *personal* unconscious and maintains against Locke (and later Hume) that the soul *always* thinks. If so, then it follows from the simplicity premise and its conclusion that *both* the identity *and* the continuity of the self are guaranteed by the unconscious (Mijuskovic, 1975); Bobro, 2004, pp. 47–48.

Leibniz's monad demonstrates a major advantage over Descartes's *cogito* because it is full; it's a plenum of varying levels of perceptual contents and monadic activities, whereas for Descartes the pure ego (I think–I exist) is absolutely clear, that is, empty. Against Locke's views, Leibniz proposes that there are continuous gradations, transitional levels of consciousness starting at conception and progressing through gestation, appetition, desire, perception, apperception, and culminating in the mind's ability to reason. As soon as the embryo is alive, beginning with conception, it is active. To be alive is to be consciously and continuously active at *some* level. For Leibniz, the temporal and developmental continuity of consciousness parallels the ontological continuity of "the Great Chain of Being" foretold in Plato's *Timaeus* and historically documented in Lovejoy's classic, *The Great Chain of Being*. Additionally, during Leibniz's time, both the telescope and the microscope were discovering infinite worlds in both directions. That the mind exemplifies both unity and continuity Leibniz holds to be essential features of self-consciousness. As he asserts, "Nature makes no leaps." There is neither a vacuum in Nature nor a void in Consciousness. Were things to appear and disappear randomly, discontinuously, human consciousness would be radically different than it is, if even conceivable. Kant will follow Leibniz in both of these assumptions (Mijuskovic, 1974c). If Leibniz is on the right track, then it follows that the self or ego is isolated from other selves.

Nevertheless, the problem with Leibniz is that the monads are *absolutely* self-contained. That's a major difficulty, to say the least. Loneliness *means* a powerful *desire*, in effect, the most imperative motivational *drive* in human beings to be with another *actual* self-conscious being, distinct but essentially related to one's self. That's an innate, *a priori* human demand. Leibniz's "solution" of a preestablished harmony orchestrated in *deus ex machina* fashion by God has no semblance of persuasion. As Hume later said of Berkeley, it's a system that admits of no refutation but produces no conviction.

Hume's Disintegrating "Self." Hume's twin masters are the skeptics Montaigne and Bayle. The roots of his skepticism are to be found in their writings. Returning once more to the materialist and empiricist traditions, we find Hume's (problematic) dual commitments to both principles. In *A Treatise of Human Nature*, Section V, *Of the immateriality of the soul*, Hume (inconsistently with his own earlier proclamations) asserts: "we may certainly conclude, that [physical] motion may be, and actually is, the cause of thought and [mental] perception." (Previously, he had entertained everything and anything as a speculative possibility.) By translating all consciousness into mental perceptions, consisting of immediate impressions (Locke's sensations) and ideas as their fainter and less vivacious copies, Hume accounts for both our *belief* in the "external existence" of the world as well as in our *belief* in the "self" along phenomenalist lines. Both, he argues, are actually *constructions* manufactured from atomistic *mental* sense impressions (or as they were later designated, *sense data* or *qualia* in terms of what subsequently commentators have described as his "atomistic psychology"). Accordingly, in the section *Of personal identity*, he argues that there is no *substantial* self, no single or unique impression of the self (and it follows of course that there is neither a Cartesian *cogito* nor a Leibnizian monad). Hume, as Locke and Berkeley before him, is a nominalist; only *particular* impressions, ideas, or, in general, perceptions exist. It is to be noted that Hume is clearly avoiding the term "sensation" because of Locke's confusion over whether they are mental or physical; accordingly, he prefers the terms "impression," "idea," and "perception" in order to mark their status as *mental* entities. Nevertheless, as an empiricist and similarly to Locke, the mind is initially only furnished by *simple, singular* impressions. The "self" is thus analyzed and described as a contingent construction or composition of distinct impressions loosely held together, if at all. Often this is described as Hume's "bundle theory of the self." The problem is that the "bundle" replaces the self; there is no self. His famous discussion *Of personal identity* follows.

For my part, when I enter most intimately into what I call *myself*, I always stumble on some particular perception or other, of heat or cold, light or shade, love or hatred, pain or pleasure. I never catch *myself* at any time without a perception, and never can observe anything but the perception. When my *perceptions* are remov'd for any time, as by sound sleep; so long as I am insensible of *myself*, and may truly be said not to exist. . . . If anyone upon serious and unprejudic'd reflexion, thinks he has a different notion of *himself*, I confess I can no longer reason with him. . . . He may, perhaps, perceive something simple and continu'd, which he may call *himself*, tho' I am certain there is no such principle in me. But setting aside some metaphysicians [i.e., idealists and rationalists] of this kind, I may venture of the rest of mankind, that they are nothing but a bundle or collection of different perceptions which *succeed* each other with an inconceivable rapidity, and are in perpetual flux and movement. Our eyes cannot turn in their sockets without varying our perceptions. Our thought is still more variable than our sight; and all our other senses and faculties contribute to this change. . . . The mind is a kind of theatre, where several perceptions *successively* make their appearance, pass, repass, glide away, and mingle in an infinite variety of postures and situations. There is properly no *simplicity* in it at one time, nor *identity in different;* whatever natural propension we may have to imagine that simplicity and identity. (Hume, 1973, i, iv, vi)

The mistaken rationalist concept of the self, as Hume concludes, is a meaningless metaphysical fiction with no foundation whatsoever in the empirical, sensory world. The erroneous notion of the self as a "simplicity and identity," Hume proposes, actually consists of a centerless, Heraclitean flux of impressions, which *succeed* each other with an inconceivable rapidity. In addition, Hume offers the metaphor of the theater to account for our illusion of the self. The mind's experiences can be analogized to watching a stage before which transitory, fleeting impressions appear and glide away as actors programmed never to repeat their roles (Mijuskovic, 1971b, 324–336). But it is this admission of a temporal succession, of an awareness of time-consciousness, however, that will provide Kant with one of his two answers to Hume's rejection of a unified consciousness and a reflexive self.

There exists for Hume, however, a *psychological belief,* a *feeling of anticipation* that the self persists; it is a natural "fiction" (as opposed to the metaphysical fiction of a permanent soul) based in the imagination that serves us practically and ethically for the purposes of life. And yet, later in Hume's Appendix to the *Treatise,* he makes frank admission of his confusion in endorsing two conflicting principles: (a) each impression is distinct and therefore separate; and *yet* (b) there seems to be a unity binding them all together in *one* and the *same* consciousness (Appendix to the *Treatise,* p. 636). And, as he himself realizes, he can't have it both ways and thus pleads the privilege of a skeptic in the end and probably would have endorsed Montaigne's celebrated motto: Que sais-je?" "What do I know?"

Three things are worth observing in Hume's critique of the self: (a) there is no permanent self, and hence there is no continuity to the self— that is, the self is not a substance; (b) perceptions are not *self*-conscious— instead, they are consciousnesses of something other than the self, namely, discrete impressions/sensations or ideas; *but* (c) there is an awareness of *succession, of a successive series of temporal changes, of perceptual movements present to the mind.* It is (c), this admission of temporal change that will allow Kant to argue that one cannot be aware of time-consciousness, of *succession* unless there is a unitary self to connect the temporal moments of past-present-future in the *same* self-consciousness.

In order to see more clearly the issue and what is at stake in Hume's phenomenalist and nominalist description of a dissolving self, we need to follow his lead by jumping ahead to our present time. Hume's misgivings about both the self and self-consciousness result in a doctrine of the "unobserved observer" or the "unscanned scanner," which strikes a sympathetic chord in the contemporary Australian philosopher, D. M. Armstrong, and similarly leads to the denial of the possibility of self-consciousness. It is also here that we can appreciate the difference between (a) Locke's, Hume's, and Armstrong's "reflection," which essentially consists of a passive observation of present and past sensory experiences and (b) Leibniz's paradigm of the activity of genuine self-consciousness or reflexion, which intrinsically unifies the self.

In the case of perception, we must distinguish between the perceiving, which is a mental event, from the thing perceived, which is something physical. In the case of introspection we must similarly distinguish between the introspecting and the things introspected. Confusion is all the more easy in the latter because both are mental states of the same mind. Nevertheless, although they are both mental states, it is impossible that the thing introspecting and the thing introspected should be one and the same mental state. A mental state cannot be aware of itself any more than a man can eat himself up. The introspection may itself be the object of a further introspective awareness, and so on, but since the capacity of the mind is finite, the chain of introspective awareness of introspections must terminate in an introspection that is not an object of introspective awareness. If we make the materialist identification of mental states with material states of the brain, we can say that introspection is a self-scanning process in the brain. The scanning operation may itself be scanned, and so on, but we must in the end reach an unscanned scanner. (Armstrong, 1968, p. 324)

Notice that Armstrong claims that self-consciousness, reflexion is impossible because "the mind is finite." But this is precisely why the idealists and rationalists posit the paradigm of the mind as *circular,* with both subject and object revolving around each other in mutual or equal co-dependence. Both the Cartesian and the Kantian unities of consciousness assume or posit the unity of the self with its own thoughts. They both go back to Aristotle's principle in the *Metaphysics:* "I think my own thoughts."

In the passage above, Armstrong is stuck, as Locke before him, by the question of whether sensations are physical or mental. Presumably he wants to say, as Locke seems to have intended before him, that as *causes* sensations are physical but as *effects* they are mental. But that won't fly because it still involves Locke and Armstrong in the mind–body paradox. In short, Armstrong has the same difficulty as Locke and Hume before him. If he defines sensations as *immediate* modes of consciousness, as mental entities directly present to or within consciousness, then, according to Montaigne's challenge, he must tell us *how* he can inferentially proceed to what is mediate, namely, the brain, which is presumably physical, not mental. If all I can directly know are my own ideas, and my ideas are *representations* of something that is not an idea, how can I claim my ideas are immediate presentations—as opposed to *re*-presentations—of something completely different from ideas, namely, the brain? And if ideas are mental alone, then in principle they cannot tell us anything about what is external and physical independently of the mind. If, in addition, both the introspecting and the introspected are mental, what justifies us in declaring that we can then go on *"to make the materialist identification of mental states with material states of the brain"*? (Mijuskovic, 1976, pp. 292–306).

A century earlier, Auguste Comte, the father of sociology, similarly rejects the possibility of "introspection" or any psychological internal knowledge of the self on the grounds that the instrument of observation (the mind) and the object of observation (the mind) cannot be the same. Differently put, if, for example, we compare the observer first to a mirror, then to a camera, and finally to a flashlight, we realize that a mirror cannot reflect itself, a camera cannot take a picture of itself, and a flashlight cannot shine on itself. But, again, without both a meaningful concept of the self and reflexivity, loneliness seems a contradiction in terms. In any case, the important point is that the notion of an unattached loneliness "out there somewhere" without a determinate mind or self to anchor it is absolutely paradoxical. If there is such an experience as loneliness, there must be *someone, a subject, a self* to experience it. How else to account for the feeling of isolation when feeling lonely in the midst of a crowd, in a teeming sea of humanity? The conclusion once again is that materialism, empiricism, and behaviorism are unable to meaningfully account for the self, reflexion, or loneliness.

And when Hume metaphorically compares the mind to the stage of a theater upon which the impressions play their roles never to reappear in their own bright costumes, he forgets the audience: *who* is watching the stage?

Finally, in order to conclude our present discussion of Hume in the context of loneliness, it's also illuminating to note that despite Hume's rejection of a substantial self, he affirms in the strongest terms possible the human affliction of loneliness, acknowledges its distress, and praises the indelible passion in human nature toward friendship as the highest intrinsic value attainable by man. He may be skeptical about the substantial reality of the self, but he expresses no doubts or hesitation about the value and need for friendship and intimacy.

In all creatures, that prey not upon others . . . there appears a remarkable desire of company, which associates them together without any advantages they can ever propose to reap from their union. This is still more conspicuous in man as being the creature of the universe, who has the most ardent desire of society, and is fitted for it by the most advantages. We can form no wish, which has not a reference to society. A perfect solitude is perhaps, the greatest punishment we can suffer. Every pleasure languishes when enyoy'd a-part from company, and every pain becomes more cruel and intolerable. (*Treatise*, II, ii, v; Mijuskovic, 1981, 69–78)

Kant, Time-Consciousness, and the Empirical Self. How do we know the self is real, substantial; indeed, that there is any such entity as the "self"? The answer to Hume—as well as to Armstrong—comes from Kant's two versions of the Transcendental Deductions (1781 and 1787) and the Second Paralogism (1781) in the *Critique of Pure Reason* (Kant, 1958). And it is Hume, by the way, whom Kant credits in his 1783 *Prolegomena to Any Future Metaphysics* for awakening him from his "dogmatic slumber," his preceding one-sided rationalist, Leibnizian convictions (Kant, 1950, p. 8).

As Kemp Smith suggests, in an epistemic context there are only three mutually exclusive plausible candidates for a secure and self-evident starting point, for an indubitable *a priori* principle grounding a theory of knowledge: the existence of the external world (materialism); the existence of the self (Descartes); and the awareness of *internal* time-consciousness (Kant). The first two are vulnerable and fall under the weight of Hume's impressive and thoughtful skeptical attacks. Therefore, by a process of simple elimination, we are left with the third, consciousness of time, of change, of succession. Even if all is appearance, an internal awareness of the passage of time cannot be denied (Kemp Smith, 1962, pp. 241–242).

In what follows I don't want to lose the reader in a barrage of technicalities. Simply what's at stake is that I am trying to prove as persuasively as I can that there must be a viable self and that it is self-conscious in order for human beings to experience loneliness. Kant's two strong arguments in behalf of the empirical self, the phenomenal subjects are dependent on two different *self-evident* premises, both of which I consider to be valid: (1) The mind experiences consciousness of temporal activities, time-consciousness; and (2) the mind is self-conscious of unifying activities.

Together they point to a doctrine of an insular, hermitic loneliness. If I'm granted that, the rest is fluff, albeit important fluff.

As we have observed in his analysis of personal identity, Hume admits to a consciousness of a *temporal succession*. Against Hume, Kant accordingly argues that one cannot be aware of immanent time-consciousness unless there is a self. In his 1781 version of the Transcendental Deduction, immanent time-consciousness is described as constituted by internal synthetic activities and structures within the mind (Leibniz), and the activity threads itself through a consciousness of "changes," which are temporally structured and recognized as such by reflexive consciousness. As we have previously indicated, this immanent consciousness of a temporal flow is diametrically opposed to the scientific conception of time as (presumably) the external and objective measure of motion based on the movement of bodies through empty space as proposed by Aristotle and Newton. Consequently, Kant grounds one of his two "ultimate" premises in the *Critique* on the mind's *internal* flow of time, on immanent time-consciousness. Hume, of course, as we have just seen, admits to a temporal succession.

Whatever the origin of our representations, whether they are due to the influence of outer [material] things, or are produced through inner [mental] causes, whether they arise *a priori* or being appearances only have an empirical origin, they must all, as modifications of the mind, belong to inner [temporal] sense. All our knowledge is thus subject to time, the formal condition of inner sense. In it they must all be ordered, connected and brought into relation. This is a general observation which, throughout what follows, must be borne in mind as quite fundamental. (*Critique*, A 99)

Kant is saying that *all* empirical self-awareness, whether internally generated or externally caused, whether illusionary or real, is subject to time; the mind is *a priori*, intrinsically permeated by time. Conscious awareness of a temporal flow cannot be denied. In effect, Kant demonstrates the existence of an indubitable unitary self through a "back-door approach" by maintaining that time-consciousness exhibits a relationally-synthesized series of temporal moments, an integrated, constitutive relation of past–present–future grounded in a single transcendental unity of apperception. This threefold-relation turns out to be universal, necessary, and mutually implicative, and consequently constitutes a synthetic *a priori* unity. It follows that there is a self and that it is self-aware of changes; it is cognizant of a temporal flow or stream of representations. More specifically, it is constituted by a threefold transcendental synthesis. The peculiar terms are unimportant. What is essential is that Kant is struggling to describe how the mind *temporally* binds something as its own, how it holds it together, and unifies it; how the mind apprehends the present in intuition, retains it in memory through the *re-productive empirical* imagination, and then synthesizes the two prior moments self-consciously by grasping, comprehending them together as its own creation in conception (*Critique*, A 99 ff.). The conclusion follows: A temporally extended self is required as a necessary and universal condition for the self both to exist and to be self-conscious. Because this temporal structure, with its unique perceived re-productive content and "empirical" awareness of changes varies from individual to individual, it follows that immanent time is (a) lonely time; and (2) this form of subjective time-consciousness cannot be shared with any other self. It further follows that personal time-consciousness points in the direction of a lonely, self-contained self. I would further submit that in the context of the infant's developmental history, the child is self-aware, in some significant sense, of time-consciousness, of changes in its field of awareness *before* it is conscious of a realm of independent objects in relation to its self.

Both Schopenhauer and Kemp Smith believe that the first edition Deduction with its grounding premise of time-consciousness is the stronger of the two editions. It's also worth recalling in this context St. Augustine's "syntheses" of past-present-future time-consciousness that we previously presented in Chapter 2. This passage in Kant undoubtedly influenced Husserl's theory of internal time-consciousness.

Kant's theory of space and time in the Aesthetic of a pure universal form of intuitional sensibility seems to have few defenders (although Schopenhauer appears to be one). It was designed by Kant to ground his theory of mathematical systems in support of Newtonian physics as consisting of synthetic judgments *a priori*, but it is clearly untenable. Mathematical and geometrical axioms are analytically valid. But by contrast, his treatment of time-consciousness, I believe, demands serious consideration (Mijuskovic, 2010, pp. 105–132).

The key to synthetic productivity is "spontaneity" *(Spontaneitat).* Kant discusses spontaneity no less than a dozen times throughout the *Critique*. It is *creative*; it produces thought and self-consciousness out of its own internal resources. In effect, it is uncaused. It is responsible for the production of the categories, the structures of relation (A 50–B 74). It creates time-consciousness (A 99), and it produces not only thought itself but it is also responsible for the unity of consciousness as well. Spontaneity-creation is not itself a pure relational or conceptual category, but it is the underlying *source,* the originator of Kant's twelve categories constituting the faculty of the understanding. Classically, the concept of spontaneity is indebted to theism: God creates the world and souls *ex nihilo.* But this spontaneity could just as well occur, as Hume suggests in our Preface, among natural physical entities or agents. For aught we know, as he speculates, anything can produce anything, and also, therefore, something immaterial can arise from something material. Reason in this universe of conceivabilities is powerless either to guide or to restrain us. Anything is imaginable, possible, or conceivable that does not entail a logical contradiction (Hume).

Before we turn to Kant's second answer to Hume, there is something worth mentioning regarding the above discussion, namely, the growing emphasis on time-consciousness eventually presenting it as a "stream of consciousness," an internal temporal flow, which essentially derives from Kant's first edition discussion of immanent time. This accounts for why not only philosophers, like Schopenhauer in *The World as Will and Representation,* C. S. Peirce in "How to Make Our Ideas Clear," Husserl in *The Phenomenology of Internal-Time Consciousness,* William James in *The Principles of Psychology,* Henri Bergson in *Time and Free Will,* Heidegger in *Being and Time,* and Sartre in *Being and Nothingness* and many others, as well as novelists like James Joyce in *A Portrait of the Artist as a Young Man* and *Ulysses,* William Faulkner in *As I Lay Dying* and *The Sound and the Fury,* and Thomas Wolfe in *Look Homeward, Angel,* to name a few, are collectively captivated in describing temporality as an immanent stream or flow of awareness. In the novelists mentioned, it is transformed into a lonely time, a temporal inner meandering of the self through its own intimate corridors and chambers within its unique residence. It's worth remarking that Wolfe, in *Time and the River* (LXXV), actually presents an impressive and sophisticated variety of philosophical insights in regard to time, an obvious indication that he was seriously concerned about its epistemological status and its relation to the novel form of narrative. And it's Kant's treatment he emphasizes in his discussion of time (Mijuskovic, 1978).

Time the form of the internal sense, and space the form of the external sense [Kant]. Within a definite limited interval of duration known as the specious present there is a direct perception of temporal relations [Bergson?]. After an event has passed beyond the specious present it can only enter consciousness by reproductive memory. Temporal experience divided into three qualitatively distinct intervals: the remembered past, the perceived specious present, and the anticipated future—By means of the tripartite division we are able to inject our present selves into the temporal stream of our own experience . . . Thus time has its roots in experience and yet appears to be a dimension in which experiences and their contents are to be arranged [structured].

Kant, the Unity of Consciousness, and the Empirical Self. The heart of the *Critique of Pure Reason* is the Transcendental Deduction, but the odd thing is that there are *two* Deductions and thus *two* hearts, two differing premises. Nevertheless, it is in these two sections that Kant "deduces," justifies, or proves the underlying conditions, the transcendental activities and structures that make both ordinary human consciousness and Newtonian empirical science possible. Crucial, of course, to his transcendental justification or "deduction" for the possibility of human experience is *the* establishment of a self-evident premise to the entire Kantian system, but, as we have just intimated, there seem to be *two* different premises and therefore two Deductions. The premise in the first edition Deduction (1781) is immanent time-consciousness as we already know. In the second edition Deduction (1787), however, it's the unity of consciousness. In terms of a Philosophy and Psychology of Loneliness, both are critical because together they confirm my theory of the self as well as acts of refelexion, since universally all *acts* are always time-structured; there is no such thing as an immediate act (presumably apart from God's creative intellectual intuition). In the following chapter, we shall also learn that Husserl's constitutive acts of meaning are similarly grounded in intentionality and thus temporally structured as well.

The second response to Hume is mired in a controversy of Kant's own making when he produces two very similar—virtually identical—versions of the Achilles or *Of Simplicity* argument (1781) *but* for two radically different purposes; first a negative one (1781) and later a positive one (1787). Consequently, the unity of consciousness conclusion appears both in Kant's first edition as the Second Paralogism (1781, A 351 ff.), which Kant rejects and exposes as a rationalist (or "dogmatist") metaphysical fallacy allegedly due to its complete absence of any possible empirical or scientific confirmation. But then, inexplicably, it resurfaces six years later, and the same "proof" or "assertion" puzzlingly reappears in the second edition Deduction in order to secure the self-evident and ultimate transcendental condition for the very possibility of human consciousness (1787, B 131). In other words, first it is a fallacy and half a dozen years later it is the indisputable, self-evident basis constituting the foundational justification for all human knowledge. But notice how the entire context for the argument is initially placed in 1781 against the possibility of "senseless matter being able to think," against materialism, the metaphysical base of behaviorism.

SECOND PARALOGISM: OF SIMPLICITY. This is the Achilles [the most powerful] of all dialectical [or fallacious] inferences in the pure doctrine of the soul. It is no mere sophistical play, contrived by a dogmatist [i.e., a *pure* rationalist, e.g., Leibniz] to impart to his assertions a superficial plausibility, but an inference which appears to withstand even the keenest scrutiny and the most scrupulously exact investigation. It is as follows.

Every [material] composite, or whatever inheres in it as thus composite, is an aggregate of several actions or accidents, distributed among the plurality of the substances. Now an effect which arises from the concurrence of many acting substances is indeed possible, namely, when this effect is external only (as, for instance, the motion of a body is the combined motion of all its parts). But with thoughts as internal [mental] accidents belonging to a thinking being, it is different. For suppose it be the composite that thinks: then every part of it would be part of the thought, and all of them taken together would contain the whole thought. But this cannot be consistently maintained. For representations (for instance, the single words of a verse), distributed among different beings, never make up a whole thought (a verse), and it is therefore impossible that a thought should inhere in what is essentially composite. It is therefore possible only in a *single* substance, which, not being an aggregate of many, is absolutely *simple* [i.e., immaterial]. (*Critique*, A 351–352)

William James boils it down in his characteristic style to its essential elements:

Take a sentence of a dozen words, and take twelve men and tell to each one word. Then stand the men in a row or jam them in a bunch, and let each think of his word as intently as he will; nowhere will there be a consciousness of the whole sentence. (James, 1950, p. I, 160)

Robert Paul Wolff, in his commentary on Kant's second edition Deduction (1787, B 131), unwittingly invokes James's version in order to positively elucidate what Kant means by the unity of consciousness as a *valid* argument, not realizing that Kant himself had earlier summoned it only to reject it. Wolff thus incorrectly attributes the words/verse trick to Brentano, when in fact Kant himself invokes it only to reject it. (I have never been able to locate it in Brentano.) (See Wolff, 1963, p. 106 Mijuskovic, 1973, pp. 156–161).

As Wolff expresses it:

The fact is that one consciousness of twelve words is not the same as twelve consciousnesses of one word each. Following Kant's terminology, we may characterize the difference by saying that the one consciousness binds them together, or conceives them as a [synthetic] unity. These descriptions are metaphorical, but whether or not they can be reduced to literal terms, the state of affairs to which they point seems undeniable. (Wolff, 1963, p. 106)

And I agree. In my view, this is an empirical argument in the respect that it is testable, just as the proposition "All colors are extended" is testable. The entire value of synthetic *a priori* relations and judgments/propositions is their applicability in telling us important features about the world which are logically independent from and "prior" to experience.

And now compare the above with the following passage, which Kant does endorse six years later in 1787.

It must be possible for the 'I think' to accompany [i.e. synthetically unify] all my representations; for otherwise something would be represented in me which could not be a thought at all, and that is equivalent to saying that the representation would be impossible, or at least it would be nothing to me . . . For the manifold representations [e.g., the single words of a verse] . . . would not be one and all *my* representations, if they did not all belong to one self-consciousness. As *my* representations (even if I am not conscious of them as such) they must conform to the condition under which alone they *can* stand together in one universal self-consciousness because otherwise they would not all without exception belong to me. (Kant, 1958; B 131–132)

Once more, I believe, this is also an *empirical* proof because it's verifiable. How else could we move from a synthetic *a priori* context to an empirical confirmation? That's the virtue of synthetic *a priori* relations; they inform us about experience independently of the experience. They tell us that "All colors are extended" and that it is pointless to empirically search for a color that is not extended.

Another simpler way of making the point about the unity of consciousness is the following: How is it—short of insanity—that I *know* that certain sensations, feelings, and thoughts are *mine* and not yours unless there is an active dynamic unity to *my* self-consciousness? How is it that I don't mistake *your* thoughts for *mine*? It follows that there is a self and that it is self-aware of its own activities and contents or "representations" in Kant's terminology. The only element missing in the second version is the reference to the verse and its single words, which I have inserted in brackets without disturbing the flow of the argument. To emphasize: The exegetical problem is that in 1781, the Achilles is a fallacy; and half-a-dozen years later, it's the first and last word on which the entire positive section of the *Critique of Pure Reason* is grounded.

At this point, it's interesting to inquire, what might Freud's solution be in terms of accounting for "the unity of consciousness"? Actually, what Freud proposes of all things is the psychic energy of Love: "the main purpose of Eros—that of uniting and binding—in so far as it helps toward establishing the unity, or tendency to unity, which is particularly characteristic of the 'ego' is accomplished by Love" (Freud, 1960, p. 35). We have replaced Isis or Athena with Aphrodite! But once more, unless we have a positive and plausible theory of human consciousness, it's futile to address the question of loneliness, its extent, its force, its motivational power, and its possible "remedies."

Beyond the foregoing self-evident dual premises—time-consciousness and the unity of consciousness—supportive of a theory of human reflexivity, Kant proceeds to argue that *both* the phenomenal/empirical self *and* the phenomenal/empirical object mutually condition or constitute each other. This result is the outcome of Kant's contention that a pure transcendental unity of apperception is mutually constituted or conditioned by an underlying transcendental object—x (A 104–110). There can be no self-consciousness without a realm of objects and no objects without a conscious self. Whether we require this "doubling" feature, I leave to others to decide. In any event, Kant reaffirms his position in the second edition *Refutation of Idealism* that self-consciousness can only occur if there is something permanent in time set against it, "a *thing* outside me" (*Critique*, B 275–276). Further, according to Kant's Copernican Revolution, the noumenal world has to conform to the synthetic *a priori* structures of the mind (*Critique*, B xvi-xvii). Self and object are thus in a mutually reciprocal synthetic *a priori* relation.

How does this reciprocal relation of self and object mesh with a psychological outlook? We recall that Mahler previously indicated and confirmed that the self is *initially* self-conscious of objects, for example, the breast, *before* and *apart* from the consciousness of other egos or selves, including the mother (Chapter 1). In saying this, I believe Mahler is confirming something Freud himself emphasizes in perfect harmony with Kant. (Freud's relation to Kant is often regarded as minimal, when in fact it may have been substantial (Brook, 2003).

Further reflection tells us that the adult's ego cannot be the same from the beginning. It must have gone through a process of development, which cannot of course, be demonstrated but which admits of being constructed [or inferred] with a fair degree of probability. An infant at his mother's breast does not as yet distinguish his ego from the external world as the source of his sensations flowing upon him. He gradually learns to do so, in response to various promptings. He must be very strongly impressed by the fact that some sources of excitation he will later recognize as his own bodily organs, can provide him with the sensations at any moment, whereas other sources evade him from time to time—among them what he desires most of all, his mother's breast [as an object]—and only reappear as a result of his screaming for help. In this way, there is for the first time set over against the "ego" an object, in the form of something which "exists outside" and which is only forced to appear by a special action. (Freud, 1961, pp. 14–15)

I take Freud to be saying here that the ego is aware of inanimate objects, including the mother's breast as an object, *before it is aware of the other self, of the mother as a person, as an independent self.* If so, this means that primordially the relation of self–object connected and constituted prior, that is, in advance to the relation of self–other–subject–mother. Since we are engaged in establishing a Philosophy and Psychology of Loneliness, this is critical. It means that the self is innately present and feels and knows its self to be alone *before* it is socially engaged with another living self. If this is the case, it follows that this initial realization of separation will follow us as the archetypal paradigm for all future separation anxieties. In the deep despair of loneliness, the self feels the entire world is a stranger, a lifeless realm of inanimate, unfeeling beings (Carazan's nightmare). Again, we recall in this context Mahler's study that indicates the infant is cognizant of objects as long as ten months *before* it is aware of the mother. It also means that the *frustration* it experiences in this stage is not yet consciously directed at a living being, and only later will it be discharged as *anger* at a definite person or indiscriminately at other selves. Accordingly, there may be a phenomenological difference between frustration and hostility. When we are frustrated it is because impersonal objects or events have thwarted our desires and goals. When we are angry, the target of our displeasure is a human subject or subjects.

As far as Kant's thoughts on human loneliness are concerned, they are more than amply confirmed by his retelling of Carazan's dream (Introduction). I am unaware of Kant having devoted as much time and space on any other passage as this one in his body of writings, a clear indication of how impressed he is at the despair encountered by rational beings when confronted with ultimate and irredeemable loneliness. Kant himself was very religious and belonged to the Pietist sect.

Recently, there seems to be a case of what for all intents and purposes is virtually a "feral child" discovered in Florida. A six-year-old girl was found living with her mother and two much older male siblings. She was neglected to an extreme degree; she was unable to feed herself; she was still wearing diapers and covered in her own feces and sores; she was unable to speak and was completely unresponsive to all efforts at communication by words or signs; she was severely withdrawn and took no notice of people around her who were trying to minister to her needs; and she displayed no apparent interest in her external surroundings. She was immediately removed from the home by Child Protective Services and although she was eventually adopted by a loving couple at the age of eight, her progress for the past several years has been very limited. It's as if that first stage of subject–object separation or possibly object–object separation never went forward developmentally (DeGregory, 2013). Apparently, she did not exhibit the usual features of autism. One can only speculate how all this may affect her further development. Harlow, of course, rather unfeelingly experimented with monkeys, which were completely isolated from other monkeys, and by report they were highly dysfunctional as a result. Obviously, an impaired or delayed transition period from the subject—object relationship to subject—subject/mother relationship is crucial in terms of healthy human development. This may suggest that children who remain neglected for extended periods of time in early childhood may display severe feelings of loneliness along with anger, anxiety, self-harm, and destructive impulses that may be irreversible. Just as there is an optimal period in children's development to learn a language and beyond that time it is much more difficult to master it, just so there is an optimal time to bond, to belong to another self. And once missed or delayed there may be severe consequences.

The Resilience of "The Achilles." In any case, it's difficult to make a plausible case for the unity of consciousness if all one has to work with are material bodies and aggregates of lifeless atoms and brain cells. How can senseless matter think? How can matter and motion *alone* cause consciousness? The point is that it is one thing to propose that minds are *dependent* on material conditions, with which assertion I wholeheartedly agree, but quite another matter to claim that minds are completely *identical with, reducible to,* or *explainable by* brain motion. I can assent to the former proposition and yet reject the latter. I openly admit no one can *think* without a brain but that is not the same as to say thought is *nothing but* the brain, that consciousness can be eliminated as a metaphysical, meaningless concept and that we can substitute thinking with "brain motion." It seems to me that thoughts exist and that they are rather different from rocks. Whoever heard of an idea or a thought six inches deep, a foot in length, and weighing seven pounds (Cudworth)?

In any case, both versions of Kant's unity of consciousness argument confirm the insularity of the mind and its reflexive activity, in short, its loneliness. Therefore, as far as our discussion of loneliness is concerned, it's irrelevant whether Kant compromised his earlier position with the later one, since both versions begin with the same premise and arrive at the same conclusion. Rather, the only important issue for our purposes is that both the Second Paralogism in the A edition (regarding the unity of consciousness), the Deductions in A (concerning time-consciousness), and/or B (regarding the unity of consciousness) all serve as a rejection of behaviorism by attributing to the mind certain activities and structures resulting in an immanent sense of time-consciousness as well as a monadic unity and insularity—in short, its loneliness. I believe materialism, empiricism, and behaviorism have no answer to the idealist/dualist and rationalist model of the mind's activities and structures.

Kant criticizes all four first edition Paralogims regarding the soul as metaphysically untenable, nonempirical, unverifiable, and hence unscientific. The four theses claim that the self is a substance; consciousness is a unity (the Achilles); personal identity is continuous; and consciousness conditions all possible human existence and awareness (idealism). All four are grounded in the Simplicity Argument, in the immaterial nature of consciousness premise (Mijuskovic, 2009, pp. 229–252). Finally, it's worth mentioning that the Second Paralogism in A comes in for special criticism by Kant because of its pivotal and singularly persuasive force in the chronicles of historical idealism and rationalism. In all this, however, Kant may have thrown out the rational baby and kept a surplus of empirical bathwater. By the way, interestingly enough, the *only* two sections of the *Critique* that were completely recast for the second edition were the Paralogisms and the Deductions. Could it be that Kant realized that he had undercut his own arguments about the unity of consciousness and thus decided to restructure them and eliminate the first edition Achilles?

One unanswered question remains: Why did Kant abandon the first edition Deduction and substitute the second in its place? We have already suggested a possibility, namely, that the involvement of an *empirical* imaginative reproductive content implicated in time-consciousness vitiates it as a pure synthetic *a priori* activity. The productive imagination is spontaneous, creative, virtually "unconditioned"; but the re-productive imagination is "compromised" by an involvement in "impure" sensuous contents. Thus, for instance, the transcendental unity of apperception and the twelve categories of the faculty of the understanding are all pure, formal, that is, nonsensuous structures. But the threefold temporal synthesis involving the *re*-productive imagination introduces a decidedly empirical element, and thus it empirically follows that each person's subjective time- sequence will be very different! But of course, for our purposes in understanding loneliness, I believe it only reinforces my contentions that we are each of us temporally alone.

In summation: In answer to Leibniz's solipsistic position, which insists on the complete independence of the monad, Kant argues on both the transcendental and empirical level that the concept of the self is *mutually constituted* or *conditioned* by the concept of an object. There can be no empirical knowledge of the self without the simultaneous contrast of a realm of opposing objects. In developmental terms, Freud states the same as we have seen. The difference is that Kant is working from the perspective of a mature person and Freud from the developmental standpoint of the infant. To highlight a further difference, whereas Kant and Freud hold that the self and the object mutually presuppose or condition each other, Hegel instead maintains that the self is mutually conditioned by other selves. This is why I claim that Kant's position is similar in this regard to Freud's intrapsychic approach rather than to Hegel's interpersonal line of argument with its dependence on the dialectic of the master-slave relationship. Again, Kant and Freud assume an intrapsychic and psychological perspective, whereas Hegel decidedly affirms more of an interpersonal and sociological perspective. But even so, Hegel likewise intimates that in the prior dialectical stages or moments of Perception, the perceiver and the object perceived constitute each other. In fact, all three prior moments of consciousness—Sense Certainty, Perception, and Understanding—seem to be singularly one-sided, and all three precede the Lordship and Bondage conflict, which produces self-consciousness.

Finally, Thomas Lennon and Edward Stainton, in their study, *The Achilles of Rationalist Psychology*, graciously credit my *Achilles* with an important acknowledgment.

What remains surprising, however, is that so little work has been done before on the Achilles argument. Ben Lazare Mijuskovic's pioneering work was the first in modern times to draw the attention to the importance of the argument, but aside from the subsequent work he has done, there is little else in print. (Lennon and Stainton, 2008, p. 2)

But the problem once more lies in their unduly restrictive manner of only considering the Achilles or Simplicity Argument in the context of its unity of consciousness application, when in fact it has multiple uses and more specifically and importantly these uses are integrally involved in a viable theory of loneliness. Unfortunately, by confining their discussion solely to considering Kant's discussion of the *Achilles* in the context of his arguments surrounding the unity of consciousness, the editors and fifteen authors have neglected the greater historical scope and its impressive distribution as well as its probative value in discussions surrounding its other vital implementations. This is why early on I switched and rechristened it from the Achilles Argument to the Simplicity Argument because in truth its real force derives from its commitment to the multiple defenses of subjective idealism and its rejection of crude reductive materialism and behaviorism. Its role in the unity of consciousness is only one of its subsets. Thus, if one views the simplicity premise and its several arguments and conclusions as *the* challenge of idealism against materialism and behaviorism, it can be shown that the multifaceted, many-faced Achilles serves as an extremely relevant factor within discussions of loneliness. Soon one also realizes how much more is at stake in this controversy between creative idealism and reductive materialism. Unless the simplicity premise is expanded to include its other uses, what is lost is its involvement in discussions concerning the transcendental conditions for self-consciousness, the unity of the self, the identity of the self, the origin and epistemological status of meanings and relations, the consciousness of freedom, time-consciousness, the unconscious, and how they all relate in understanding the dynamics of loneliness. These are all implicated issues originating from the Simplicity Argument, and therefore I believe they warrant serious reconsideration. Accordingly, I think the difficulty with Lennon's and Stainton's line of thought is that the editors unfortunately restrict themselves by exclusively focusing on the unity of consciousness theme alone. What is lost is the incredible versatility of the argument from simplicity throughout the history of Western philosophy. At the start of this study, I mentioned the History of Ideas discipline. One of its great advantages is that it crystallizes, unifies, and identifies principles and arguments that appear and reappear time and again in multiple guises throughout the history of Western thought in various disciplines and guises and are reiterated, deepened, and expanded but also vigorously challenged and criticized by many, many scholars and writers of different persuasions and principles. Today unquestionably materialism, empirical science, behaviorism, psychiatric medications, and technology hold the field of battle in mental health in the United States. Nevertheless, I am convinced that the roots of behaviorism are shallow, that the trunk is soft, and that it bears little edible fruit.

REFERENCES

Aaron, R. (1955). *John Locke.* Oxford, UK: Clarendon Press.

Armstrong, D. M. (1968). *A Materialist Theory of Mind.* New York: Routledge & Kegan Paul.

Bobro, M. (2004). *Self and Substance in Leibniz.* Dordrecht: Kluwer.

Brook, A. (2003). Freud and Kant. In *Psychoanalytic Knowledge.* Cheung, M. & Feltman, C. (Eds.). New York: Macmillan.

DeGregory, L. (2013). The girl in the window. *Tampa Bay Times,* October 15.

Descartes, R. (1955). *The Philosophical Works of Descartes.* Haldane, E. & Ross, G. R. T. (Trans.) New York: Dover, I, *Meditations of First Philosophy*, Meditations I and II.

Freud, S. (1949). *An Outline of Psychoanalysis.* New York: W. W. Norton.

Freud, S. (1960). *The Ego and the Id.* New York: W. W. Norton.

Freud, S. (1961). *Civilization and Its Discontents.* New York: W. W. Norton.

Hegel, G. W. F. (1968). *Hegel's Lectures on the History of Philosophy.* London: Routledge & Kegan Paul.

Hume, D. (1973). *A Treatise of Human Nature.* Oxford, UK: Oxford University Press.

James, W. (1950). *The Principles of Psychology.* New York: Dover.

Kant, I. (1950). *Prolegomena to Any Future Metaphysics.* New York: Liberal Arts Press.

Kant, I. (1958). *Immanuel Kant's* Critique of Pure Reason. Kemp Smith, N. (Trans.). London: Macmillan & Co.

Kemp Smith, N. (1962). *A Commentary to Kant's* Critique of Pure Reason. New York: Humanities Press.

Leibniz. (1968). *The Monadology and Other Philosophical Writings.* Latta, R. (Trans.) London: Oxford University Press.

Lennon, T. & Stainton, E. (Eds.). (2008). *The Achilles of Rationalist Psychology.* New York: Springer.

Locke, J. (1959). *An Essay Concerning Human Understanding.* New York: Dover.

Mackie, J. (1976). *Problems from Locke.* Oxford, UK: Clarendon Press.

Mijuskovic, B. (1971a). Descartes's Bridge to the External World: the Piece of Wax. *Studi Internazionali di Filosofia,* III. Reprinted (1996). In *Descartes: Critical Assessments,* Georges Moyal (ed.). Longon: Routledge.

Mijuskovic, B. (1971b). Hume and Shaftesbury on the self. *The Philosophical Quarterly,* 21:85.

Mijuskovic, B. (1973). The premise of the transcendental analytic. *The Philosophical Quarterly,* 23:91.

Mijuskovic, B. (1974). *The Achilles of Rationalist Arguments: The Simplicity, Unity, and Identity of Thought and Soul from the Cambridge Platonists to Kant.* The Hague: Martinus Nijhoff, Chapter Four.

Mijuskovic, B. (1974a). *The Achilles of Rationalist Arguments: The Simplicity, Unity, and Identity of Thought and Soul from the Cambridge Platonists to Kant.* The Hague: Martinus Nijhoff, Chapter Two.

Mijuskovic, B. (1974b). *The Achilles of Rationalist Arguments: The Simplicity, Unity, and Identity of Thought and Soul from the Cambridge Platonists to Kant.* The Hague: Martinus Nijhoff, Chapter Five.

Mijuskovic, B. (1974c). The general conclusion of the argument of the transcendental analytic. *The Southern Journal of Philosophy,* XII:3.

Mijuskovic, B. (1975). Locke and Leibniz on personal identity. *The Southern Journal of Philosophy,* XIII:2.

Mijuskovic, B. (1976). The simplicity argument *versus* a materialist theory of consciousness. *Philosophy Today,* XX:4.

Mijuskovic, B. (1977). Hume on space and time. *Journal of the History of Philosophy,* XV:4, 387–394.

Mijuskovic, B. (1978). Loneliness and time-consciousness. *Philosophy Today,* XXII:4.

Mijuskovic, B. (1981). Loneliness and human nature. *Psychological Perspectives: A Journal of Jungian Thought,* 12:1.

Mijuskovic, B. (2009). The argument from simplicity: A study in the history of an idea and argument. *Philotheos,* 9.

Mijuskovic, B. (2010). Kant's reflections on the unity of consciousness, time-consciousness, and the unconscious. *Kritike,* 4:2.

Peirce, C. S. (1957). *Charles C. Peirce: Essays in the Philosophy of Science.* New York: Liberal Arts Press.

Plato. (1966). *The Collected Dialogues of Plato.* Hamilton, E. & Cairns, E. (Eds.). New York: Pantheon. *Theaetetus.*

Snyder, L. (1994). It's all necessarily so: William Whewell on scientific truth. *Studies in the History and Philosophy of Science,* 25.

Webb, T. E. (1885). *The Veil of Isis: A Series of Essays on Idealism.* Dublin: Dublin University Press.

Wolff, R. P. (1963). *Kant's Theory of Mental Activity: A Commentary on the Transcendental Analytic of the* Critique of Pure Reason. Cambridge, MA: Harvard University Press.

Chapter 4

Loneliness and Phenomenology

As a waiver for the ensuing discussion, I intend to put aside Sartre's technical distinction between "reflective" and "pre-reflective" consciousness and instead confine myself to what I consider to be the traditional historical meaning of the term "self-consciousness" or "reflexion" as I have outlined it throughout the present study, which provides me with the advantage of accessing a span of two-and-a half millennia covering the ancient, modern, and contemporary discussions on the subject.

The threefold goal in the present chapter is to show: (a) that Husserl's phenomenological method inevitably leads to a substantial ego; (b) how his constitutive acts of intentionality contribute a vital insight into the temporal acts that terminate in an isolated, lonely self; and (c) that both intentionality and reflexivity are necessary to understand the dynamics of loneliness. Before beginning, however, one of the obvious hurdles to my interpretation is that Husserl *initially* in his writings brackets and "puts out of gear" any and all considerations that the ego is a substance, something I am concerned to assert. Indeed, the preposition *of* or *about* in phenomenology fundamentally implies *nonreflexive* intentionality.

An essential feature of the representational theory of knowledge is that the world and other selves are *inferred*. Husserl's epistemic program instead focuses on the immediate, intuitive "givenness" of meanings, the "things themselves." His overall purpose then is to ground his phenomenological method in a presuppositionless beginning (as was Hegel's before him). Whereas Leibniz and Kant presuppose *a priori* mediate concepts, categories, judgments, and principles (in opposition to the presuppositions of empiricism and phenomenalism regarding the immediacy of sensations or impressions), Husserl begins with the immediately present to consciousness by emphasizing the active principle of intentionality. In pursuing this interpretation, I also expect to show that Husserl's intentionality eventually will lead him to accept self-consciousness or reflexivity as well in his description of the dual constitutive acts of the mind. Thus, as his view of the phenomenological method develops, I argue that he progressively becomes constrained to turn inwardly toward transcendental subjectivity, the ego, and its contribution to the constitutive acts generative of consciousness, meaning, and loneliness.

A helpful contrast can be drawn between Husserl and Sartre. Sartre accepts the principle of intentionality but rejects Kant's and Husserl's structural activities emanating from the undisclosed ego in *The Transcendence of the Ego*. Sartre's answer is *Being and Nothingness*, wherein the ego is presented as a "nothingness" without either Kantian or Husserlian structures contributing to the opacity, the distortion of the "seen." But in terms of our interest in tracking the import of phenomenology in the context of a Philosophy and Psychology of Loneliness, Husserl's concentration on Kantian constitutive, structural *acts* emanating from the ego presents an important shift in favor of *both* the reality of the self *and* the synthetic *a priori* relation holding between intentionality and reflexion. In effect, Husserl's thought evolves from initially seeking to phenomenologically "discovering" the truth to later "spontaneously creating" it along more "idealist" and Kantian lines (Ricoeur, 1966).

Husserl's debt to Descartes is twofold, and we will acknowledge them in the same order as they are presented in Descartes's *Meditations*. First, the universal doubt, the classic skeptic's "suspension of judgment," which he announces in Meditation I: *Of the things which may be brought within the sphere of the doubtful,* his hyperbolic doubt. This includes the existence of the external world, the "objective" reference of his sensations, mathematical certainty, and even his own existence. Husserl's own version follows.

We can now let the universal epoche (abstention) in the sharply defined and novel sense we have given to it step into the place of the Cartesian attempt at universal doubt.... If I do this, as I am fully free to do, I do not then *deny* this "world," as though I were a sophist, *I do not doubt that it is there* as though I were a sceptic; but I use the "phenomenological" epoche, which *completely bars me from using any judgment that concerns the spatio-temporal existence (Dasein).* (*Ideas* [1962], Section 32; cf. *Crisis* [1970], Section 17)

The second "borrowing" from Descartes is addressed to the theme of intentionality. Again, in Descartes's Meditation II, titled *Of the Nature of the Human Mind; and that it is more easily known than the Body,* Husserl argues in agreement with Descartes for a direct access to the contents and acts of consciousness. It is in this sense that the cogito will "lend" its indubitable certainty, its absolute truth-value to the entire synthetic *a priori* structure of ego-cogito-cogitatum. Thus, Husserl declares:

It is intentionality which characterizes *consciousness,* in the pregnant sense of the term, and justifies us in describing the whole stream of experience as at once a stream of consciousness and unity as *one* consciousness. . . . Intentionality the unique peculiarity of experience "to be the consciousness *of* something, maybe a thing." It was in the explicit *cogito* that we first came across this wonderful property in which all metaphysical enigmas and riddles of the theoretical reason lead us eventually back; perceiving is the perceiving of something, maybe a thing; judging the judging of a certain matter; valuation; the valuing of a value; wish, the wish of the content wished, and so on. . . . In every wakeful *cogito* a "glancing" ray from the pure ego is directed upon the "object" of the correlate of consciousness for the time being, the thing and so forth." (*Ideas,* Section 84)

Husserl's hallmark description is seconded in the following commentary by Maurice Natanson:

The essence of consciousness is directionality [or intentionality]. All perceptual acts, according to Husserl, have one dominant characteristic; they point toward, or intend, some object. Thus, all thinking is thinking *of* something; all willing is willing *of* something; all imagining is imagining *of* something. Perception is not a state but a mobile *act*-ivity. In its essential dynamic, perception (in the widest possible sense) projects itself toward its intended object but that object is not to be understood as a "thing" but rather as the correlate of its attending act or acts. (Natanson, 1973, p. 85)

But in the beginning there is no possibility of accessing or intuiting the ego itself. Intentionality is not *of* or *about* the ego itself. There can be no self-conscious eidetic intuition of the ego *by* and *for* its self. Consequently, I wish to show that although Husserl begins by "bracketing" the ego as a substance and stresses intentionality at the expense of reflexion, in the end he will depend on both for their theoretical advantages in fully accounting for the consciousness of loneliness. In effect, I will show that *both* reflexivity *and* intentionality are compatible through their common source: the *activity* of consciousness. We recall that during our earlier discussion of first principles, I stated that differing ultimate assumptions cannot be combined or synthesized and that is true. But *both* reflexion *and* intentionality are *activities* of consciousness, and that is their grounding basis of compatibility and synthesis. Together, they constitute an *a priori* synthetic relation. It's analogous to the same person enjoying the capacity both to see and to hear as residing within the same individual; both are predicates attributable to human sensation, both are sensory but distinct experiences in the identical and unified subject. Just so, intentionality and reflexivity will be shown to be mutually constituted. I am concerned to validate both the acts of reflexivity and intentionality because otherwise the self will be trapped in a cocoon of loneliness. Intentionality offers the *only* means of escape.

Let us continue following our historico-conceptual thread. Whereas Descartes's pure cogito is completely empty—it's a pure act without content—Leibniz undertakes to fill the void of consciousness with a plenum of mental activities and contents but concludes that the monad is absolutely solipsistic and alone (apart from the existence of God). Kant undertakes to correct Leibniz by demonstrating that both the transcendental and the empirical self are mutually conditioned or constituted by, paired with, or co-dependent upon the concept of the object, while at the same time he insists that there exists an unknowable noumenal sphere of "things in themselves," which allows us to *conceive,* to *assume*—but not to experience or know—for ethical purposes the possibility of God's existence, the immortality of the soul, and the freedom of the will in *The Critique of Practical Reason*. In short, there are two worlds for Kant—one of an inaccessible reality for human beings and a second one in which we empirically live, occupy, and share together with other selves. Husserl, however, rejects Kant's metaphysical separation between the two completely independent realms of noumena (ultimate reality) and phenomena (ordinary human consciousness and empirical science). He is also unsympathetic to Kant's unquestioning acceptance of Newtonian science when he summons it as his starting presupposition. Instead, Husserl believes that "the things themselves" are immediately evident in consciousness and directly accessible through intuitive or eidetic insight. Nevertheless, there is a continuous line of paradigmatic congruence and agreement between Descartes, Leibniz, Kant, and finally Husserl on the existence and nature of the mind and its fundamental *activity* and *ideality*. Indeed, it's the shared commitment to the activity of consciousness that essentially binds the quartet of thinkers together as members of the same club and opposes them to reductive materialism, simplistic empiricism, and crude behaviorism. As we have shown, there are numerous examples of the uses of the Simplicity Argument, as well as references to it, throughout the history of Western philosophy. It is the vessel that carries us across the ocean of consciousness. In the present case, I also wish to contend that Husserl will eventually end his journey on the shores of loneliness.

In the previous chapter, I proposed that Descartes's position, in Meditation II, anticipated Husserl's appeal to the intentionality principle or premise. Confirmation of this reading comes in the following citation from Paul Ricoeur.

The first radical reflection on the priority of consciousness over its objects must be attributed to Descartes. By virtue of this, he is the originator of the transcendental motif, which alone is capable of destroying the naivete of naturalism [which accepts things at their face value]. . . . His doubt [the epoche] initiates every imaginable criticism of the sufficiency [without proper foundation] belonging to mathematical, physical, and sensuous evidences. . . . Going almost to the end of the universal "suspension" of being, he made the "apodictic [i.e., necessary] foundation" emerge: ego cogito cogitatum [self-intentional act<>meaning/object]. This *fully elaborated* formula indicates that the world [and other physical selves], lost as the disclosure of an in-itself, can only be reaffirmed as "that which I think"; the cogitatum of the cogito is the sole indubitable being of the world. In *enlarging* the sphere of the cogito, which is impervious to doubt, to the cogitatum, which he called ideas [i.e. meanings], *Descartes implicitly posited the important principle of intentionality* and by this means undertook to bring all objective evidence back to the primordial evidence of the cogito. (Ricoeur, 1967; emphasis added)

Ricoeur is saying that Husserl, in adopting Descartes's cogito as the "priority of consciousness over its objects," and then *extending, enlarging, expanding, elaborating* it is able to bring in intentionality and thus address the mistaken natural and naïve attitude of the empirical sciences, which can then be challenged and corrected. The mind's activity underlies a tripartite relation of ego-noetic act-noema; or self-intentional act-meaningful target. Through this maneuver, the entire scientific world is returned within the immanent sphere of the cogito. Thus, it is able to bestow the same quality of certainty to "scientific objects" and laws that is accorded to the cogito itself, thereby greatly expanding the status of universality and necessity to heretofore *contingent*, that is, *non*-necessary empirical concepts and laws. In any case, Ricoeur's pregnant interpretation bears full fruition in Husserl's larger *Crisis*.

"Intentionality" in Descartes: Accordingly, the foundation-laying first meditations [I and II] were a piece of psychology: but one element remains to be brought out expressly as highly significant though completely undeveloped: *intentionality*, which makes up the essence of egological life. Another word for it is *cogitation* [thinking *of* or *about* something], *having something consciously* [directly before one's mind] e.g., in experiencing, thinking, feeling, willing, etc.; for every *cogitatio* [thinking] has its *cogitatum* [object, meaning, target]. (Section 20; see also III B, Section 68; emphasis in the original)

Here we must avoid confusion by making some distinctions. Descartes's cogito is its own and sole *cogitatum*; it is reflexive and absolutely *a priori* self-evident. Again as before, in Descartes it *means* "I think my own thought." In the quotation above, however, Husserl has expanded the cogito to include the activity of thinking (*cogitation*) *beyond* the ego by invoking the *intentional* object/meant (the *cogitatum*). According to Ricoeur, then, Husserl by "enlarging," extending, and expanding the cogito to what it is thinking about, Husserl has brought in intentionality. Descartes's inferences, however, concerning the "bracketed" existence of the piece of wax, the external world, other selves, and other minds—the *cogitata*—although they are conceived by Descartes as *mediate, non*-intuitional forms of thought that actively "move" from the self to an "existential" proposition *beyond* the self, thus can be interpreted as essentially modes of intentionality. My strong suspicion is that Husserl "locked in" on the same passages I did in interpreting the wax example in Meditation II as an instance of intentionality. Again, it's to be noted that Cartesian reflexion (the cogito) is a perfectly self-referential act, whereas by contrast Descartes's "intentionality" refers to something *beyond* the self, the piece of wax, other men, and other minds, and so on, but they remain in the intentional field of immanent consciousness. In effect, then, Descartes had already expressed a relation of cogito-cogitatum. Assuming that Husserl is correct (and I believe he is), namely, that Descartes is committed to intentional acts, then we should be able to show how Descartes's "inferential judgment" is consistent with Husserl's intentionality. One major difference, of course, is that Descartes will eventually need God to ensure the validity of the connection between the cogito and its inferences/intentions, whereas Husserl's constitutive intentional acts are presumably self-validating when they result in eidetic intuitions. But if the entire world is bracketed, that problem can be circumvented. In other words, both Descartes's inference and Husserl's intentionality are (a) *contained, enveloped* within the epoche and (b) they are both acts—Descartes's is an inferential act and Husserl's an intentional act. As acts, nevertheless, they are identical in the sense that they are temporally structured. Neither says anything about the real existence of the external world. (It's only in Meditation III that Descartes proves the existence of God and in Mediation V that God is not a deceiver.)

Beyond that it's important to realize that if one is willing, as Husserl obviously is, to attribute intentionality to Descartes, he cannot then simply reject acts of genuine *self*-reflexion; that is, the Cartesian cogito as a substance, since Descartes's entire epistemological principle, as well as his methodological goal, is to ground not only the self but *all truths* in reflexive acts, which would correspond to Husserl's eidetic intuitions. It's not open to Husserl to pick and choose what he will accept, namely, Descartes's "principle of intentiuonality" but reject Descartes's concept of the self as a substance. Husserl cannot simply remove the lemon from the lemonade. Descartes's "I think = I am" provides the criterion not only for the self but for *every* proposition that is clear, distinct, universal, and necessary.

In any event, for Husserl meanings are the outcome of constitutive acts. As such, they are temporally structured. It's the essence of an act to take place through time. There is no such thing as an immediate act. Although Husserl's constituted meanings, the eidetic noema, can be intuitively "seen," the constituting *acts* take place in time, within the framework of time-consciousness. Thus, the noetic acts by which a noematic object/meaning is built up in consciousness, as well the manner in which it is constituted, essentially involve activity. It's the intentional constitution that "achieves" the completed act (Spiegelberg, 1965, p. I, 146–147). In *The Phenomenology of Internal Time-Consciousness,* Husserl undertakes to phenomenologically describe the acts and meanings constitutive of time apart from any involvement by a self (Husserl 1966). If we are to identify Descartes's inferences/intentionalities, Kant's transcendental mediate categories, and Husserl's constitutive intentional acts, it can only be done if we ascribe the *activity* of temporal consciousness to all three. In summary, then, all three thinkers, Descartes, Kant, and Husserl, join in agreeing that consciousness is active. Further, both Kant and Husserl stress the involvement of temporal factors in all consciousness. In any case, all these considerations are absolutely antithetical to the principles of materialism, empiricism, and behaviorism, which interpret "consciousness" as a passive event, as *caused* by the interaction of the human body and brain with a world of material objects.

In addition, what Ricoeur's interpretation implies is that one may begin with self-consciousness (Descartes); or with synthetic *a priori* categories and the unity of consciousness (Kant); or with intentionality (Husserl), but sooner or later each activity will fall upon the other as essential to the other. Simply put, reflexivity and intentionality *a priori* mutually constitute each other.

During the period under discussion, Husserl, along with many others, was engaged in questioning the very foundations of the natural and mathematical sciences, as Descartes had over two and a half centuries previously; hence the new challengers placed the alleged and vaunted "scientific certainty" in serious doubt.

The progress of science has now reached a turning point. The stable foundations of physics have broken up: also for the first time physiology [with its concentration on the brain in the manner of the Vienna Circle of philosophers] is asserting itself as an effective body of knowledge.... The old foundations of scientific thought are becoming unintelligible. Time, space, material, ether, electricity, mechanism, organism, configuration, structure, pattern, function, all require reinterpretation. What is the sense of talking about a mechanical explanation when you do not know what you mean by mechanics? (Whitehead, 1925, p. 23)

The key term "explanation" is critical here. Explanations are considered to be external physical events, causal events, and what Husserl desires are insights into meanings constituted by the intentionality of consciousness. One can give "explanations" without understanding the full or even superficial meaning of what they are observing. One can describe human behaviors without insight into motives underlying the behavior. Given that the naïve or "realistic" acceptance of the natural world is suspect, Husserl elects to provisionally turn away from it and seek certainty within the mind, from the standpoint of intentional consciousness. But then the problem is not to permanently lose the world in the process of turning so radically within, so solipsistically inward. Rather, the world outside is to be fully reinstated within the mind as an intentional meaning. But this is not only Husserl's problem, but it is related to mine as well, since I insist the self as a subject or thinking substance is epistemologically and ontologically alone. This difficulty of the separation of the world and other selves from the ego is something we will be unable to address until the last chapter when we discuss Husserl's dependence on the meaning of empathy in connection with the problem of solipsism and human loneliness. For although I believe the self is alone, I am also convinced it is able to forge a limited *affective* connection with and to other selves under certain conditions.

Meanwhile, Ricoeur offers the following interpretation of the Husserlian self:

[The ego] is given rather in absolute selfhood and in its unadumbratable unity is to be grasped adequately in reflection upon itself as a functional center in an adequate insight.... As pure ego it conceals no hidden internal domain; it is absolutely simple and lies entirely open. All domains lie within the cogito and in an adequately apprehended manner of functioning (*Ideas*). (ibid., p. 54)

At this juncture in *Ideas,* Husserl is still not willing to admit the ego to full reflexive and substantial status, but as Ricoeur points out there is already an internal strain in his thought.

This ego which is not an object at all [not a substance, not a reflexive self], which is in no way an intended noematic unity, is it, therefore, a point-like I? Certain expressions suggest this conviction. It is called a "functional center" (hence the image of the center of radiation), the *terminus a quo*, or the counterpole of the object, to which the analogue is the body as center of orientation and vision. (ibid., p. 54, Note 1, pp. 164–165)

This description may remind us of both Plotinus and Kant except for the reference, of course, to the body.

Further, Ricoeur emphasizes in his commentary that "The psyche is not extended, it does not fill a space, and it is not spatially divisible. But it is 'localized' in space, which is not the same thing, or, so to speak, it is ordered to space" (p. 42). This means that although my consciousness, with all its attendant meanings remains "simple," unextended, indivisible, immaterial, and unified, yet I am located for myself and others in a particular spatial dimension because my mind is "housed" in my body; I can find myself, and so can others at *some* place in the physical world we share. But the relevant question is not who can find whom, or "me," or the "other," and where, but rather do I have any access to other minds; or do they to my mind? If not, then the stakes for loneliness have increased greatly, and the danger of solipsism lurks behind every thought.

And even much later, in his lecture on May 7, 1935 at the University of Prague, titled *The Crisis of Philosophy and European Man,* even after the *Cartesian Meditations,* Husserl still repeats something similar, namely, that ideas or meanings as intentionalities are not in space as *naïve* physical science simply assumes the natural world and brains to exist. Hence, they are not reducible to the behavioral, mechanistic view of the cerebral cortex as a complex set of electrochemical reactions occurring between molecules and cells in the cranium. Rather, Husserl suggests that in terms of subjective, psychic consciousness, ideas or meanings are non-spatial in *individual* consciousnesses.

Ideas, within individual persons as sense[-meaning] structures that in a wonderfully new manner secrete themselves as intentional infinities *are not in space* like real things, which *later*, entering as they do into the field of [communal] human experiences do not by that very fact as yet signify anything for the human being as a person. (Husserl, 1965, p. 160; emphasis added)

As Kockelmans interprets it:

We have shown that the psychical enters the spatial world by means of a "bond of annexation." The psychical is by its self not extended, although it acquires extension through the bodiliness to which it remains tied. (Kockelmans, 1967)

One may well ask, how "tied"? What exactly is the "bond of annexation"? Notice, however, that *initially* the psychic is nonphysical, and it is only "later" that it becomes "embodied' in the person. Again, according to Husserl, as *individuals, as subjects, as egos* our minds, consciousnesses, and meanings are not in space, although they must persist through time, as he demonstrates in *The Phenomenology of Internal Time-Consciousness* (Husserl, 1966). However, as a *person* functioning in a *social* environment, one's mind can be located by the position of his body, for it is our body *qua* person that "houses" our mind. Thus, Husserl makes a distinction between the *individual* and the *person*. The individual is in direct contact with his own feelings and thoughts, whereas the person always exists in a social milieu, and his mind, "adjunctly" located in the presence of the body, is situated physically among other selves with their bodies.

I must confess these distinctions and the commentator's defense of them do not seem very plausible or persuasive to me and rather appear to beg the question. As far as I am concerned, the salient point remains: Ideas and meanings are not extended, not material, and therefore are not reducible to physical brain states. But again despite my exegetical difficulties and reservations with how Husserl transitions from Descartes's "intentionality" to his own version of embodied persons with minds, it's important to my theory that *both* reflexion *and* intentionality constitute consciousness in order for me to be able to mount a fully adequate theory in accounting for loneliness. Husserl cannot use the bracketing procedure as both shield and sword, first in order to exclude metaphysical dualism (shield) and then posit "embodied minds" in the *Crisis* (sword).

One of Husserl's clearest rejections of "psychologism," including behaviorism as a naturalistic, physicalist science, is formulated in Section 11 of his posthumous larger *Crisis,* where he criticizes Hobbes's materialism and Locke's sensationalism.

Naturally as soon as Descartes had proclaimed the idea of a rational philosophy and the division of nature and spirit, a new psychology was an immediate requirement, and it had already made its appearance in Descartes' contemporary Hobbes. It was . . . a psychology of a sort completely unknown to earlier times, designed concretely as a psychophysical anthropology in the rational spirit. . . . The naturalism of Hobbes wants to be a physicalism and, like all physicalism it follows the model of physical [causal] rationalism . . . but the physicalist view of nature makes it obvious that a further-developed physics would in the end "explain" all these concrete entities in a physicallistically rational way. . . . This naturalism of the psychic comes down through John Locke to the whole modern period up to the present day. Locke's image of the *white paper* is characteristic—the *tabula rasa* on which psychic data come and go, somehow [inexplicably] ordered

like the events of bodies in nature. This novel physicalistically oriented naturalism is, in Locke, not yet consistently worked out, not thought through to the end
as positivistic sensationalism. But it spreads rapidly, and in a way which is fateful
for the historical development of all philosophy. (Husserl, 1970)

Like myself, Husserl rejects all efforts to "psychologize," to materialize
consciousness through "physicalist," empiricist, and behaviorist approaches.

In Locke's great work this is the actual intent from the start. It offers itself as a new
attempt to accomplish precisely what Descartes's *Meditations* intended to accomplish: An epistemological grounding of the objectivity of the objective sciences. . . .
Locke senses nothing of the depths of the Cartesian epoche and of the reduction
to the ego. He simply takes over the ego as soul, which becomes acquainted . . . with
its inner states, acts, and capacities. Only what inner self-experience shows, only
our own "ideas," are immediately self-evidently given. Everything in the external
world is inferred, (ibid., Section 22).

In the larger *Crisis,* composed around a year after the *Cartesian Meditations,* Husserl holds that every self is "embodied" (Sections 47, 69, 70,
72). In all these passages, as well as in others, Husserl is depending on his
concept of "empathy," as formulated in the *Cartesian Meditations* (1931),
to carry the day for him and demonstrate the intersubjective nature of *persons* sharing a communal life—indeed, ideally a communal life of dedicated
phenomenologists all working on an infinite number of phenomenological tasks. But meanwhile, as we shall see, there are significant problems in
the manner in which Husserl expresses his concept of empathy and
attempts to use it as an interpsychic suffusing force to guarantee intersubjectivity. In fact, throughout the larger *Crisis,* Husserl is completely silent
about the *Cartesian Meditations*; it's as if they were never written. And yet
he invokes, indeed virtually exploits, the notion of empathy by presenting
it in the larger *Crisis* as if it were a completely unproblematic meaning
grounding the entire scientific intersubjective world of socially connected
persons within a communally lived world, the *Lebenswelt.*

But setting aside the larger *Crisis* for the time being, I intend to demonstrate that as Husserl's theory develops, he will progressively move closer
to affirming the reality of the self and self-consciousness, culminating in
the *Cartesian Meditations.*

For Husserl, an essential difference and significant advantage of the
mind over the body is that the acts and the resultant meanings produced
by our minds are completely unhidden, "open" to unobstructed viewing,
and lie ready to be uncovered because, unlike physical objects, they exhibit
no hidden sides, aspects, or perspectives. Part of the synthetic *a priori*

essence or meaning of our thoughts is that they are given completely when they occur at all. A thought has no hidden sides or aspects as, for instance, a physical chair does. The chair exhibits an inside and an outside; left and right; a part-to-part relation; and can only be viewed perspectivally, in parts, incompletely, and never as a whole. We are unable to see the entire chair all at once. A thought or meaning, however, displays no such restricted spatial dimensions or unobservable aspects. That also makes ideas and meanings advantageous in terms of the possibility of providing (relatively) exhaustive phenomenological descriptions, since we can "see" meanings as a whole and never through alternating perspectives and partial views. Further, our minds—psychically—are extended in time but not in space, whereas physical objects are essentially *meant* to be and are spatially extended both *as meanings* and as physical realities (*Ideas,* Section 86).

If we are to be aware of immanent objects, claims Husserl, they must be spread out in a time flow. This is the necessary structural form that all immanent objects must have if they are to be objects of experience, if we are to be conscious of them.

That this identification is possible, that an object is constituted here, depends on the structure of experiences: namely, that each phase of the stream [of temporality] turns into retention "of" and that this phase then turns again, etc. *Without this, a content (viz. a sensation) would be inconceivable as experience.* Otherwise an experience, in principle, would not and could not be given as a unity to the subject, and thus would be nothing. [Kant would say "as good as nothing."] One of the reasons why immanent objects must be extended in time is that such extension gives them individuality [i.e.,identity] and unity, which they must have in order to be experienced. (Sokolowski, 1970, pp. 82–83; emphasis in the original).

Recall in this context Kant's discussion of immanent time-consciousness and the unity of consciousness in the two Deductions. Thus, Husserl affirms Kant's foundational premise concerning the "I think."

Husserl therefore reasserts the Kantian proposition that "*I think* must accompany all my representations." In *Ideen* [1913] the ego remains an empty form, impossible to determine (Section 57b). This conception has changed in the course of the evolution of Husserl's thought that forthcoming publications will make accessible to the public. In these studies Husserl considers the self in all its concrete aspects, giving the beginning of a phenomenological clarification to the old problems of personality. In these studies, the ego is no longer reduced to an empty, purely formal point from which acts originate; it is considered as "personality." (Levinas, 1973, pp. 50–51)

I would further argue that Husserl's theory of ideas, as ideal or "irreal" meanings, is indebted to the influence of his revered teacher, Franz Brentano, whose lectures he attended from 1884 to 1886 and Brentano's commitment to the Simplicity Argument. The two marks of the psychic for Brentano are immateriality and intentionality (Mijuskovic, 1978, pp. 315–324). However, Brentano remained a metaphysical dualist.

The old tendency finds its most modern impress in Brentano's separation of the "psychical" from the "physical phenomena." . . . Brentano himself remained a stranger to phenomenological ground, and although with his sharp distinction he failed to reach that for which he searched, namely, the separation of the empirical domains of psychology and the natural sciences. (*Ideas*, Section 85)

Undoubtedly, under the influence of Heidegger's *Being and Time* (1927), Husserl sought to go beyond the subjective idealism of the *Cartesian Meditations*. But the question that remains is whether he was legitimized in doing so. Still, for Husserl, meanings remain *ideal* unities: "A meaning is an ideal unity that can be realized in many different expressions; the meaning is an ideal unity over and against all the particular acts of meaning that realize it whether they are performed by one person or by other persons" (Sokolowski, 1974, p. 113). Similarly, "Two speakers cannot perform numerically the same act of judging, but they can possess numerically the same judgment for a judgment is an ideal entity, identically the same no matter when, where or by whom it is expressed" (ibid., p. 207). As the Simplicity Argument dictates, meanings are nonspatial and consequently can be communicated and shared, whereas particular sensations cannot; they are essentially private. It follows that we can communicatively share ideal meanings but not individual experiences such as loneliness, since the latter are chock-full of different qualitative sensations and feelings and therefore absolutely idiosyncratic.

Whereas for Kant, the emphasis falls on the unity of consciousness, for Husserl it centers on the unity of meaning. Nevertheless, Husserl also affirms that "We must likewise describe the *unity of consciousness* which is demanded *by the intrinsic nature of the cogitations*, and so necessarily demanded that they could not exist without this unity" (Husserl, 1962, p. 105).

Further:

Consciousness, considered in its "purity," must be reckoned as a *self-contained system of Being*, as an *Absolute Being*, into which nothing can penetrate, and from which nothing can escape [Leibniz's monad?]; which has no spatio-temporal exterior, and can be inside no spatio-temporal system: which cannot experience [external] causality from anything nor exert causality upon anything, it being presupposed that causality bears the normal sense of natural causality as a relation of dependence between [external, physical] realities. (ibid., Section 49; emphasis in the original)

I consider this statement with its strong Leibnizian undertones to be a clear rejection of behaviorism and the naturalistic attitude.

Later, in *Formal and Transcendental Logic* (1929), Husserl will continue to characterize ideas, meanings, thoughts, and intentionalities as immaterial or unextended in conformity, either wittingly or unwittingly, with the Simplicity Argument as having been suggested by Brentano:

[T]houghts do not make their appearance in consciousness as something "external." They are not real objects, not spatial objects, but irreal formations produced [created?] by the mind; and their peculiar essence excludes spatial extension, original locality, and mobility. Like other products of the mind, they admit, however, of a physical embodiment, in their case an embodiment by the sensuous verbal signs; and thus they have a secondary spatial existence (that of the spoken or written sentence). (Husserl, 1962a, Section57b)

Thoughts, as meanings, are nonspatial; but when they are "transformed" from intentional meanings within consciousness and "translated" physically into spoken words or written sentences, they "take on," they manifest a "material" and "localized" aspect. But of course, this doesn't help us when we assure another, "I know how lonely you feel." The mere sound of the verbal utterance does not assure the other that I experience anything close to an eidetic insight or an empathic feeling into *his* emotions and *his* thinking. (By the way, the term *eidos* is related to the Greek meaning for "seeing," as in Plato's use of the term "Ideas," which signifies intuitively *seeing* the Forms with our mind's eye.)

In 1929, Husserl becomes increasingly aware of the problem of solipsism and the problematic status of other minds in *Formal and Transcendental Logic.*

Whether convenient or inconvenient, and even though (because of no matter what prejudices) it may sound monstrous to me [the Cartesian "I am"] *is the primal matter of fact to which I must hold fast,* which I as a philosopher, must not disregard for a single instant. For children in philosophy, this may be the dark corner haunted by the specter of solipsism. . . . The true philosopher, instead of running way, will prefer to fill the dark corner with light. (ibid., Section 95)

Whether ideas are ultimately dependent on the brain and, if so, how and to what extent is one question. But again whether they are *completely* reducible to, explainable by, or identical with physiological motions contained in the skull is a totally different issue, the possibility of which Husserl categorically denies after 1900. As we have repeatedly shown, the thesis that ideas are unextended is a direct consequence of the Simplicity Argument. Husserl's account of the mind, its intentional cognitive acts, and the in-dwelling meanings "inhabiting" consciousness, if not consciously borrowed or modeled from Kant's unity of apperception, is at least very similar to it in many important respects. Thus, in the *Cartesian Meditations,* for instance, in his discussion of the unity and identity of meaning found in all constitutive *acts* of intentional consciousness, he finds that there is a triadic synthetic *a priori* relation between the *ego-cogito-cogitatum.* These, he contends, are directly displayed within the mind as unifying structures that in turn make possible multiple connections between intrinsically related, synthetic *a priori systems* of intentional meanings (Gallagher, 1972, pp. 341–352). I have presented Kant as holding that the subject and the object mutually constitute each other, but one can also claim that their *relation* is the third and indeed active factor connecting the subject to the object.

Originally, these unities are grounded in the transcendental ego, the center and source of any and all monadic constitutive intentionalities. Again, in this fashion, Kant's unity of consciousness becomes transformed for Husserl into a unity of meaning that includes direct access to an immanent ego as well as "intentionalized" objects thetically posited as transcendent *meanings* existing beyond and independently of the self. For Husserl, the meaning of a unicorn can be bracketed, intended, and described, whether or not unicorns exist. Indeed, Husserl contends that there is a valid intentional meaning in the idea of a square circle, even if it cannot exist in any possible sensuous or hyletic image (Ricoeur, 1967, p. 204).

A set of continuous links thus leads from Leibniz's monadic theory of apperception/self-consciousness/reflexion to Kant's more refined version of the transcendental unity of apperception as mutually conditioned by the transcendental concept of an object=x (*Critique,* A 109–A 110), and finally ending in Husserl's unity and identity of meaning. Although, properly speaking, Hegel's form of idealism is out of bounds in the present chapter, still we see the same *active* dynamic in the *dialectical* play of the in-itself, for-itself, and the in-and-for itself; or consciousness, self-consciousness, and reason. The mind is active; it is self-conscious; one cannot be self-conscious apart from possessing a mind, self, or ego. That's what it *means for the mind to be reflexive.* And this active reflexivity is solitary.

I can lift the same table with you, but I cannot intuit the same self with you. The ego is essentially, universally, and necessarily lonely.

But the "problem of other minds" forms a special difficulty for Husserl because it seems by definition inconceivable and contradictory to immediately, directly apprehend or "see" the mind of another distinct self, if for no other reason than the very *meaning* of "other self" signifies it *as* "other than self" and/or "a different self."

As we shall see in the next chapter, loneliness will be constituted by a "multiplicity of emotions in unity," including anxiety, guilt, shame, abandonment, and betrayal, all constituted as synthetic *a priori* meanings and relations within the "umbrella" concept of loneliness. Furthermore, these rich and teeming intentionalities, as Husserl indicates, will emanate from a single source, the ego, transcendental subjectivity.

The fact is that the constituting multiplicities [and intentionalities] of consciousness— those actually or possibly combined to make the unity of an identifying synthesis— are not accidental but, as regards the possibility of such a synthesis, *belong together for essential reasons.* Accordingly, they are governed by *principles* thanks to which our phenomenological investigations do not get lost in disconnected descriptions but are essentially organized. Any "Objective" object . . . points to a *structure within the transcendental ego that is governed by a rule.* (Husserl, 1960)

As Husserl proceeds in his description of the ego's functions, he credits it with formulating universal objective *rules.* Kant says the same. The categories are rule-directed activities for unifying representations within awareness. The difference, Husserl believes, is that Kant's are mediate and his immediate; Kant's are purely formal, whereas Husserl's are constitutive. But they both occur within the structure of time-consciousness. For Husserl, the result of these constitutive acts is eidetic intuitions, Platonic essences. These ideally will form a *system* of synthetic *a priori* meanings. In parallel fashion, the "field" of loneliness, like a gravitational field, would then constitute such a coherent, interlocking system of universal knowledge in the strictest sense. For Kant, the result is empirical consciousness and phenomena. The difference appears to be more verbal than real.

In Kant, the constitutive synthetic acts are mediated by the relational categories. The pure concepts or structural forms of substance and accident, cause and effect, and so on, for instance, are mediate and relational; they go *beyond* the immediate forms of passive sensibility (the pure intuitions of space and time) that are innate to the human mind. (Extraterrestrial *rational* beings may not intuit in the forms of pure sensibility of space and time, but if they are rational, they will be constrained to think within the categorical form of causality according to Kant.) In Husserl, however, meanings and relations are directly, immediately "seen," "exhibited," and it is the task of the phenomenologist to virtually exploit the phenomenological method in order to "see" and describe these meanings and their implicated relations. William James, coming from a different perspective, in his "radical empiricist" period, holds that relations are immediately *given* in experience (James, 1962, pp. 222–240).

In any case, the phenomenological task in terms of a Philosophy and Psychology of Loneliness is twofold: (1) to emphasize the active role of intentionality in constitutive acts; and (2) to describe the various possibly infinite connections implicated in all the synthetic *a priori* meanings constitutive of loneliness. Successful therapy will then depend on insight into the complexity and severity of the sense of loneliness being clinically addressed. This may well turn out to be an infinitely varied field of exploration as directed toward and in behalf of the therapeutic subject, whether it is one's own self or that of another self. There is nothing in principle which dictates that loneliness therapy cannot be self-conducted or self-administered. After all, Freud essentially practiced many of his discoveries and investigations on himself. Such therapeutic enterprises may well be life-long simply because the struggle against loneliness is lifelong. To repeat: It's innate. Thus, for our purposes the Phenomenology of Loneliness is a portal leading to a corridor in which many doors and rooms are readily available for entry; one room is marked depression, another jealousy, another anxiety, another revenge, and all are *essentially* connected as interior chambers in the same house, the abode of loneliness and isolation.

If we are on the right track, then, what would these intentionalities and relations look like? They would certainly involve synthetic judgments *a priori* as instantiated in such propositions as "All colors are extended"; "All sounds have pitch, timbre, and intensity"; "All physical objects display sides"; and "All psychic phenomena are given as a whole or a unity." This notion goes all the way back to Plato's *Meno* when he proposes that the Forms of Virtue and Knowledge are related in a similar fashion as Color is to Extension in the judgment, "Virtue is Knowledge (of the Good)" (Mijuskovic, 1970, pp. 13–23). Indeed, according to Husserl, in the example just proposed of a synthetic *a priori* relation stating that all colors are extended, Husserl further enriches the meaning by adding that color indicates *quality* while extension implies *quantity* (Berger, 1972, p. 25). Kant, Hegel (though he criticizes Kant for his "static" Table of Categories as devoid of development in comparison to his own dialectical synthetic *a priori* ones), Schopenhauer, Husserl, and Sartre are all committed to *a priori* synthetic meanings and structural relations as well. It follows that the relation of things to thoughts is grounded in synthesizing *a priori* acts. Both meanings and structural activities dualistically exist as intentionalities side by side, and it is not possible to think of one without the other; hence they are universal and necessary, that is, *a priori*. The advantage of this is that the clinical phenomenologist can explore as yet undisclosed but hidden interrelated meanings that are present within the consciousness of the therapeutic subject through the meaning of loneliness. Hence, if someone states that she is lonely, the therapist *already, a priori* knows that there is a trove of feelings and thoughts engrained in the mind of the subject waiting to be excavated and explored. As Husserl declares at the conclusion of *The Paris Lectures*:

[T]he necessary path to knowledge which can only be ultimately justified in the highest sense . . . is the path of *universal self-knowledge,* first in monadic and then in an intermonadic sense. The Delphic expression, *know thyself* has acquired new meaning. Positive [naïve] science is lost in the world. One must first lose the world in order through the *epoche* so as to regain it in universal *self-examination.* "*Noli foras ire,*" said St. Augustine, "*in te redi, in interiore homine habitat veritas*"; "Do not wish to go out; go back into your self. Truth dwells in the inner man." (Husserl, 1964, pp. liv, 4, 11, 34–35, 38, 39; emphasis added)

In this passage, it is manifestly clear that Husserl distinguishes monadic self-consciousness, that is, *intra*subjective consciousness from intermonadic awareness, and it follows that the two modes of knowledge must be quite differently grounded. Husserl's determined effort to secure intermonadic consciousness occurs in the Fifth Cartesian Meditation. But the important admission is that there is *first* a solitary, monadic consciousness and only subsequently a (possible) connection to and with other selves.

The synthetic *a priori* serves two essential functions for Husserl. First, it binds; it unifies distinct essential meanings to each other, as, for example, "psychic" and "physical" phenomena:

Thus, for instance, "material thing" and "soul" are different existential regions, and yet the latter has its grounds in the former, and there follows therefrom the grounding of the theory of the soul in the theory of the body. (*Ideas,* Section, 16)

Although Husserl brackets or suspends *real* metaphysical dualism, he readily "accommodates" it within the "phenomenological" sphere of consciousness. But precisely how vital for existential thought the synthetic *a priori* is can be readily established by considering that Sartre's ontological dualism summons it in *Being and Nothingness* as *the* essential grounding for his entire ontological system, since at the very Conclusion to the entire work he maintains that the relation between Being (the in-itself) and Consciousness (the for-itself) is a synthetic *a priori* one (Sartre, 1966, pp. 760–761). Although both Husserl and Sartre posit the validity of synthetic *a priori* relations, as well as intentional acts of cognition, Sartre nevertheless rejects Husserl's position on the bracketing procedure as applied to the transcendental ego and along with it the assumption that self-consciousness and structural acts in the Cartesian or Kantian sense are possible in the *Transcendence of the Ego* (1936). Indeed, he criticizes the whole line of thought that leads from Descartes through Kant and on into Husserl. And yet, when we consider Sartre's own ethical insistence that each one of us is *alone* responsible for our radically free choices, for our decisions in the investment of value in our lives in his 1949 essay, "Existentialism Is a Humanism," it appears quite questionable for him to assign moral responsibility if there is no self. For "who" or "what," then, is ethically responsible? Can there be ethical imputability if there is no "self"? Sartre, of course, later repudiates the essay, but it illustrates how difficult it is to disown the ego in ethics as well as in the Philosophy and Psychology of Loneliness. So although Sartre describes the human condition as doomed to freedom as well as to forlornness, one wonders just *who* is it that is free and lonely? And when he describes the existential category of forlornness, exactly who is it that is forlorn?

As an aside, if one is a behaviorist or a psychoanalyst, normative ethical principles or commands—oughts and shoulds—are completely meaningless or at best translate into mere expressions of subjective emotions. Morality can only be relative and subjective for the behavioral clinician, the empirical anthropologist, and the psychoanalyst. Freud promises happiness—or at least relief from a repressive and punitive conscience—but not morality. Neither behaviorism nor psychoanalysis permits judgments of intrinsic ethical (or aesthetic) value. All such value judgments can be simply reduced to cultural relativism, subjective feelings, and thus skepticism. For Sartre, self or no self, value judgments are "absolute" for the individual alone; by contrast, for Kant the categorical imperative is conceived as universal for all rational beings.

For my purposes, it's vital to show that Husserl's developing phenomenological position on the self and reflexivity, culminating in the *Cartesian Meditations*, directly leads to the loneliness of the self. As such, the ego neither requires nor admits of inferential proof. Rather, it is constituted in awareness as a phenomenological given. It is directly, immediately present within "transcendental subjectivity." Consequently, the vital connection between the phenomenological method of Husserl and his turn to the lonely ego is doubly interesting for our discussion of loneliness because of his "paradigm shift" from initially advocating for the intentionality principle without any possibility of truly reflexive acts. But eventually, he moves to assigning a *dual* supporting role to genuine acts of reflexive consciousness, which leads him to a *qualified* or *provisional* solipsistic commitment, while at the same time it fruitfully exposes an entire theoretical field of monadic and lonely consciousness lying in wait. In saying this, I am contending that his implementation of the phenomenological method, when fully exploited at its roots, the absolute givenness of the active subject, necessarily uncovers the primordial feature of reflexivity along with the transcendental actuality of human isolation, of loneliness. This in turn opens an access to an infinitely fertile field of exploration of synthetic *a priori* meanings and relations within the subject matter of loneliness, which are directly applicable to gaining insight into individual human loneliness.

But let us track more closely how all this came about. First, we must distinguish Husserl's reflection from the empiricist's notion of reflection. For Husserl, reflective *acts*—as opposed to mere observations—are designed to elicit eidetic intuitions, to discover essential meanings. They are related to what he describes as the process of "free imaginative variation," which we will discuss in the next chapter. By contrast, Locke's, Hume's, and Armstrong's concept of reflection consists of a passive observational introspection of Lockean sensations or Humean impressions. In *Ideas* (1913), Husserl stresses the concept of active "reflection." However, although the ego can "reflect" on its intentional experiences, it still cannot reflexively capture or target its self. Consequently, the subject and the object can never coalesce or fuse or unify. In short, the two terms—Husserl also refers to them as ego pole and object pole—cannot form a unity as in the traditional idealist and rationalist reflexive tradition. The ego is like an archer whose arrows only shoot forth. Husserl's *intentional* reflection is like a camera that focuses and captures eidetic meanings but fails to acknowledge the directional role of the cameraman as an active subject. Under these circumstances, it follows that no matter how well or how deeply or how resolutely we accomplish the phenomenological reduction,

We shall never stumble across the pure Ego as an experience among others within the [temporal] flux of manifold experiences which survives as transcendental residuum. . . . The Ego [or cameraman] appears to be permanently, even necessarily, there, and this permanence is obviously not that of a stolid unshifting experience, of a fixed idea. On the contrary, it belongs to every experience that comes and [temporally] streams past, its "glance" goes "through" every *cogito* [or act] and towards the object. This visual ray changes with every [act of the] *cogito,* shooting forth afresh with each new one [i.e., snapshot] as it comes, and disappearing with it. But the Ego remains self-identical. In principle, at any rate, every cogitation [structural act] *can* change, come and go. . . . But in contrast, the pure

Ego appears to be *necessary* in principle, and as that which remains absolutely self-identical in all real and possible changes of experience, it can in no sense be reckoned *as a real part or phase* of the experiences themselves. (Husserl, 1962; Section 57); emphasis in the original)

At this point, Husserl's "pure Ego" sounds identical to Kant's pure, universal "transcendental unity of apperception," a purely formal unity without its own content. The ego is necessary, but it is not a substance reflexively, empirically, or otherwise aware of its self. The intentional arrows radiate forth but do not return to the archer or the cameraman. And yet it is the archer or the cameraman who *selects,* who decides what he intends to "shoot," and presumably he must know what he is about, he must have selected one target rather than another, and he must have reflexively thought about *it.* The cameraman cannot function passively in the manner of a mechanically disengaged surveillance camera that merely records events that happen to cross the camera's "field of vision" or exposure. That would be tantamount to denying the activity of human selectivity. For who is it that selects the phenomena to be investigated?

In any case, the concession that the ego is necessary, albeit not its self open to eidetic insight serves as a welcome shift in direction and actually marks an advance over Husserl's earlier skeptical theory of the self formulated in *Logical Investigations* (1900–1901). In other words, in his prior work, as in the *Phenomenology of Internal Time-Consciousness*, Husserl pursued his phenomenological mission of describing "the things themselves" without implicating transcendental subjectivity, the pure ego. Thus, as just indicated, in *Ideas,* Section 57, note 1, he confesses that previously "I took up on the question of the pure Ego a skeptical position which I have not been able to maintain as my studies progressed." Hence, *Ideas* affirms the existence of a limited ego that performs reflective acts that are intentional and not merely observational and passive as in the empiricist model. As an intentional act, it presents the ego as always receding into the background as it scrutinizes its respective phenomena or noemata. This is similar to Sartre's description of running to catch the streetcar. While I am immersed, consumed, and absorbed by the activity, there is no "I"; there is only the streetcar; but afterward when I reflect, I tell myself a third-person narrative about "me" (George Herbert Mead's "me") sprinting after the conveyance, but the ego is not there; it always recedes into the background (Mead, 1934, p. 174). Once more, the ego cannot catch its self. In short, it is able to intentionally reflect on objects in its field of vision or attention but it cannot reflexively capture the functional source or the agent "in its self" that is performing the act or survey.

Husserl's *Formal and Transcendental Logic,* however, expresses a growing tendency toward a genuinely reflexive model of consciousness on more

historical and traditional lines. It also inevitably ushers in the issue of knowledge of other minds. Indeed, Husserl confesses: "I have experience of myself
with primary originality; of others, of another's psychic life, with merely
secondary originality, since another's psychic life is essentially inaccessible to
me in direct perception" (Sections 94–95). This admission, of course, not
only introduces the problem of other minds but also obviously presents
implications in terms of solipsism as well. Thus, one cannot meaningfully
discuss or even refer to "an other's *psychic* life" without implying that one's
own is different, separate, and distinct from that of other selves or minds.

An absolute existent is existent in the form, an intentional life—which, no matter
what else it may be intrinsically conscious of, is, at the same time, consciousness
of itself. Precisely for that reason . . . it [i.e., transcendental subjectivity, the
ego] has at all times an essential ability to make itself thematic and produce
judgments, and evidences, relating to itself. *Its essence includes the possibility of
self-examination*—a self-examination that starts from vague meanings and, by a
process of uncovering [i.e., insight], goes back to the original self. (Husserl, 1962a;
Section 103; emphasis in the original)

And in the *Cartesian Meditations,* where Husserl undertakes to present
a full-blown monadology or egology, thus emulating Descartes's egocentric revolution, the ego is more explicitly credited with the essential structure of *ego-cogito-cogitatum.* So here, finally, he definitely summons the
traditional idealist-rationalist paradigm of a self-conscious existent while
accommodating his earlier intentionality principle. Therefore, in this later
work, Husserl contends that the ego-pole is just as securely and surely
given as the object-pole through a process of self-constitution that can be
recaptured in cognition. In fact, in this thoroughly idealistic study, Husserl goes so far as to confess that transcendental subjectivity constitutes
the most *primary* datum within human consciousness and that it is dis-
coverable after the bracketing procedure has been instituted.

If I keep purely what comes into view—for me, the one who is meditating
[reflexively]—by virtue of my free epoche with respect to the being of the experienced world, the momentous fact is that I, with my life, remain untouched in my
existential status, regardless whether or not the world exists and regardless of
what my eventual decision concerning its being or non-being might be. (Husserl,
1960; Section 11)

The Ego grasps himself not only as a long life, but also as I, who live with this and
that subjective process, who live through this and that *cogito as the same.* (ibid.,
Section 31)

I regard these passages as evidence of reflexive acts of consciousness intrinsic to the self. This interpretation is in full agreement with Professor Kockelmans's perspective:

On the basis of this synthesis of [self and object] the ego appears and reappears as an identity [i.e., unity] pole in regard to all that which appears as object. In the explicit reflection upon the self, however, I am both subject and object at the same time. (Kockelmans, 1967, p. 175)

We are back to Kant's principle that in consciousness self and object constitute each other.

In Husserl's *Preface to the English Edition,* written for W. R. Boyce Gibson, his English translator, in 1931, the same year as the *Cartesian Meditations,* Husserl offers frank admission that he could no longer deny the principle of reflexivity, of "self-comprehension," of "apperception":

It develops as a course of self-reflexion taking place in the region of the pure psychological intuition of the inner life. . . . It leads eventually to the point that I, who am here reflecting upon my self, become conscious that under a consistent and exclusive focusing of experience upon that, which is purely inward, upon what is "phenomenologically" accessible to me, I possess in my self an essential individuality, self-contained and holding well together in its self, to which all real and objectively possible experience and knowledge belongs. . . . I my self as this individual essence, posited absolutely, as the open infinite field of pure phenomenological data and their inseparable unity am the "transcendental Ego"; the absolute positing means that the world is no longer "given" to me in advance [naively], its validity of a simple existent, but that henceforth it is exclusively my Ego that is given (given from my new standpoint). (*Ideas,* 10–11)

But Husserl's final attempt to solve the problems of solipsism and other minds will have to be postponed until our discussion of the Fifth Cartesian Meditation, which we will treat in Chapter 8 in order to evaluate his final success or failure. But for the time being, as Peter Koestenbaum states in his Introduction to the lectures, "The ego is lonely. Not withstanding his rejection of solipsism, Husserl confesses, in his *Crisis of the European Sciences,* that the ego, which he is, is unremittingly lonesome" (liv). Again for Husserl as for Kant: How is it that I *know* that certain sensations and thoughts are *mine* and not yours unless there is an active dynamic unity to *my* self-consciousness? How is it that I don't mistake *your* thoughts for *mine*? It follows that there is a self and that it is self-aware of its own activities and contents or "representations" in Kant's terminology. Accordingly, Husserl concludes that the ego is pure subjectivity, a solipsistic monad.

In spite of Husserl's promise to slay the solipsistic dragon in the *Cartesian Meditations*, other critics have already pronounced the issue resolved to Husserl's disadvantage.

If Husserl doubted the existence of the world with its mountains, rivers, trees, plants, and animals, how could he help doubting his own existence in this specific body? He then went on from human loneliness to transcendental loneliness. "I have become," he said, "the transcendental Ego"; and this was true. He did not talk as his own natural self, but as an anonymous transcendental Ego . . . in Kant's sense. Here we have reached the central point, *Husserl's philosophy of the lonely transcendental self*. . . . We have simultaneously reached the point where we can fix Husserl's position in the history of modern self-estrangement. Husserl's method is of interest to us an expression of self-estrangement. (Heinemann, 1979, p. 53)

And another commentator agrees:

The phenomenological reduction places subjectivity within the shell of its transcendentality, from which it can no longer escape. The ego, as soon as it recognizes itself as transcendental, sets ablaze all bridges that could lead it back to actuality. To borrow a metaphor . . . if one likens the transcendental ego to a house, then one would have to say that this house [grounded in self-consciousness] has no windows, no doors, no walls. (Geniusas, 2012)

Like Leibniz's "windowless monads, Husserl has drawn all the curtains and sealed all his exits.

Finally, no more sympathetic and able a commentator on Husserl than Paul Ricoeur, in his article *Kant and Husserl,* while discussing the Fifth Cartesian Meditation, concludes with the same reservations as the above commentators:

Did not Kant basically demonstrate the limits of not only the pretensions of the phenomenon, but of the limits of phenomenology itself? I am able "to see," "to feel" the appearance of things, of persons, of nature, but the absolute existence of the other model of all existence [i.e., the other, alien self], cannot be sensed; it is announced as a stranger to my experience by the very appearance of the other in his behavior, his expression, his language, his work. But this apparition of the other does not suffice to announce it as being-in-itself. (Ricoeur, 1966, pp. 164–167)

Interestingly enough, Ricoeur tries to bail Husserl out by invoking Kant's second formulation of the categorical imperative, which legislates that we ought to ethically treat others as ends-in-themselves and never as means to our own ends. But this can't work for Husserl as Ricoeur himself realizes; it presupposes a noumenal realm of moral beings, of rational souls. Thus, Ricoeur concludes his essay with the pronouncement that "Husserl does phenomenology but Kant limits and grounds it." In short, Husserl fails to eidetically confirm the existence of other selves within his own self.

Can Husserl pull it off: Can he reach, or is he able to access the other self phenomenologically? The dynamics through which the other is significantly, meaningfully created within consciousness must be founded in the freedom of consciousness, the capacity which the mind exhibits of transcending the moments of loneliness and thereby escaping past the walls of solipsism. Both the idealist and the phenomenological traditions insist on the existence of such an *intentional* force immanent to consciousness. Much of this again follows from Kant (and Fichte). According to Kant, the entire faculty of the understanding is grounded in creative, spontaneous, productive acts since the mind has the ability to forge structures from its own internal resources (*Critique*, A xvii–xviii; A 51–B 74). The mind generates and creates relations spontaneously; it inserts relations into our reflexive experiences through the *agency* of spontaneity (Pippin, 1987, pp. 449–475); or, if one prefers, the empirical content provided by the "external world" *conforms* to the structural activities of the categories (Kant's Copernican Revolution). But still, the categories themselves are spontaneously generated. Husserl's ego similarly displays a spontaneity, a freedom, a creative transcendence that enables it to intentionally, to thetically posit meanings and spheres of interlocking relations beyond the entrapped self. He even refers to these syntheses as "creative beginnings" (*Ideas*, Section 122).

But *each* act of whatever kind can start off in this *spontaneity modus of a so-to-speak creative beginning*, in which the pure Ego steps on the scene as subject of spontaneity. (emphasis in the original)

But the unresolved question in terms of loneliness still remains, namely, whether Husserl's principle of intentionality and empathy will be able (a) to create, to thetically posit, and to successfully *mean* the other self *qua* other; and *next* (b) to meaningfully *enter into, to reach into, fuse with,* and *penetrate* the other as a self *identical* to my self in a persuasive or convincing enough manner. He has the tool, the device—spontaneity—but will he be able to fashion a truly existing affective and/or cognitive relation to the *other self* who is sufficiently constituted in me so that I can *directly, immediately* feel and understand *his* loneliness and (to some extent) unburden him of his distress? We shall see how all this fares in the last chapter.

In the preceding, I have obviously focused on the *Cartesian Meditations* because I believe it's directly and singularly relevant to my speculations about loneliness. It is in the later and larger work, *The Crisis of European Sciences and Transcendental Phenomenology: An Introduction to Transcendental Philosophy,* however, that Husserl's criticisms of materialism, the physical sciences, and psychologism, by which he essentially means his contemporary scientific world, are most clearly laid bare. It is here we learn that it is due to Galileo's "abstraction" from nature and his "mathematization" of objects, thus denuding all our experiences from their human context, that the entire abandonment from everything truly human, ethical, and spiritual first began, which has led to modern and contemporary science's universal reduction of reality to bodies, which in turn institutes the entire downward spiral and moral downfall of European man and his values. No less responsible is Hobbes with his "materialistic naturalism" and "physicalist" interpretation of psychology as well as Locke's sensationalism and his ensuing identification and confinement of consciousness to mere perceptions. Hume's nominalist and atomistic psychology comes in for some very rude treatment as well (Sections 9–13). Ensemble all these naïve reductivist doctrines only assure us that the Veil of Isis will remain forever secure *unless* we are able to apply phenomenological methods of investigation. This is Husserl's criticism of behavioral psychology with which I deeply agree. In Section 60 and throughout, however, he defends the notion of "embodied" souls in the "lived world." With this I would disagree and instead choose his *Cartesian Meditations* as his final and most consistent view of the matter. Perhaps one might be inclined to suggest that in the *Cartesian Meditations,* Husserl defines the problem of loneliness, while in the *Crisis* he solves it. But that would be far too generous. And that is precisely because in the *Cartesian Meditations* he never successfully resolves how the other self can be intentionally constituted by *indirect* "appresentational and analogical" acts. In Chapter 8, we shall consider how Husserl's conceptual flaws in his notion of empathy can be addressed and whether they can be sufficiently corrected to allow the soul or self or mind an egress from the confinement of loneliness.

REFERENCES

Berger, G. (1972). *The Cogito in Husserl's Phenomenology.* Evantson, IL: Northwestern University Press.

Descartes, R. (1955). *Philosophical Works of Descartes.* New York: Dover.

Gallagher, K. (1972). Kant and Husserl on the synthetic *a priori. Kant Studien,* 63:1–4.

Geniusas, S. (2012). The origins of the horizon in Husserl's phenomenology. In Embree, P., & Nennon, T. (Eds.). *Contributions to Phenomenology.* Dordrecht: Springer.

Heinemann, F. H. (1979). *Existentialism and the Modern Predicament.* Santa Barbara, CA: Praeger Press.

Hume, D. (1973). *A Treatise of Human Nature.* Oxford, UK: Clarendon Press.

Husserl, E. (1960). *Cartesian Meditations,* Second Meditation, Section 22.

Husserl, E. (1962a). *Formal and Transcendental Logic.* Cairns, D. (Trans.). The Hague: Martinus Nijhoff, Section 57b, Section 95.

Husserl, E. (1962b). *Ideas: General Introduction to Pure Phenomenology.* Gibson, A. B. (Trans). New York: Collier Books, Section 34.

Husserl, E. (1964). *The Paris Lectures.* Koestenbaum, P. (Intro.). The Hague: Martinus Nijhoff.

Husserl, E. (1965). *Phenomenology and the Crisis of Philosophy.* New York: Harper & Row.

Husserl, E. (1966). *The Phenomenology of Internal Time-Consciousness.* Bloomington: Indiana University Press, *Introduction.*

Husserl, E. (1970). *The Crisis of European Sciences and Transcendental Phenomenology: An Introduction to Phenomenological Philosophy.* Evanston, IL: Northwestern University Press, Section 11.

James, W. (1962). A world of pure experience. In Barrett W. & Aiken, H. D. (Eds.). *Philosophy in the Twentieth Century.* New York: Random House

Kockelmans, J. (1967). *Edmund Husserl's Phenomenological Psychology: A Historico-Critical Study.* Pittsburgh, PA: Duquesne University Press.

Levinas, E. (1973). *The Theory of Intuition in Husserl's Phenomenology.* Evanston, IL: Northwestern University Press.

Mead, G. H. (1934). *Mind, Self and Society: From the Perspective of a Social Behaviorist.* Chicago: University of Chicago Press.

Mijuskovic, B. (1970). The synthetic *a priori* in Plato. *Dialogue,* 12:1.

Mijuskovic, B. (1978). Brentano's theory of consciousness. *Philosophy and Phenomenological Research,* XXXVIII:3.

Natanson, M. (1973). *Edmund Husserl: Philosopher of Infinite Tasks.* Evanston, IL: Northwestern University Press.

Pippin, R. (1987). Kant and spontaneity. *Canadian Journal of Philosophy,* 17:2.

Ricoeur, P. (1966). Kant and Husserl. *Philosophy Today,* 10:3.

Ricoeur, P. (1967). *Husserl: An Analysis of His Phenomenology.* Evanston, IL: Northwestern University Press.

Sartre, J-P. (1966). *Being and Nothingness.* New York: Washington Square Press.

Sokolowski, R. (1970). *The Formation of Husserl's Concept of Constitution.* The Hague: Martinus Nijhoff.

Sokolowski, R. (1974). *Husserlian Meditations.* Evanston, IL: Northwestern University Press.

Spiegelberg, H. (1965). *The Phenomenological Movement: A Historical Introduction.* The Hague: Martinus Nijhoff.

Whitehead, A. N. (1925). *Science and the Modern World.* New York: Macmillan.

Chapter 5

Psychological Roots of Loneliness

In the previous three chapters, we sought the cognitive roots of loneliness. Basically, as Kant inquired, "How is human consciousness itself possible; what are the conditions that make human thinking actual?" (*Critique of Pure Reason*, A xvii); just so we have inquired, "How is loneliness possible and indeed universal, necessary, and actual?" Assuming we have shown on cognitive grounds that loneliness is innate, it is now time to turn to its affective dimensions, its motivational dynamic, and its practical implications.

A helpful approach is to ask how does the self "enter" into the world? To repeat, loneliness is meaningful only if there is an actual self and that self is actively self-conscious and intentional. We initially suggested that primarily there are two compatible and mutually supportive elements for establishing the relationship of the self to the world as well as to other selves: (1) cognitively, philosophically, and phenomenologically, which we have just considered at length, but now we are prepared to move forward with (2), the self's psychological and developmental entrance into the sphere of human existence. But this time we shall focus primarily on the emotional and motivational factors as opposed to the previous cognitive ones involved in loneliness. Both methods, however, incorporate the legitimacy of the self and together they are able to account for reflexivity and intentionality.

What now follows is the psychological birth of loneliness. At first, the new born is incapable of distinguishing the internal from the external sphere. When the infant begins its first period of post-partum existence, it experiences what Freud calls, in *Civilization and Its Discontents*, an "oceanic feeling," an immediate, seamless identification with all that exists; it is a state of pure chaos, of indeterminate, shifting sensations and feelings during which "it" is unable to distinguish its "self" from a surrounding world of independent, external objects. At this stage of non–self-awareness, the infant's mind spontaneously and aimlessly wanders to and fro toward whatever happens to attract and stimulate its attention. Dreams and waking states are indistinguishable. These are the initial moments of primordial consciousness (Freud, 1961a, p. 15). Similarly, William James, in the *Principles of Psychology,* describes how "The baby, assailed by eyes, ears, nose, and entrails at once feels it all as one great blooming, buzzing confusion," an amorphous chaos of colors and sounds, smells and tastes, pains and pleasures (James, 1950, p. I, 488). *This primary, spontaneous, disorganized pursuit of transient sensations and feelings and thoughts, this arbitrary freedom of perspective and attention will later in life be mimicked by all kinds of soothing fantasies, unbounded daydreams, free-floating reveries, as well as nightmarish terrors, anxieties, and frightening visions, a jumble of the pleasant and the unpleasant, all motivated by both unconscious and subconscious desires and fears. This dynamic is never left behind. It forever lurks unattended, seething, and simmering in the depths of a truly irretrievable subconscious as opposed to the theoretically retrievable unconscious.* Its latent content may at times appear in the distorted guise of nightmares, but even there it is veiled in obscurity as we shall see.

At the next developmental level of awareness, the child begins to distinguish its self from an independent realm of objects. In its crib, it initially reaches for the moon, thinking it is an attainable part of its body like its hand, only to discover its independent ontological status. It self-generates relations, forms of thought between self and not-self; it recognizes and reinforces a distinction between self and objects as it attains an increasing sense of discrimination between an internal and an external reality. It begins to sense its limitations and objective constraints in relation to its desires. This represents the first moments of self-consciousness; it cognizes and eventually recognizes and reaffirms its separate individual existence as distinct from a *general* sphere of objects. This developmental stage reflects Kant's and Freud's cognitive assertion that the empirical concept of the self is mutually constituted by the presence of phenomenal objects or, in psychoanalytic terms, "object relations." And at a still later juncture, the infant's consciousness intersects with a special "object," and it begins to realize that there is a certain independent but very active object (the mother) within its unique field of self-concern that exhibits a powerful and highly significant relation of *"self–other self–to itself."* This is the beginning stage of primary narcissism as well as the incipient, dawning moment of social consciousness. Additionally, the other self displays a dominating power over the physical nourishment the child requires as well as the emotional nurturance it demands. It also realizes and recognizes that this forceful other *person* can both bestow and withhold the sustenance it needs and the care it craves. Consequently, a conflict of opposing desires is engendered; the child demands attention and the mother imposes restrictions. This is the next developmental stage of overweening narcissism in the child, of unlimited entitlement fantasies, which maternal solicitation, on the one hand, and society's impersonal socialization, on the other hand, will have to curb and control as the infant's ego develops (Mijuskovic, 1979–1980, pp. 479–492).

Interestingly enough, a similar dialectical progression, which moves forward only to return to itself enriched, occurs in Hegel's description of individual and social consciousness in the *Phenomenology of the Spirit* as it captures the cognitive and affective progression of human development. First, there is Consciousness, the temporal moment or stage of Sense-Certainty (Plato's *Theaetetus*); then Perception (Locke's *Essay*); next Understanding (Kant's first *Critique*); and, finally, Self-Consciousness, the Lordship and Bondage relation, the struggle for dominance over the other self as instantiated in the works of Hobbes and later Marx and Sartre (Hegel, 1977, pp. 58–118). Long before Darwin's theory of biological evolution, Hegel formulates a theory of individual development as well as philosophical evolution. It is to be noted that unlike Kant (and later Freud), who contend that the self and the object mutually condition each other, Hegel maintains that self-consciousness instead awaits to be dialectically constituted by a struggle for dominance with another ego. In a moment, we shall suggest a very similar structural progression, which occurs in Margaret Mahler's *The Psychological Birth of the Human Infant*.

What is loneliness? Whatever it is, it presupposes both a genuine self and the activities and structures of reflexivity and intentionality. But it cannot be fully understood unless both the cognitive and the emotional factors are given their due. In my original *Psychiatry* article, I offered the following definition:

Loneliness is something that we can "observe" reflexively within ourselves. Just as the manifestations of physical gravity are externally observable, so I contend loneliness in a psychological medium appears sometimes as a gentle force but also often as a violent one moving us internally. As a sensation or feeling, it is indefinable just as the quality of the color yellow cannot be communicated to one congenitally blind. But as a meaning, it consists in the desire to be intimately related to another self-conscious being but being unable to be so related. In this respect and to this extent, we can share it as a *meaning*. In what follows, I shall treat loneliness as a psychological drive—one whose internality or immanence, its *meaning* is essentially independent of physiological factors, although they are peripherally present. As every significant proposition must have a meaningful opposite, intimacy serves as the contrary to loneliness. (Mijuskovic, 1977, p. 114)

With the lapse now of some three-and-a-half decades of peering and squinting into the recesses of the human mind, I currently believe loneliness is much more than that. The earliest article of which I am aware devoted solely to loneliness as a topic in its own right is by a psychoanalyst, Gregory Zilboorg, who pleads for an intrinsic, *a priori* connection between the concepts of narcissism–entitlement–loneliness–hostility. He further argues that in extreme or pathological cases, this complex relation often leads either to suicide or to murder, the former because the person blames himself or herself for not being desirable to others; and, in the second instance, the individual blames others for not desiring him or her (Zilboorg, 1938, pp. 45–54). Essentially, Zilboorg is proposing that both cognitively and emotionally narcissism, entitlement, loneliness, and hostility issues are mutually implicative, that *all* cases of loneliness, by their very nature, universally and necessarily, entail varying degrees of aggression; that whenever and wherever one finds loneliness one will also discover anger as its invariable companion. Every instance of hostility merely disguises an underlying loneliness. Thus, I am contending that the relation between the meanings of loneliness and the affective feelings of aggression constitute what I have previously characterized as a synthetic *a priori* connection. To repeat, just as color and extension, two totally different concepts, are *a priori*, that is, universally, necessarily, and thus inseparably related, so are loneliness and hostility. Whenever we feel lonely or abandoned or betrayed we tend to regress within the self by retreating toward the sanctuary of the womb or even more symbolically toward death through extended periods of sleep. In Greek mythology sleep is the brother of death. Both states represent a time when there was neither self nor other nor loneliness.

As we become alienated from other conscious beings, we inevitably become resentful and angry. Hostility is an emotion that signals not the abnormality of the few but instead the desperate isolation of all of us who are "human, all too human" (Nietzsche). Zilboorg's penetrating analysis goes far to provide an accurate and balanced picture of the dynamics between loneliness and anger. Often we tend to think of lonely people as sad or depressed. They are, but they are also angry. As Freud correctly remarks, depression is internalized anger; it is self-conscious loathing turned within, and it is always potentially poised to intentionally discharge internally toward the self or externally toward others. The sense of intense or prolonged isolation inevitably engenders resentment, which, when it escalates, becomes directed destructively against either the self or others. In its milder forms, it appears disguised through commonplace phenomena as "our universal and protean propensity toward gossip" (p. 45), in our need to pry into the affairs of others merely so that we can criticize them and thereby enhance our own narcissistic self-image by comparison. Indeed, just as boredom signals loneliness in its less virulent form (Pascal, Schopenhauer, and Nietzsche), in a similar fashion gossiping betrays evidence of an underlying hostility born of narcissistic impulses, according to Zilboorg.

At the other end of the social spectrum, loneliness can fuel a powerful need to submit one's self to aggressive leaders or groups just so that one can experience a sense of security, of belonging, of false superiority. Loneliness frequently fuels resentment toward others who are perceived as undeservedly more fortunate than themselves. Religious and political fanatics are twin beneficiaries of men's fear of isolation and their consequent immersion in violent and prejudiced groups animated by feelings of resentment against other groups, or sects or even the world at large.

We try to drown the essential meaning [of loneliness] in the din of revolutionary explosions, the rattle of machine guns, and the roars of infuriated crowds—masses of human beings who don't know how lonely they are, applauding prostate before "leaders" ready to let them be destroyed. (p. 48)

This passage, written during the darkest years that Europe had ever known, readily summons to the imagination the specter of a lonely and paranoid leader promising recognition to a terrified, humiliated, and angry populace by the promise of military actions aimed toward the rest of mankind, the world, and civilization in general; by offering a mistaken sense of redemption, a distorted sense of belonging—political, nationalistic, ethnic, economic, all in the name of the "master race," it matters not—to those who feel disenfranchised and alienated from the rest of humanity. This sort of global hostility can only be generated by the envy of others who are perceived as undeservedly fortunate.

Hannah Arendt, in her famous and classic work, *The Origins of Totalitarianism*, targeting German Nazism, Italian Fascism, and Russian Communism, blames loneliness and a sense of alienation for the ills of the world current during her own time. She categorically states:

Loneliness, the common ground for terror, the essence of totalitarian government, and for ideology or logicality, the preparation of its executioners and victims is closely connected with uprootedness and superfluousness which have been the curse of modern masses since the beginning of the industrial revolution and have become acute with the rise of imperialism at the end of the last century and the break-down of political institutions and social institutions in our own time. To be uprooted means to have no place in the world recognized and guaranteed by others; to be superfluous means not to belong to the world at all. . . . Taken in itself, without consideration of recent historical causes, and its new role in politics, loneliness is at the same time contrary to the basic requirements of the human condition *and* one of the fundamental experiences of every human being. (Arendt, 1976, p. 475)

As I write this book, terrorism, suicide bombers, public beheadings of innocents, mass murders of uninvolved civilians and children are rampant throughout the Middle East with Al Qaida and ISIS in Iran, Syria, and Iraq. At the same time, ironically and tragically enough, the same groups who are disenfranchised and persecuted are willing recruits for indoctrination into the identical violent causes that threatened their own existence but a short while ago. It brings to mind Orwell's prophetic novel, *1984,* of a world divided into three parts, each in conflict with another part. How often does the fear of loneliness and exclusion from their kind drive men to fanatically align themselves with violent extremism, to bond and subjugate themselves at whatever cost and to whatever cause lest they be left behind and alone? It's not only misery that loves company but terrorism and aggression, too.

On a more individual scale, we notice how often divorce leads to anger and recrimination; how often parental abuse and abandonment lead children into "acting out" behaviors and juvenile delinquency. Beneath all this lies the specter of loneliness, isolation, alienation, estrangement, failed communication, and misunderstanding.

How does all this happen? Initially, the child is ushered into a world of warmth, affection, and attention.

He is played with, amused, taken care of, attended to, talked to, cuddled, and otherwise made to feel that the universe is ready to serve its pleasure. It learns the joy of being admired and loved before it learns anything about the outside world. . . . Here we have the quintessence of what later becomes the narcissistic orientation: a conviction that life is nothing else but being loved and admired. (p. 53)

All this attention in turn stimulates in the child a false feeling of security and self-sufficiency, a narcissistic sense of well-being, omnipotence, and megalomanic entitlement. But as the infant's desires for unending gratification are increasingly challenged and thwarted by the mother's recalcitrance, it is compelled to realize its utter dependence on a powerful other self. In a short time, it learns to recognize its complete dependence on the mother, which is inevitably accompanied by feelings of inferiority against the background of an emerging conflict between its desires and the mother's directive expectations and insistent demands (Adler). This once more precipitates an aggressive reaction—the moment of Hegelian negativity, of opposition as the child realizes its desires and wishes are in conflict with those of the other self. It is here that the frustration brought about by the dialectical conflict with the other self occurs. As Zilboorg warns:

Here is the nucleus of hostility, hatred, impotent aggression of the lonely and the abandoned. Here is the beginning of intolerant anger which some day civilization will have to subdue, or mental illness will discharge again into the open. And if we continue from the crib to the nursery and to the kindergarten, we can observe scene by scene the enactment of the story entitled narcissism, megalomania, and loneliness. (p. 53)

But notice how in the last sentence, the author substitutes the term "loneliness" for hostility. We all too often blame others for our loneliness. We hold them responsible both psychologically and ethically for our isolation. Consequently, we respond by exhibiting various degrees of displeasure and then anger and finally hatred. Even boredom, as we earlier suggested, is symptomatic of loneliness in its more subtle form, and when it is amplified and intensified, it soon turns into irritation, eventually hostility, and even death (Ibsen's *Hedda Gabler*). In fact, there is a certain irony in our institution of punishment. In order to penalize individuals, we incarcerate them and place them in solitary confinement, with the result that their intolerable loneliness only reinforces a mounting hostility. Instead of reducing aggression in the world, we only add to it. In *Loneliness in Philosophy, Psychology, and Literature*, I refer to Schopenhauer's description of the hopeless misery that attends incarcerated prisoners; subjected to the boredom of solitary confinement in the American prison system, they frequently resorted to suicide.

From the very beginning of our realization of separation, from the moment we recognize the extreme schism between self and other, we are maneuvered either into a desperate struggle to master and dominate the other; or to obsequiously please the other self. When we fail in our efforts, loneliness and hostility intervene, eventually to be discharged toward the self or against others. This is as true of the personality disorders that are commonly classified as narcissistic, antisocial, avoidant/obsessive/compulsive, borderline, dependent, and histrionic as well as of the common man.

Almost four decades later, the studies of Margaret Mahler et al. amply confirm the same dialectical structure, a dynamic interplay between narcissism, loneliness, and hostility as foreseen by Zilboorg. Indeed, in their work, the authors view aggression as a direct consequence of separation anxiety. For Mahler, there is initially a sense of "symbiotic oneness," an undifferentiated unity between the child's consciousness and the entire universe, which she terms primary narcissism—Freud's oceanic feeling— and the barriers separating infant and caretaker are nonexistent (Mahler et al., 1975, pp. 8, 18, 153). Next, the infant develops the capacity to distinguish its self cognitively first from other things and objects and later from the other self (generally the mother), and thus it is able to separate its emotions and thoughts initially from other selves and subsequently from other minds by recognizing emotions not concordant with its self and those of the others. This is a momentous cognitive distinction, namely, the realization that the other person is not only a separate bodily self but more significantly a self-conscious being with often unpredictable emotions and demands that need to be deciphered in order to be anticipated. This constitutes a further developmental stage, a process of "separation-individuation" during which the nascent ego continues to aspire toward explicit *self*-consciousness (pp. 42, 75, 116). Along with the separation from the mother it experiences a feeling of freedom, transcendence, and intentionality, but the child also realizes that this independence arrives at a high price as Mahler strongly confirms Zilboorg's endorsement of the relation between loneliness and hostility. Once more, the sense of isolation frightens the ego, and jointly anxiety and anger together result, suggesting a more complex relation between loneliness, anxiety, and anger. When we are frightened, we are also angry (pp. 149, 160, 178, 181). Again, Mahler's work parallels Hegel's Lordship and Bondage section, which describes the dialectical, triadic interplay of consciousness as it progresses through position-opposition-reconciliation. Conflict is characteristic of the second developmental stage of opposition according to Mahler. In his Lordship and Bondage section, Hegel describes it as a *desire for recognition,* as a confrontation between two egos literally engaged in a battle to the death in which, in Hegel's words, "each seeks the death of the other" (Kojeve, 1969). Marx based his entire (dualistic) dialectical struggle between the capitalists and the proletariat on this conflict, and Sartre exploited the same dynamic in his description of the hostile engagement between two egos pitted against each other in his famous keyhole passage in *Being and Nothingness.* Each self seeks to reduce the other's freedom and turn the other into an unfree object.

James Lynch, in *The Broken Heart* (1977), chronicles how single, divorced, widowed, and in general lonely adults suffer from five times the frequency rate of heart attacks than their married counterparts. Later, in a second study, *A Cry Unheard* (2000), he demonstrates the consequences of loneliness for vulnerable school children by the "bullying" of peers and the neglect and unresponsiveness of teachers who discourage their wards from verbal expression and participation in the classroom, thus destroying and inhibiting the children's sense of confidence by ignoring them. Personally, as a Child Protective social worker, I often noticed while visiting elementary schools that all too frequently teachers seemed unaware that Hispanic children by culture are taught the value of cooperation as opposed to competition, and often they felt intimidated in contrast to the Anglo kids who waived their arms in eager response to the teacher's questions. All too often our teachers no longer live in the neighborhoods or communities where they teach, and so they are forced to travel long distances through crowded traffic conditions just to get to their schools. By the time they arrive, they are already in no mood to deal with "hyperactive boys." The energetic offender is summarily marshalled into the principal's office, and his mother is called to report to the school and advised to put her son on Ritalin, Cylert, Adderall, and the like. Lynch also goes on to show how being raised in dual settings, in joint custody situations by divorced parents, in dysfunctional broken homes, and in single-parent households inevitably produces lonely children and teenagers. There are "latch key kids" left to their own devices while both parents work—ironically enough—in order to provide a "higher quality of life" for their emotionally neglected children. Similarly, in three closely related articles, I have tried to emphasize the toxic results of loneliness in children and adolescents (Mijuskovic, 1986a, pp. 941–951, 1986b, pp. 227–240, 1988, pp. 503–516). In the psychological sphere as in the physical sphere, each action produces a reaction. Abused children often become abusers as adults. Children of divorced parents frequently resort to divorce as adults. Collectively, all forms of neglect, abuse, prejudice, and cruelty directed against the self will predispose and induce the victims themselves to produce either self-directed- or other-directed anger or both.

Culturally, America is a very individualistic and atomistic society, as opposed to organically structured communities. This means that competition prevails over cooperation, and an intrinsic *a priori* feature of competition is aggression. No one competes without a goal of besting the other. If one wishes to understand American society, one could do no better than to look at the National Football League; at the end of the season there are thirty-one losers and only one winner. And in the winning team a good portion of the players, the "stars," will move on next fall coaxed away by more lucrative contracts (Mijuskovic, 1992, pp. 147–162).

During my extended period of studying loneliness, I have found that the deepest *expressions* of loneliness are rooted in literature, not philosophy or psychology. In fact, it clearly starts with the novel form of narrative first instituted in Murasaki Shikibu's eleventh-century *The Tale of Genji*, Miguel de Cervantes's seventeenth-century *Don Quixote*, and Daniel Defoe's eighteenth-century *Robinson Crusoe* (Mijuskovic 2012). There seems to be an intimate connection between the first- and the third-person narrative style of writing and loneliness. In terms of philosophy, there is certainly a concentration on loneliness to be found in the existential works of Kierkegaard and Nietzsche, but that comes fairly late in the game. Basically, philosophers have been unconcerned about loneliness. Literature, on the other hand, as I understand it, following a tradition that goes back to Aristotle, offers universal truths about mankind as opposed to history, which rather dwells on the particular (*Poetics*, IX, 5–8). It is in this spirit that I offer the following two literary works in further confirmation of the synthetic *a priori* relation between loneliness and hostility. In his short story, "The Laughing Man," J. D. Salinger recounts how a young man assigned to minister to a group of nine-year-old boys after school entertains them with episodes concerning the exploits of a lonely hero, whose isolation is symbolized by a facial disfigurement, a sort of incongruous mask, which makes him appear as if he were always grinning or smiling, while his true, innermost feelings and thoughts are quite the opposite from his exterior appearance. And "Every morning, in his extreme loneliness, the Laughing Man stole off to the deep forest. . . . There he befriended any number of animals." The serialized installments are told daily at the end of the group's athletic outings by a young man, the Chief, who is in charge of the group calling itself the Comanche Club. One day, the storyteller introduces the boys to an attractive young woman who is obviously dating him. The girl is as friendly as she is attractive and in a short while becomes a welcome participant in the Club's excursions and athletic activities. At the end of each day, the sessions are topped off with another adventure of the Laughing Man and his faithful companion, Wolf. Unexpectedly, one afternoon during a baseball game, the Chief and his girlfriend argue, and she abruptly leaves, weeping. After her departure, the Chief relates the final episode of the Laughing Man to the bewildered children, which describes the mutilated death of their favorite hero and his trusted canine, and the boys are left upset and crying. (Salinger, 1953).

The story demonstrates on two levels how quickly loneliness can be transformed into hostility and an indiscriminate displacement of undeserved anger toward innocent bystanders. The aggression is not only turned against the unprepared children, but at the same time it is symbolically and unconsciously self-directed destructively through the Laughing Man at the Chief himself. Feelings of aggression—as well as affection, interestingly enough—are often indiscriminate; they either destroy or enhance their surroundings with an equal suffusing force of evil or goodness. The children, having trusted and loved the Chief with all their hearts and experienced a strong sense of attachment are now left with a deep sense of abandonment, betrayal, fragmentation, and separation, all symptoms of loneliness. And we can generalize that whenever we experience a comparable loss of trust in those closest to us, we also experience a "loss of innocence" and we will never again feel the same; the lost trust can never be regained or recaptured. It is akin to a close friend lying to you or a spouse committing adultery. It is a betrayal directed at the very heart of our vulnerability.

Beyond all this, the spectrum from annoyance to rage generated by sexual disappointment, frustration, and denial, with its consequent deprivation of anticipated erotic pleasure, undoubtedly underlies a great deal of hostility prevalent in the world (Mijuskovic, 1987, p. 15–22). At my current county mental health clinic, endless subjects complain about their inability to control their anger, and quite often with men it's in the context of sexual frustration leading to physical abuse, molestation, rape, and incest.

With this theme in mind, I now wish to draw on a remarkable passage in Jerzy Kosinski's *The Painted Bird* in order to graphically illustrate the terrible anger generated by unrequited sexual passion and its consequent feelings of loneliness, abandonment, and betrayal. (Graham Greene, more than any other writer, has explored the theme of betrayal of others, of values, and of the self in his novels.) The story depicts a young boy of six abandoned by his parents for his own safety as they are being transported to a concentration camp by train during World War II. As he is forced to wander throughout the countryside of Eastern Europe from village to village among the conflict's devastation, he is subjected to various abuses and humiliations from the peasant populations where he has sought sanctuary. He continues to survive alone, unloved, and misunderstood. At one point, he secures shelter from a professional bird catcher. The peasant, Lekh, maintains a prolonged series of sexual encounters with a buxom, long-haired woman called Stupid Ludmilla, herself the victim of sexual atrocities by her townspeople. Generally, the two lovers meet daily, but one day she fails to appear and as her absences become prolonged.

Lekh would become possessed of a silent rage. He would stare solemnly at the birds in the cages mumbling something to himself. Finally, after prolonged scrutiny, he would choose the strongest bird, tie it to his wrist, and prepare stinking paints of different colors which he mixed together from the most varied pigments. When the colors satisfied him, Lekh would turn the bird over and paint its wings, head, and breast in rainbow hues until it became more dappled and vivid than a bouquet of wild flowers. Then we would go into the thick of the forest.

There he would take the painted bird and order me to hold it in my hand and squeeze it lightly. The bird would begin to twitter and attract a flock of the same species which would fly nervously over our heads. Our prisoner hearing them, strained toward them, warbling more loudly, its little heart, locked in its freshly painted breast, beating violently. When a sufficient number of birds gathered above our heads, Lekh would give me a sign to release the prisoner. It would soar, happy and free, a spot of rainbow against the backdrop of clouds and then plunge into the waiting brown flock. For an instant, the birds were confounded. The painted bird circled from one end of the flock to the other, vainly trying to convince its kin that it was one of them. But dazzled by its brilliant colors, they flew around it unconvinced. The painted bird would be forced farther and farther away as it zealously tried to enter the ranks of the flock. We saw soon afterwards how one bird after another would peel off in a fierce attack. Shortly the many-hued shape lost its place in the sky and dropped to the ground. When we finally found the birds, they were usually dead. Lekh keenly examined the number of blows which the birds had received. Blood seeped through their colored wings, diluting the paint and soiling Lekh's hands.

As Ludmilla's absences become more prolonged, Lekh's hostility becomes more intensified.

Stupid Ludmilla did not return. Lekh sulking and glum removed one bird after another from the cages and released them into the air to be killed by their kin. One day he trapped a large raven, whose wings he painted red, the breast green, and the tail blue. When a flock of ravens appeared over our hut, Lekh freed the painted bird. As soon as it joined the flock a desperate battle began. The changeling was attacked from all sides. Black, red, green, and blue feathers began to drop at our feet. The ravens ran amuck in the skies and suddenly the painted raven plummeted to the fresh-plowed soil. It was still alive, opening its beak and vainly trying to move its wings. Its eyes had been pecked out, and fresh blood streamed over its painted plumage. It made yet another attempt to flutter up from the sticky earth but its strength was gone.

Lekh grew thin and stayed in the hut but more often swigging home-made vodka and singing songs about Ludmilla. At times he would sit astride his bed, leaning over the dirt floor, drawing something with a long stick. Gradually the outline became clear; it was the figure of a full-breasted long haired woman. (Kosinski, 1977, pp. 43–45)

During the ensuing course of the story, the child, who is never named, never recognized as a human being by the peasants, becomes electively mute because he is either unable or unwilling to share his thoughts with others. There is no point in even trying to communicate. No one will understand what he is feeling and thinking. His absolute loneliness is complete, and it results in the loss of any desire to express himself.

Every one of us stood alone, and the sooner one realized that . . . the better for him. It mattered little if one was mute; people did not understand one another anyway. They collided with or charmed one another, hugged or trampled one another, but everyone thought only of himself. His emotions, memory, and senses divided him from others as effectively as thick reeds screen the mainstream from the muddy bank. (ibid., p. 212)

The symbolism of muteness representing loneliness is also reminiscent of Carson McCullers's *The Heart Is a Lonely Hunter,* where one of the main characters, a mute, commits suicide following the death of his companion, another mute. Often loneliness is represented in novels by a physical handicap, like blindness, deafness, or even lameness, as in Somerset Maugham's *Of Human Bondage.*

At a later point in the story, the boy forms an association with another mute boy, and together they collaborate in derailing a train transporting peasants to market, killing and injuring an untold number of victims. It's in retaliation for a wrong done to the boy, but the failed reprisal is not only unsuccessful but it also turns out to be essentially and tragically anonymous and indiscriminate. By anonymous and indiscriminate, I mean that more often than not, lonely and angry individuals lose their "sense of proportion" and indiscriminately lash out through *displacement* at innocent bystanders. Frequently, the public becomes aware through newspaper headlines and the media that spouses of athletes engaged in violent contact sports become innocent "objects" of frustration by partners who simply "take it out" on them.

The boy is represented in the novel by the raven. At the conclusion of the work, when he is finally reunited with his parents, who in the meantime had adopted a younger boy, and after a short failed attempt to reintegrate him within the family because of his violence, he is sent away to live with a stranger in the hills. Having survived the entire war and having been painted in all the hues of loneliness and aggression, he is incapable of returning to his own kind, and at the end the novel closes with a premonition of his suicide. Still a child in human development, he realizes he will never fit in again within the loving and protective arms of his parents and that he has already been displaced. (Kosinski himself committed suicide.) It's not a stretch to compare the child in *The Painted Bird* with the U.S. servicemen returning home from their engagement during World War II, Korea, Viet Nam, Iraq, and Afghanistan. The government upon which they relied so trustingly in so many cases was often unable to discharge the trust. A case in point is the felt betrayal generated by the response of the U.S. military and the Veterans Administration hospitals by denying that Agent Orange, a toxic defoliant prolifically used in the Viet Nam conflict, had a negative impact on returning American servicemen.

Along with hostility, there is *always* a sense of failed communication as one experiences loneliness and a sense of forced or unwanted isolation; a feeling that others not only don't understand but they don't even care.

In my experience in the social work field as a Child Protective Services worker ministering to countless children and teens, I often had the occasion to witness the placement of children with foster parents, who were trained not to bond with their charges in the event they were returned to their natural parents. The result was that they frequently attained their eighteenth year of age and maturity while being shuttled from one foster home to another or one group home to another. One can imagine the atmosphere of desolation in these surroundings and the distorted sense of family "unity" they developed in these settings. I especially remember one girl who was removed from her mother's custody because of positive toxicology screens for both mother and infant at the hospital and eighteen months later "freed" for an adoption that never transpired. She was very pretty, bright, and incredibly rebellious. She was shuttled from foster home to foster home until she was eighteen. Her level of anger was constant and extreme. Another female released from Camarillo State Hospital at eighteen years of age promptly produced five children in five years by a quintet of fathers and taught her children not to speak to anyone unless she explicitly gave them permission. Needless to say, home visits were difficult and unproductive. I could only imagine how it would go when they had to start school—assuming she was going to allow them to attend school. The agency provided her with forty hours a week "respite care" in the home, probably until the fifth child would turn eighteen and assuming she had no more children.

I offer the following two newspaper documents in the spirit of empirical evidence. They appeared as separate incidents in a syndicated column by Bob Greene in a *Los Angeles Times* edition dated January 2, 1980. The first document concerns two individuals, a young woman whose loneliness elicited self-destructive impulses and a man whose sense of isolation prompted a vow to begin indiscriminately killing Los Angeles County residents because of his intense feelings of "depression, frustration, and loneliness." The following quotations are excerpts from their correspondence to the columnist. The young woman poignantly asks the reader: "So why do I find myself playing with razor blades, wondering how much I would bleed if I slashed my wrists?" She continues:

You once asked in your column why any person would bare his soul to a complete stranger, why would anyone be willing to read painful embarrassing things. I think people do this because the emotions build up inside them until they reach a breaking point. At this point, a person has to share their problems or break down into sobs of pain. Sometimes it's easier to confide in a stranger than your closest friend. Another reason I wrote is because I would like to know if there are other people out there who know how I feel. Is there someone who understands the torment of fear and isolation? Can you understand what it's like to be so lonely for companionship and understanding?

It's clear from her epistle that this nineteen-year-old girl is struggling to reach someone *beyond* herself, through an act of *intentionality*, someone, anyone who will acknowledge her existence and pain; to establish even an indirect contact with a person "out there," someone to recognize how she feels; to break through the barriers of her isolation. The worst fate a human being can experience is to be ignored, unrecognized, unacknowledged: not to exist in the eyes of others, as Ralph Ellison writes in *The Invisible Man.* It's the ultimate indignity; to be lonely and unnoticed. Like the lonely and angry graffiti writers who express their sense of isolation on vacant buildings and freeway overpasses, who desperately wish that someone, anyone, even nameless strangers would acknowledge their existence; anything to force others to admit their individual being, their unique existence.

The second newspaper letter, dated a few days later, is from "Molded to Murder":

Dear Bob Greene: The disintegration of a mind is a terrible thing to experience, especially when it's your own mind. That is what a 19-year-old girl wrote to you in her article. Well, she is right. I know because my mind is slowly disintegrating due to my being lonely, isolated, and unwanted. . . . Do you know what it is like to be lonely all your life long? I do. Do you know what it's like to be always on the outside looking in no matter what you do, not being able to get in? Do you? I do. I can't remember when I didn't feel empty or alone. In my early years, it was not so painful but it builds up as time goes by until it becomes unbearable. I always tried to make friends all my life but failed . . . have kept trying to have friends—have meaningful relationships—all my life I have failed. I tried to find a young woman—someone to be a partner and share my life. . . . All I ever wanted was friends, a good wife, children, love, affection, understanding, truth. I never really got much of any of them. I differ from the girl who wrote to you. She mentioned suicide—many times. I do not think about suicide. For the last year or so I have been thinking about hatred—murder and revenge. I have been a good person all my life and I have never hurt any one physically. . . . But I think about all the pain and loneliness I have received all my life from cool, unkind, thoughtless people and I feel I must do it.

Hostility and envy are the constant companions of loneliness. When prolonged or severe, they are the ready fuses fated eventually to discharge and explode into aggression toward the self or others as Zilboorg warns.

Lest we tend to consider these cases as isolated instances of pathological aggression, it may be helpful to place the thesis of the universality of loneliness and its connection to anger in a more explicit expression.

The whole conviction of my life now rests on the belief that loneliness, far from being a rare and curious phenomenon, peculiar to myself and to a few other solitary men, is the central and inevitable fact of human existence. When we examine the moments, acts, and statements of all kinds of people—not only the grief and ecstasy of the greatest poets, but also of the huge unhappiness of the average soul, as evidenced by the innumerable strident words of abuse, hatred, and contempt, mistrust, and scorn that forever grate upon our ears as the manswarm passes us in the streets—we find I think, that they are all suffering from the same thing. The final cause of their complaint is loneliness. (Wolfe, 1968, p. 146)

The second important article focusing solely on the topic of loneliness is by another psychoanalyst, Frieda Fromm-Reichmann, who describes her initial frustration in trying to communicate with an institutionalized psychotic patient until she finally asks, "That lonely?" and thus suddenly establishes the basis for a dialogue. As in the preceding literary example of the boy in *The Painted Bird,* loneliness invariably involves the sense of failed communication, the fear that no one is listening, no one wishes to understand, and hence no one cares and so we might just as well doom ourselves to a self-imposed silence. Why bother trying to reach the other? When others don't listen to us, it usually means that they don't care.

In a similar vein, J. B. Hoskisson proposes that *all* cases and situations involving forlornness and loneliness are grounded in the inability to communicate, that "all loneliness is due to a lack of communication or a total breakdown in communication." Accordingly, he further believes we shall always discover a compelling connection between loneliness and unsuccessful communication, thus pointing to an essential underlying substratum of loneliness when we feel misunderstood, unappreciated, disrespected, and unheard. "Whenever we feel 'misunderstood,' we feel the other has not listened to us; our words have fallen on deaf ears" (Hoskisson, 1965, pp. 37–38; Mijuskovic, 1980, pp. 261–270). "You're not listening to me" is a common refrain when matters deteriorate in a relationship and we feel we are not being "listened to." Virginia Satir founded an entire therapeutic treatment on just this principle. Having worked with psychotic individuals in acute psychiatric hospitals, institutional settings, outpatient, and inpatient mental health clinics for thirty years, I can attest to this profound speculation. It's extremely difficult to gain the trust of many psychotic individuals, and one can readily observe how much energy it takes for them to carry on a "social" conversation, to appear normal before they feel overwhelmed and suddenly break off the dialogue. They want to communicate, to be "listened to" so desperately that the tension and pressure of making themselves understood often proves too much for them to bear.

Further in the course of her seminal, groundbreaking article, Fromm-Reichmann goes on to emphasize that loneliness and anxiety are inseparable, and at the conclusion of her essay, she proposes that loneliness and anxiety are *identical* concepts. In effect, she validates a powerful intrinsic connection, a synthetic *a priori* relation between loneliness and anxiety (Fromm-Reichmann, 1959, pp. 1–15).

Erich Fromm, her ex-husband, in *The Art of Loving*, echoes similar sentiments when he states:

Man is gifted with reason; *he is life being aware of itself;* he has [self-conscious] awareness of himself. . . . The awareness of his aloneness and separateness, of his helplessness before the forces of nature and of society, all this makes his separate, disunited existence an unbearable prison. He would become insane could he not liberate himself from this prison and reach out and unite himself in some form or other, with men, with the world outside. The experience of separateness arouses anxiety; it is indeed the source of all anxiety. The deepest need of man, then, is the need to overcome his separateness, to leave the prison of his aloneness. The *absolute* failure to achieve this aim means insanity, because the panic of complete isolation can be overcome only by such a radical withdrawal from the world outside that the feeling of separation disappears—because the world outside, from which one is separated, has disappeared. (Fromm, 1970, pp. 6–7)

If one puts the above suggestions together, what begins to appear is an underlying, *a priori* conceptual relationship between the affective feelings of entitlement, hostility, failed communication, and anxiety as vital, constituent elements of loneliness and all emanating from the natural narcissistic needs and demands of the self. At first, narcissistic egoism *is* the self. It all begins with narcissism and feelings of entitlement. Sociologically, it's only much later that Auguste Comte coins a term for the opposite motivation—altruism as a concern and care for the other. That is not to say it's weaker or inferior but only that it's different.

All the foregoing being said, one begins to realize that loneliness, as a dynamic concept, is actually an "umbrella concept" whose painful extended spokes are generated from a central nucleus of narcissism. Indeed, I would postulate that in *all* negative emotions, there are underlying conscious and unconscious coloring shades of loneliness. In sum, the concept of loneliness actually forms an extended *system* of synthetic a *priori* meanings, relations, and Husserlian intentionalities. The nucleus of loneliness is haloed by horizons and fringes of inextricably attached and interdependent meanings within consciousness.

Having arrived at this intriguing thought, I began to explore its possibility with one of my female clients. I currently work at a large public mental health facility. She is a young adult, and I diagnosed her as having Posttraumatic Stress Syndrome (309.81) and Major Depression (296.33). (We are not allowed to open cases without assigning a *Diagnostic Statistical Manual of Psychiatric Disorders (DSM)* diagnosis for insurance purposes and funding.) She was incestuously molested for three years from the ages of six through eight by her father. When it was finally discovered, the case went to court, and she was removed from school for six months so that she could testify against him. She was subjected to intense harassment by the father's extended family members, who aggressively defended him and accused her of lying. Found guilty, the father was sentenced to prison. At the age of ten, her mother attempted to commit suicide. At the age of twelve, her mother left her with a maternal aunt and took her younger sibling to live with her and another man. After her father's release from his incarceration eight years later, he moved to Mexico and began a second family. At sixteen she started acting out, dropped out of school, started using drugs, and became victimized in a physically abusive and stressful relationship with a young man for four years (Mijuskovic, 2014, pp. 44–53).

According to Erikson's chart, the first developmental stage of life is concerned with trust versus mistrust issues. During the second stage, from ages three to five, the key crises revolve around initiative *versus* guilt and shame dynamics, and the child experiences a desire to emulate the parents and takes formative steps in creating play situations. The child makes up stories, playing out roles in a make-believe world of fantasy and what it means to be an adult. The child also begins to ask questions about that magic word—why? The most significant relationship occurs within the basic family unit. The goal is to conceptualize and forge purposive commitments for the self and to pursue close and intimate relationships. Ideally, Erikson's next stage, from ages six through twelve, involves the maturational stage of industry versus inferiority. The child learns new skills, the ability to create and incorporate knowledge and to develop a sense of accomplishment, attend school, and master educational skills (Erikson, 1963, pp. 247–261). Up to the age of six, the child successfully negotiated the stages. But it was at this third stage, at the age of six, that everything went wrong with my client and a sense of deep betrayal, of emotional abandonment, and a consequent loss of trust now permeates her entire sense of being, a loss from which she has yet to recover—and most likely never will. Whatever developmental gains she had accrued were soon lost beginning at the age of six. During those three years of incest, sexual exploitation, and molestation by her father, her mother's failure to protect or even recognize what was occurring, she was driven violently backward to Erikson's initial developmental crisis stage of trust-mistrust and all her previous achieved progress was completely undone. Her IQ remained the same when she was six, when she was eight, and when she turned twenty-two (her present age), but emotionally and in terms of maturity she remains six years old and vulnerable to frequent hysterical crying fits at the slightest reminiscence of her father. She now consistently and habitually avoids situations in which she feels pressured to perform even standard requests or normal expectations from others. She is unable to show up for appointments at the clinic, complete her school work, or follow through on volunteering assignments at the clinic, and she acknowledges severe and debilitating performance anxiety issues going back to her past when she was forced to fulfill impossible sexual demands by her father.

At this point, it is important to draw some diagnostic distinctions applicable to this particular case and situation. Phobias are simple, concrete fears. One simply cannot make a mistake about what one is afraid of. Further, they seem readily amenable to treatment through desensitization by a gentle, safe, and graduated exposure to the feared object, person, or situation. By contrast, Freudian anxiety is essentially grounded in internal, unconscious conflicts between opposing positive and negative emotions, as in the case above, for example, experiencing ambivalent feelings and thoughts between trust and mistrust, love and disgust, desire and fear, nurturance and abandonment, affection and abuse, and so on. And clearly this is the case in the example we are currently considering. But if the reader will recall our earlier discussion of Freud's and James's infant "assailed" by endless and boundless multiplicities of sensations, feelings, desires, frustrations, thoughts, distractions, pains, and pleasures, one can then begin to see how impoverished it is simply to characterize PTSD as merely a reliving, reexperiencing, or revisualization of the original trauma. In severe cases of PTSD, the victim is overwhelmed by powerful and conflicting emotions which destroy the individual's ability to make decisions and follow through on practical or even simple survival plans. Rather, in the young woman described above, the waves of emotion, *feelings* of fear, depression, anxiety, hostility, remorse, resentment, longing, revenge, abandonment, betrayal, guilt, shame, jealousy, even complicity, as well as issues of likely failure—conscious as well as unconscious—flood over her, overwhelm her, and threaten to drown her in continual series of undulations, repetitive phobias, anxieties, posttraumatic terrors, and so on. Many of these painful, enmeshed feelings and meanings are at bottom bound together through synthetic *a priori* relations that need to be first clinically distinguished and then addressed as elements of a constituted whole in order to be addressed, understood, and dealt with. It's critical to distinguish these terrors and sources. Unless this therapeutic probing occurs, insight into her sense of isolation will not be achieved. To be sure, although there are *unconscious* conflicts still functioning that are connected to the original series of incest events, for example, a desire for love and nurturance *versus* fear and disgust, it is also the case that she vividly remembers the multiple molestations and she currently experiences night terrors as a result. In short, there are graphic memories as well as unresolved unconscious conflicts all operating at once. Her mind is "assailed" (in James's sense) by terribly painful and disturbing recollections; she cannot sleep on a bed that is raised from the floor in fear that someone may be hiding under it; she is obsessed in looking in the back seat of cars before getting in dreading that there may be someone hiding; and she frequently becomes paralyzed and confused by uncertainties and fears of failing in her current plans and goals. Invariably, she avoids situations, runs away, and physically disappears for varying and extended periods of absence. Indeed, a psychiatrist in Germany, Michael Linden, who works extensively with Holocaust victims, has proposed that in extreme cases PTSD should be re-classified as PTED—Posttraumatic Embitterment Disorder—because the emotional damage is so severe that the key sense of *trust*—Erikson's first and most critical stage—immobilizes individuals from acting or even attempting to follow through on plans. The sufferers *cognitively* know what to do, but in terms of *motivation* they cannot do it, they cannot *act*. Subjects become angry, anxious, and feel helpless. They have lost all trust in others. They do not believe that if they change matters will improve for them. Rather they feel the problem is the world and human nature, and they cannot change that. They are simply enervated. This internal conflict produces anxiety and obsessive-compulsive thinking, and finally culminates in systematic avoidant behaviors and constitutes, in the present case we are discussing, a prime example of the violent clash between cognition and motivation, which is so pervasive in cases of PTSD. For example, one can cognitively *know* that smoking is self-destructive, even deadly but not emotionally *believe* it. She intellectually *knows* she should finish high school but cannot bring herself to believe she will ever be able to do it and hence repeatedly drops out. This form of extreme loneliness paralyzes and enervates the will, it crushes all positive, outwardly motivated desires and intentions. The individual even realizes that the avoidant tendencies, based on multiple negative emotions, are self-defeating and self-destructive, and only lead to a downward-spiraling retreat into further loneliness. But the prospect of disappointing others and personally failing in her plans is overwhelming. Time and again her remedy is to request postponements, to procrastinate, or simply physically disappear altogether for varying and extended periods of time, strategies which are so relieving to her that it systematically prevails over any healthy, pragmatic prudence, over positive functional choices (Mijuskovic, 2014, pp. 44–53).

Now with many returning servicemen diagnosed with PTSD, the treatment recommended is "flooding"—subjecting the sufferer to vivid graphic exposures to the original trauma in order to desensitize the subject. I believe, however, that PTSD is not simply a form of fear, a phobia for the reasons given above. Instead, I elected to focus pretty much entirely on her trust-mistrust issues; to return to the original issue.

In any case, my point is that the dynamics of loneliness as an emotional and cognitive phenomenon constitutes what I wish to call an *umbrella concept.* This in turn reminds me of Edmund Husserl's method of teasing out essential synthetic *a priori* meanings by applying the phenomenological method of "free imaginative variation" (*freie Variation in der Phantasie);* of testing which feelings and meanings are *essential* to loneliness, which are synthetically *a priori* related to each other, as opposed to those that are merely contingently connected in the individual case. Is it possible or conceivable, for example, to imagine loneliness without anxiety; or depression; or hostility; or a sense of failed communication; or shame; or guilt, or jealousy; or envy; and so on? As therapists, when dealing with the dynamics of loneliness, we should make it a common practice to inquire about these feelings and thoughts and to elicit meaningful responses from the subject. If, for example, we cannot separate or imagine the feeling of envy from loneliness, then we know that their synthesis is an *a priori* relation and that they must both be addressed.

Obviously, when people are lonely, there are elements of hope, a meaning that the loneliness will not last. But that is another matter. Hope has its own structure of intentionalities that is completely different from loneliness. And in therapy it should be explored as well. The stronger the hope the better. Intimacy is another concept that serves as a goal in overcoming, transcending loneliness, but again that is a completely different set of meanings. In this study, we are focusing solely on loneliness as a meaning, although we will propose some positive strategies for alleviating loneliness in the last chapter.

Loneliness consists of a *system* of interrelated negative emotions attached to a central, nuclear meaning, and all these feelings emanate from the narcissistic self. By freely imagining whether certain feelings and meanings are either (a) necessarily implicit or (b) merely contingently associated, the therapist is able to discover and anticipate in advance the direction the treatment should pursue. Loneliness is like a solar system constantly surrounded by revolving planets tracing circumscribed paths around a central sun, the narcissistic self; it is a gravitational field consisting of fiery mercurial bodies and dark plutonic masses circulating endlessly in transcribed paths around the ego. Thus, although each person's loneliness is unique to the individual, it is also the case that there are uniform laws to its circumscribed revolutionary trajectories. Just as each particular circle may display greater and lesser surface areas, nevertheless all circles, large or small, will show a circumference of 360 degrees.

Husserl's most extended discussion of free imaginative variation occurs in *Experience and Judgment* (Husserl, 1975). By freely imagining various and differing affective permutations to be *either* universally *or* contingently tethered to key psychological concepts and relations, we can discover and anticipate *a priori* connections, we can have an advance notice and preliminary *insight* into what persons are feeling and thinking about their loneliness independently of their own awareness.

We are asking what is invariant in the object or event as imagined, what the minimal conditions are for something to be presented or represented, and what alterations in some aspect of what is fantasized can make a change in the thing imagined . . . the method of free variation is not directed toward concrete objects as such but toward the possible exemplification of types of objects. (Natanson, 1973, pp. 67–68)

Again:

In this process of free variation we become aware of an identity [of meaning] that persists in all the cases we can imagine. It is the invariant, the essence, which is the basis of the similarity of all the examples we contrive . . . It is one and the same eidos in all the examples we imagine and so it does not matter which of the infinite possibilities we begin with or actually contrive; any one of them serves as well as any other to display the eidos. (Sokolowski, 1974, p. 63; cf. Spiegelberg, 1965, pp. II, 680–681)

The foregoing consideration assures us that if some people are lonely, we already know a great deal about them; in effect, as condescending as this may sound, at this point in time, we know them better than they know themselves. As a theoretical tool, this provides the therapist with an incredible advantage in helping those who feel isolated and lonely, disenfranchised, abandoned, alienated, and estranged. All these constitutive elements and meanings need to be addressed.

In the case presented above, the young woman will likely continue to experience the thoughts as well as the emotions of fear, anxiety, hostility, ambivalence, and fantasies of revenge for the rest of her life. Her sense of loneliness and betrayal and her feelings of unfulfilled longing will persist endlessly because of her conscious and unconscious exposure to her father's outrage. In suggesting that loneliness is an umbrella concept, I mean that it incorporates multiple negative emotions as well as intermittent fantasies of relief. If the latter are lacking, then feelings and thoughts of hopelessness and suicidality become the constant companions of the afflicted. The progression is often tragically simple: abandonment; betrayal; loneliness; rejection; and suicide (de Maupassant, "Two Little Soldiers"). Tragically enough at our clinic a few years ago, a schizophrenic patient, who was tardy for her med appointment was turned away and later that night killed herself and her parents.

Consider for a moment, the term "suicide" in relation to depression. Is the conceptual difference merely a matter of degree, or is there a qualitative difference between Major Depression and suicidality that bespeaks of final hopelessness. As it now stands, suicidal feelings and thoughts are simply coded under the *Diagnostic Manual of Psychiatric Disorders'* code 296 in terms of intensity/degree/measurement (e.g., 1, 2, 3, and 4). But the term "suicide" or "suicidality" is not in the *DSM* as a diagnosis. That is why, by contrast, the impoverished set of symptoms offered in the *DSM* is woefully inadequate to address and deal with the complexities of loneliness.

It is also both significant and interesting to note that the term "loneliness" itself nowhere appears in the *DSM*—nor should it—and that is simply because the reference catalogue artificially delineates and reduces the disorders into lifeless, component, analytic parts; it overanalyzes and ends by reducing complex wholes into separate, disjointed elements. Instead, loneliness is an umbrella concept or meaning that includes clusters rather than separates constituent elements. Frankly, in the end, *I believe all human feeling and thinking can be "charted" between two poles: loneliness and the desire to belong. The only human absolute is loneliness, and all else emanates from it and is dependent on that source.*

REFERENCES

Arendt, H. (1976). *The Origins of Totalitarianism.* New York: Harvest Publishers.
Descartes, R. (1955). *Philosophical Works of Descartes.* New York: Dover.
Erikson, E. (1963). *Childhood and Society.* New York: W. W. Norton.

Freud, S. (1961a). *Civilization and Its Discontents*. New York: W. W. Norton.

Fromm, E. (1970). *The Art of Loving*. New York: Harper & Row.

Fromm-Reichmann, F. (1959). Loneliness. *Psychiatry: Journal for the Study of Interpersonal Processes*, 22:1.

Hegel, G. W. F. (1977). *Phenomenology of Spirit*. Oxford, UK: Oxford University Press.

Hoskisson, J. B. (1965). *Loneliness*. New York: Citadel.

Hume, D. (1973). *A Treatise of Human Nature*. Oxford, UK: Clarendon Press.

Husserl, E. (1975). *Experience and Judgment*. Evanston, IL: Northwestern University Press, Section 87.

James, W. (1950). *The Principles of Psychology*, New York: Dover.

Kojeve, A. (1969). *An Introduction to the Reading of Hegel*. New York: Basic Books.

Kosinski, J. (1977). *The Painted Bird*. Boston: Houghton Mifflin.

Lynch, J. (1977). *The Broken Heart: The Medical Consequences of Loneliness*. New York: Basic Books.

Lynch, J. (2000). *A Cry Unheard. The Medical Consequences of Loneliness*. Baltimore, MD: Bancroft Press.

Mahler, M., Pine, F., & Bergman, A. (1975). *The Psychological Birth of the Human Infant*. New York: Basic Books.

Mijuskovic, B. (1977). Loneliness: An interdisciplinary approach. *Psychiatry: A Journal for Interpersonal Processes*, 40:113–122; reprinted in: *The Anatomy of Loneliness* (1980). Hartog, J., Audy, R., & Cohen, Y. (Eds.). New York: International Universities Press.

Mijuskovic, B. (1979–1980). Loneliness and narcissism. *The Psychoanalytic Review*, 66:4.

Mijuskovic, B. (1980). Loneliness and communication. In *Man and His Conduct*. J. Gracia (Ed.). Rio Piedras: Editorial Universitaria.

Mijuskovic, B. (1986a). Loneliness: Counseling adolescents. *Adolescence*, XXI:84.

Mijuskovic, B. (1986b). Loneliness, hostility, anxiety, and communication. *Child Study Journal*, 16:3.

Mijuskovic, B. (1987). Loneliness and sexual dysfunctions. *Psychology: A Journal of Human Behavior*, 24:4.

Mijuskovic, B. (1988). Loneliness and adolescent alcoholism. *Adolescence*, XXIII:91.

Mijuskovic, B. (1992). Organic communities, atomistic societies, and loneliness. *Journal of Sociology & Social Welfare*, XIX:2.

Mijuskovic, B. (2012). *Loneliness in Philosophy, Psychology, and Literature*. Bloomington, IN: iUniverse.

Mijuskovic, B. (2014). Loneliness and PTSD. *Psychology Journal*, 11:1.

Natanson, M. (1973). *Edmund Husserl: Philosopher of Infinite Tasks*. Evanston, IL: Northwestern University Press.

Salinger, J. D. (1953). The laughing man. In *Nine Short Stories*. Boston: Little, Brown & Company.

Sokolowski, R. (1974). *Husserlian Meditations.* Evanston, IL: Northwestern University Press.

Spiegelberg, H. (1965). *The Phenomenological Movement: A Historical Introduction.* The Hague: Martinus Nijhoff.

Wolfe, T. (1968). *The Hills Beyond.* New York: Signet.

Zilboorg, G. (1938, January). Loneliness. *The Atlantic Monthly.*

Chapter 6

Loneliness and Language

In Chapter 2, we had the occasion to mention the historical emphasis in the idealist and rationalist tradition on reason as an essential feature of self-consciousness—indeed as the primary identifying characteristic of humanity. By contrast, British materialism, beginning with Hobbes and continuing with the empiricists, Locke, Berkeley, and Hume, introduces a definite paradigm shift in viewing the special characteristic in humans as grounded in the ability to use language and speech. Words thus become signs for complexes of sensations, ideas, and thoughts, and the stress now turns to making our thoughts—and therefore "meanings"—clearer through the refinement of words; their significance; the criteria for their use; and their relation to consciousness—not to say their frequent *substitution* for consciousness. Empiricism easily lends itself to nominalism as exhibited in Locke's view that words are basically signs used in place of things for facilitating communication; in Berkeley's criticism and rejection of general or abstract ideas; and in Hume's position that words are reducible to particular sensory impressions. All three tendencies contribute to the prospect that all our thoughts are in the last analysis composed of single sensations. Indeed, James Burnett (Lord Monboddo), a contemporary and fellow countryman of Hume, drawing on the "Great Chain of Being" theme that there is a continuous link from the highest to the lowest species of conscious beings, develops an anthropological, early pre-Darwinian theory of evolution and speculates that there is a solid empirical connection between men and apes and he believes that "Ourang Outans" have an inherent capacity to learn speech. Apparently, he thought, they could be trained as servants and to be responsive to verbal commands. We recall Locke's fascination with Prince Maurice's conversant parrot. All of these trends in the English-speaking philosophers and scientists directly lead in a new direction in language studies toward man's natural endowment of speech and away from "reason" as the defining essence of man.

Although the previous chapter concentrates on the motivational factors in loneliness, it also introduces a concern with the vocabulary that is involved in ferreting out and describing the feelings and especially the affective meanings of loneliness, their conceptual clarifications in relation to each other, and the question of their practical and/or legitimate use in the *DSM*. But now we need to delve more deeply into what precisely is the relationship of loneliness to consciousness and language? What is the connection between certain feelings and thoughts of loneliness and their attached verbal counterparts or signs? How effective is the language enlisted to describe and express man's sense of forlornness? In what follows, we shall explore the relation between loneliness, consciousness, and language, their relative primacy, and their role in addressing man's sense of isolation and expressing it. Specifically, what is the goal of the vocabulary of loneliness? Is it (1) to confirm a contractual consensus between clinician and patient; to aid in objectively measuring and charting the outcomes of treatment progression (behaviorism); or is it (2) to enhance any and all uses of expression, whether verbal, figurative, pictorial, or metaphorical as a means of penetrating through the husk of the individual's sense of isolation (insight)? Perhaps words—as opposed to the richness of feelings and meanings—are mere external shields forbidding entry into the inner sanctum of loneliness, while the reality remains forever artificially cloaked. Perhaps we feel and mean more than we can ever say.

Before we begin, we need to draw a vital distinction between two theories of truth in philosophy. The coherence theory holds that truth "grows," "develops"; there are different levels of truth, some more comprehensive than others, but the criterion of their validity is always judged in relation to each other, within the interconnected system as a whole. The "lower order" truths must be consistent; they must *cohere* with the "higher order" truths. Sometimes this is referred to as the "doctrine of internal relations." There would be a hierarchy from the most comprehensive to the less general and on downward. In the field of psychology, the Law of Loneliness would be at the top in our system, whereas presumably for Freud it would be the Law of Libidinal Energy. Ultimately, it would result in something comparable to Einstein's desideratum of a Unified Field Theory for the Human Sciences. Ideally, it would be completely comprehensive. Likely proponents of the coherence theory are Spinoza and Kant, but certainly and foremost Hegel and Dewey. The relevance here would be that I have argued in behalf of a *system* of intrinsically related synthetic *a priori* feelings and meanings in relation to understanding and treating loneliness. If I am right, then the coherence paradigm would be directly applicable. This is where the Philosophy and Psychology of Loneliness would live and thrive.

By contrast, the correspondence principle maintains that a proposition is true if and only if it corresponds to an external state of affairs. It's often referred to as the "doctrine of external relations," the mind on one side and objects on the other side. Thus, the statement, "The cat is on the mat," is true if and only if it is factually the case that the cat *is* on the mat. Obviously, this theory also entails the mind–body problem. Proponents are Russell, Wittgenstein, and Ryle as well as language philosophers and linguists in general.

Given these distinctions, we can see that behaviorism and the *Diagnostic Statistical Manual of Psychiatric Disorders* both separate symptoms and diagnoses from each other as well as from relevant conceptual implications. For instance, the *DSM* offers diagnoses as "definitions" attached to a number of different symptoms. If the patient exhibits, say, four out of six symptoms, the diagnosis is "confirmed." But this makes it appear that at least some symptoms are separate, removable, and nonessential "parts." Plus they can be moved around to other diagnoses. Like complex machines that have parts, often some parts can be removed without disabling the entire operation—for example, an automobile doesn't need fenders in order to run—but minds, feelings, and thoughts are not like that. There are no unessential "parts" to loneliness if its meaning, its eidos, is grasped *adequately*. The meaning can be deepened but not disassembled. For instance, if anxiety and anger are essential meaning components within the larger meaning of loneliness, it would not be possible to be lonely but not anxious or angry.

Language as the primary tool of behaviorism is impoverished in its efforts to adequately express the dynamics of the active mind. In fact, according to Husserl in *The Idea of Phenomenology,* consciousness *precedes* language. By contrast, for the linguistically oriented English-speaking thinkers and behaviorists, it is exactly the reverse: Language *precedes* consciousness—or even more radically, language *is* consciousness. This is an interesting and critical difference. Hence, the relevant question becomes whether we need language in order to experience loneliness, and even if we do, what are the limitations? Can we feel and think we are lonely without being able to verbally express it? Are higher order animals that do not possess what we would qualify as a language capable of feeling lonely? Is the preverbal infant capable of experiencing loneliness and feelings of abandonment without being able to express it with words? (Mijuskovic, 1978, pp. 14–20).

According to empiricism, a synthetic proposition is a meaningful state-ment that is either true or false. In order to test its alleged factual mean-ingfulness, we must be able to specify the conditions under which it can be confirmed or disconfirmed. Generally speaking, this is referred to as the "principle of verifiability." In short, a proposition must be open to empirical testing or confirmation. Accordingly, such propositions as "God exists" in order to be meaningful must be verifiable. What would the world be like if God did not exist? If there is no conceivable difference, if one cannot specify the difference, then it is a meaningless statement; it's empirically unverifiable in principle. In order for something to *be* a differ-ence, it must *make* a difference. Incidentally, this not only discredits meta-physical claims but religious, ethical, aesthetic, and poetic expressions as well (Ayer, 1936). Expressions of feeling, such as experiencing pain, for instance, and simply saying "Ouch!" are regarded as noncognitive as well. But "Ouch" can be incredibly meaningful. It means "I hurt," "I'm in dis-tress," or at the very least it signifies "a self-conscious being is in pain." The problem with the reductivist theory of language is that it risks losing the nuances and ambiguities, on the one hand, and the depth and complexity of the emotions on the other hand. Most often, loneliness surfaces as a vague but permeating *mood*, alternating between fading and intensifying, from shifting moments and states of discomfort, from boredom, uncanni-ness, and vague hypervigilance at one end and terror, hopelessness, panic, and suicidality at the other extreme. By contrast, behaviorism in the last analysis ultimately seeks to define or resolve extreme loneliness, for exam-ple, as a species of panic disorder, of fear in terms of physiological effects, as for instance galvanic reactions in the brain with measurable physical symptoms, electrochemical responses, difficulty in breathing, heart palpi-tations, contraction of the pupils, sweating palms, tightness in the chest, and so on. In doing so, it strips the flesh from the emotion and leaves a lifeless skeleton. Behaviorism concentrates on the physically measurable. It strips meanings into words and then dissects words into immediate sensations and physical reactions. Physical reactions can be objectively mea-sured; they are quantitative. Therefore, they are "scientific." Indeed, many scientists define science as the "art of measurement."

Both behavioral treatment and cognitive therapy are basically commit-ted to establishing clear linguistic formulations through verbal contracts—and a corresponding compliance with specific psychiatric medication regimens—in order to insure behavioral compliance. The premise is that clarity of language adequately grasps human feeling and thinking. Ana-lytic and linguistic philosophies similarly strive to reduce language to single, clearly defined terms, which, in turn, can be decomposed and resolved into collections or aggregates of discrete sensations, all in the spirit of clarity and the goal of discrediting metaphysics, avoiding ambiguity and vagueness, and promoting the rigor of the empirical sciences. These twin reductions serve as the primary methodology employed by the contemporary movements of Logical Atomism (the early Wittgenstein), Logical Positivism, Conceptual Analysis, Linguistic Analysis, Ordinary Language theory (the later Wittgenstein), and so on. The overall purpose is to eliminate any vagueness and ambiguity in the interests of clarity of communication, and consequently the focus shifts to concrete, overt, and publicly observable criteria with the practical interest of documenting successful treatment. In this context, specificity of communication and patient-therapist concordance on the desired behavior, with improvement in target symptoms is paramount. Again, this oversimplification and reduction of consciousness to simple words and their further analysis into atomistic sensations are abundantly supported in the *DSM* by pursuing "diagnoses" that are "objective" and "scientific," by pinning down emotional terms to lifeless criteria for hundreds of psychiatric disorders so that they can be conveniently and conventionally labeled and then behaviorally addressed. It's like affixing dead butterflies on a board so that they can be more readily classified. But the life of the species is no longer present. The consequence is that the deeper feelings, thoughts, and meanings of loneliness are nullified. Rather, the reality is that there are living, complex, and extensive weblike synthetic *a priori* meanings and relations within loneliness that are intrinsically interwoven within the fabric of the mind and need to be grasped before one can even begin to know other selves or indeed even one's own self when one is lonely.

The error of the analytic, linguistic, and scientific communities consists in separating and crystalizing the feelings and meanings within consciousness in order to address them singly and behaviorally, "to divide and conquer." In fact, this method of vivisection only reduces, destroys, and eliminates the very organic and synthetic qualities and structures one is trying to penetrate and understand. It's comparable to Heisenberg's dilemma of attempting to observe the motion of subatomic particles by isolating them and then exposing them to powerful magnifications, which only distorts what one wishes to observe.

Loneliness operates in a social field in an analogous manner as physical objects operate in a gravitational field. By that I mean, if a single cognitive or affective element shifts or adjusts, other constituent elements are altered as well. For example, if one sibling in a family unit becomes less lonely, another may become more lonely or jealous or feel neglected. Or, instead, the altered family dynamic may positively affect the other sibling and bring the two closer. The point is that it will have *some* meaningful effect. Unlike machines, which exhibit mechanistic principles and operations, where one can simply remove a part of the engine, repair it, and then replace it so that the vehicle will run, human beings display dialectical, organic, that is, interlocking synthetic relations in which any change affects all the other members of the unit. Human relationships because they continually transform themselves through feelings and meanings that are constantly shifting and interpenetrating are not readily susceptible to verbal and behavioral specificity. They are too fluid.

The mechanistic use of psychiatric medication is analogous to repairing a motor. Often the psychiatrist rather than moving from a "correct" diagnosis and proceeding to the "right" prescription works backward, in reverse. By a trial-and-error method, various medications are prescribed until the patient in complete exhaustion says he feels better and the diagnosis is "confirmed" and charted as a successful "outcome measure." Frequently, different psychiatrists will offer different diagnoses and prescribe different psychiatric medications. Many have their favorite medications and routinely prescribe the same ones pro forma.

The related error of empiricism is the prejudice that in order to understand something, one must reduce it to its simplest components. Russell and Wittgenstein are no less guilty of this nominalistic prejudice than are Hobbes, Locke, Berkeley, and Hume (Mijuskovic, 1976, p. 85–103). It is the attempt to understand life by tearing it asunder into inanimate pieces. In order for loneliness therapy to have a chance of success, however, one must address the complexity of the underlying cognitive, affective, and motivational filaments emanating like electrical rays from the active ego. I don't know why we think physical reality is infinitely complex and yet we reduce mental processes to a finite set of simple sensations and robotic behaviors.

Consequently, one of the more interesting and controversial topics in the Philosophy and Psychology of Loneliness is the issue of the relation between consciousness and language, which receives exposure in Husserl's *Idea of Phenomenology* (1964a, p. 31; see also pp. xxi–xxii, 24, 40–41). There he argues that *we can intend, intuit without language;* that consciousness and *phenomenological,* that is, immediate experience is primary and original, while language is secondary and derivative. Language only serves as a crude tool in its efforts to describe the rich tapestry of consciousness. The same conviction is summoned in Husserl's *The Paris Lectures* where he describes the absolute primacy of immediate consciousness over what any language could possibly convey, though to be sure language will continue to be a practical but impoverished handmaiden to consciousness in describing loneliness. In this connection, we can also turn to Peter Koestenbaum's "Introductory Essay" for a helpful critical distinction.

The first premise is that there are two current philosophical methodologies: philosophy is either the description and analysis of *language;* or, correlatively that of *experience.* . . . To understand Husserl one must first grant that this distinction is actual and legitimate. The second premise is consequent to the first. It establishes the logical and ontological primacy of experience over language. The phenomenological method is the descriptive analysis of experience. The necessary presupposition, therefore, is that language embodies experiences, i.e., that the structure of language is parallel to and representative of experience. The semantic or language oriented approach assumes the converse to be true. . . . The assumption inherent in the semantic approach is that at least some, and perhaps all, philosophical problems are logical consequences of quasi-grammatical errors or of ambiguities in the use of language. Husserl must be understood to assume that language reflects the structure of experience, or, if it does not, that we can examine experience independently of language. It follows that analyses of experience, with all their subtleties is the presuppositionless beginning of philosophy. (Husserl, 1964b, pp. xii–xiii)

A related conviction is expressed in Heidegger's *Introduction to Metaphysics* where he maintains that "along with German, the [ancient] Greek [language] is in regard to possibilities of thought at once the most powerful and most spiritual of all languages" (Heidegger, 1959, p. 57). The clear implication is that in both the original Greek and current German languages one can *mean* things *beyond* what someone is able to express in English. Rather than being an advantage, English with its abundance and proliferation of technical terminology becomes a disadvantage not only because of its distorting precision by dissecting thoughts into unattached parts but more importantly because of its prejudice that it has captured reality in its net or words, that it has lifted the Veil of Isis with words alone. For practical and technological purposes, a precise and "concrete" language may be preferable in many cases. But for the communication of human feelings and thoughts and loneliness, this is not the case. For example, think of how one would describe a *mood* in precise, technical terms. The essence of a mood is essentially to be vague, undulating, or imprecise. Or, imagine describing a painting, an aesthetic experience, in terms of splotches of colors, "refining" the hues into visual, quantitative intensities, and finishing by decomposing the colors into points of colored dots in the manner of Seurat. When I look at Seurat's painting, "A Sunday Afternoon at La Grand Jatte," I don't want to focus on the little specks of color. Instead, I wish to feel the vivacity of life, the laziness of the afternoon, the tranquility and humanity of the gathering, the vital subtle unspoken sense of interaction among the figures, and so on. Otherwise, the painting would soon lose its sense, its qualities of human feeling and meaning, as well as its aesthetic qualities. It would be devoid of the flow of life, the flesh of existence. The experience of loneliness is elusive and fluid as well as complex and deep because of its essential panorama of feelings extending from malaise, uneasiness, boredom, and often, all too often terminating in thoughts of desperation and suicide.

The assumption throughout this study is that the "subjective nature of consciousness" dictates that there is a genuinely private sphere of privileged access within the ego, a hidden entry to one's own thoughts This is the primary residence of loneliness, which is often hidden when unconscious and opaquely obscured when subconscious forces are involved and "at work" as we shall show. This latter sphere is especially impervious to simple linguistic descriptions. Nevertheless, through exploration and insight into subjective, deep-seated feelings, thoughts, and phenomenologically excavated meanings, much can be learned—although not everything—about the sources of one's own loneliness as well as those of others. Thus, two critical implications follow: (1) the *meaning* of loneliness is universal; but (2) it also exhibits a personal, idiosyncratic dynamic. Just as "orangeness" has a determinate universal meaning but my affective reaction to the color orange is uniquely personal. The task of phenomenological investigation is twofold: first to understand the universal meaning and conceptual ramifications of loneliness; and second, to respect the unique dynamic of an individual's struggle with her or his loneliness. All instances and situations of loneliness will exhibit the same universal constellation of interrelated meanings, but it is also the case that there will be enormous personal *qualitative* variations on *how* and *why* each person feels lonely. This is why loneliness, as a therapeutic target, is so complex and difficult to unravel. It also means that the Philosophy and Psychology of Loneliness is constituted by concepts and laws that are universal and necessary and yet, as a therapist, one must always take into account the shifting situations, adjustments, and nuances within the individual as each subject copes with their unique loneliness in various ways. Therapy performed on others or one's self is a lifelong process. There is no vaccination for loneliness. One of the main problems with cognitive behaviorism is that it often assumes that complete success can be attained. That loneliness is like a broken arm; that there is a cure for it.

Cognitive psychologists and behaviorists argue in behalf of a state of affairs in which language is viewed as environmentally and socially conditioned, a learned behavior rather than conceiving its structures as innate (Chomsky). Language accordingly is viewed as basically a behavioral and social enterprise. For example, Wittgenstein adopts a position, in his *Tractatus* period, which assumes a natural *correspondence* between language and facts—"Language reflects reality." Subsequently, he holds that thinking can be *meaningful* only if it occurs in the context of a shared and corrigible language use, his Ordinary Language theory. As we have seen, for the positivists, a proposition is true if and only if it corresponds to or factually describes an external state of affairs. Similarly, the *use* of language in behaviorism is viewed analogously. It is seen as a *learned* response. As such, the meanings we put into "use" and develop are learned through social intercourse and interaction. It follows, according to the behavioral paradigm, that the meaning of loneliness, as well as its application to the self, is therefore an *acquired* mode of language behavior without any necessary innate mental anchor or structure within the mind or self required to ground it. Further, a word must await social acceptance before it can operate meaningfully. As one hears and uses the term "isolation" or "loneliness" or "longing" by seeing and hearing it employed by others ("look and see" or "listen and hear"), just so one discovers how to apply it to one's self. Loneliness, then, is a "reality" that can only appear subsequent to social training and the learning of a language. According to this view, there must always be a public criterion for the correct usage of language when one is using a word or making a declarative statement. The ultimate presupposition, then, behind the foregoing naïve and objective view is that "mental" phenomena are actually grounded in the premise that language precedes consciousness. Again, the unexamined assumption is that "language reflects reality," that the two are isomorphic. Indeed, anthropologists have long sought to show that the use of certain words depends on their pragmatic employment in particular societies. But that has to do with behaviors and practical needs, not feelings and not thoughts. Not all consciousness is pragmatically oriented. Perhaps most of it is not. I agree that if we are going to measure a house we need to agree on a common criterion of measurement. But if you and I are going to "measure" our feelings with and against each other, there is no standard measure.

One wonders if there could be a society in which the term "loneliness" was completely deleted. What a wonderful world that would be! No more loneliness!

But are language and reality really isomorphic? Again, consider for a moment loneliness as a *mood, as malaise, a vague sense of discomfort, a sense of not knowing what to do with one's self.* Are the italicized words adequate to the feeling I am trying to convey? I think not.

Further, ordinary language-oriented and behavioral proponents, most notably Ludwig Wittgenstein and Gilbert Ryle, argue that the purported state of affairs, allegedly occurring hidden within self-consciousness, which asserts that there are mental events transpiring in a private theater called the mind and only accessible to the individual, can be readily refuted.

Accordingly, Wittgenstein criticizes such claims as "Only I can know I'm in pain; you can only infer it" (Wittgenstein, 1965).

Ryle likewise objects that the Cartesian "myth of the ghost in the machine," the mistaken notion of the self as haunted by an immaterial mind, commits us to the absurd thesis that "Absolute solitude is on this showing the ineluctable destiny of the soul" (Ryle, 1949, p. 15; see also pp. 25, 60–61, 83, 115). But this is quickly and bluntly corrected by Ryle: "Only our bodies can meet" (ibid.). Further, as far as the "mind" is concerned, Ryle holds that "there are just things and events" (p. 249). And I suppose the argument would then proceed that only bodies have brains, vocal chords, voices, and therefore words. And, *voila,* we have reduced everything to an artificial and conventional, that is, social language. Presumably, Ryle would go on to contend that Robinson Crusoe could not have written a diary on his island because he had no means of checking if the words he used were correct. But there actually was a real Robinson Crusoe, Alexander Selkirk, who was marooned alone for four years on a desert island, and after his rescue he related his narrative to Daniel Defoe. Are we to believe that until Selkirk met Defoe, he could not have been lonely on the island?

Wittgenstein and Ryle basically reject the conceivability of a private language by denying the possibility of self-consciousness. *If* they are right, it follows that all sensations and feelings are inherently public because they can only be experienced, conveyed, and expressed behaviorally through objectively determined, linguistically shared words, and public meanings, significances that only lend themselves to the empirical principle of verifiability or confirmation. If that is so, then no feeling uniquely belongs to me alone. Further, if this is the case, how can I ever distinguish between my feelings from yours? If the state of affairs that is being depicted by Wittgenstein and Ryle is to obtain, then not only would it be impossible to differentiate my realm of experience from yours, but "me" and "you" would dissolve into an amorphous public "one." We would then have to radically change our statements not to read "*I* am lonely," but rather "*We* are publicly lonely." If we follow Wittgenstein and Ryle, it would seem that no one can be lonely in the sense we usually *intend* to say, "I am lonely; I feel lonely" unless one is able to check his feelings publicly for confirmation. It follows that loneliness can only occur in a social context, since language is essentially a socially learned behavioral product. If my sensations, feelings, and thoughts must always conform to a public-usage criterion and the principle of verifiability, loneliness seems peculiarly elusive and problematic. It is as if I were unable to refer in any meaningful sense to Central Park in New York as mine alone. But on the subjectivist interpretation, it *is* mine alone; it exhibits feelings and meanings that are unique to me and un-shareable. To repeat: Loneliness as a *conceptual meaning* is universal, but as an essentially *affective* and *qualitative* experience, it is purely subjective and thus intimately private.

The emphasis on the subjective nature of consciousness is also true for Henri Bergson, who regards language as a second-order function and hence an artificial tool of the scientific "intellect" in opposition to the immediacy of intuition. According to Bergson, we express ourselves in terms of words, but we think of words in terms of space. We think of words as analogous to things, objects with sharp outlines. This is useful and practical. We thus translate the unextended to the extended; we move from quality to quantity. But self-consciousness as immanent time-consciousness is a nonmeasurable flow or stream of duration. Intuition directly, immediately *apprehends the quality* of human being, human existence, whereas the discursive intellect *comprehends the quantity* of nature in relations of part to part as, for example, in the practical interest of classifying animal genera and species. By contrast, intuition is motivated by instinct rather than intellect; it is endowed with the ability to undercut all the practical needs of life and directly connect with the seamless flow of time as *duration.* It thus reaches absolute being, as opposed to relative being, which latter is always guided by practical concerns and is always relative or contingent to those pragmatic needs. Bergson accordingly maintains that there is a deep self, *le moi profond,* which is only accessible through the immersion of self-consciousness in *duration.* Like Husserl, he envisions a realm of being that is qualitatively different from the world populated by ordinary tasks pursued in the interests of comfort, of accommodation, and of naïve science. And similar to Husserl, for the French philosopher, this realm refers to a reality unattainable by the instruments and tools of language. After all, a stop sign is a mere flat symbolic image of the *full* meaning of "stop." Thus, intellect and intuition are two very different ways of "knowing" versus "seeing" things. Notice that the visual term "seeing" in and of itself implies immediacy, direct contact, whereas knowing implies a system and an analytic operation of connecting parts to parts (Mijuskovic, 1977, pp. 43–58). Feelings of loneliness are by their very nature subjective, intimate, and personal.

Marcel Proust is strongly influenced by Bergson (Bergson was his uncle or cousin by marriage). In his novel, *Swann's Way,* he enlists Bergson's early views, from *Time and Free Will,* on the immaterial nature of consciousness, reflexivity, and time-consciousness, and transforms them into his unique stream of consciousness narrative style. As Proust envisions it, the individual can directly *feel* (Bergson's intuition) the past *as present,* as immediately given to consciousness through what he describes as "involuntary memory" when we are unexpectedly carried backward in time to repeat a prior qualitative event. It's a complete immersion of the self in the temporal flow of the past. But one cannot intellectually or conceptually reproduce it. If he tries, it will be a different "past." To analytically conceptualize an object or an event involves dismembering it, reducing it to mere frozen words, dissecting it for practical purposes, placing it in an objective causal sequence. Imagine the difference between having the identical experience in memory, capturing the past exactly as it was as opposed, as Proust suggests, to testifying in a criminal trial (Camus's *The Stranger,* the murder *versus* the trial). These are very different functions and states of consciousness. But we destroy a feeling or a memory when we diagnose it or analyze it into its constituent parts. It's like writing a clinical description of panic while we are experiencing it; it can't be done (Spinoza.) On the other hand, when we genuinely experience a feeling, when consciousness is invaded by *qualitative* existents, when we are captured by the very qualities that constitute our being, then we are immersed in the reality of a unique isolation, one in which our very experience becomes indistinguishable from the self. This is what Proust means when he declares that the "essence was not in me, it was myself" (Proust, 1956, p. 55; see also pp. 25, 60–61, 83, 115, 162). And yet for Proust it is exactly this self-conscious, reflexive ability which rests on an immaterialist interpretation of awareness for its very possibility, since only if the mind is immaterial can consciousness be reflexive.

When I saw any external object, my consciousness that I was seeing it would remain between me and it, enclosing it in a slender, incorporeal outline which prevented me from ever coming directly in contact with the material form; for it would volitalise itself in some way before I could touch it. (p. 104)

Following Montaigne's "way of ideas" limitation argument (Chapter 2), Proust correspondingly maintains that we are never in direct contact with objects in the external world because our ideas, as modes of consciousness, mediate and interpose themselves between physical objects and our immaterial minds. Consequently, material entities become present within the diaphanous medium (Descartes) of self-awareness as immaterialized (Proust's "volatilization"), as qualitative feelings. After all, a *feeling* of pain, in terms of extension, is dimensionless. Nevertheless, we are cognizant of these immanent "objects" as they flow through awareness and preserve their identity within the form or structure of subjective time, *within* the ego. And, actually, even visual qualities, for example, colors, are conceived as essentially unextended, since the instrument of apprehension, the mind, is immaterial, spatially unextended. Put differently, colors *qua* qualities, are nonquantitative. (In both Leibniz and Hume, the qualitative *minima sensibilia* are unextended [Mijuskovic, 1977c].) Because of this immersion in qualitative being, Proust then conceives the true self as an immaterial pinprick of intensified consciousness, a dimensionless point, which is not in space and yet exists apart, separated from both things and other minds. Hence we are each of us alone. And yet it is an isolation that *intentionally* strives to reach the consciousness of the other.

> For even if we have the sensation of being always enveloped in, surrounded by our own soul, still it does not seem a fixed and immovable prison; rather do we seem to be borne away with it, and perpetually struggling to pass beyond it, to break out into the world, with perpetual discouragement as we hear endlessly, all round us, that unvarying sound which is no echo from within. Sometimes we mobilize our spiritual forces in a glittering array so as to influence and subjugate other beings who, as we very well know, are situated outside ourselves, where we can never reach them. (pp. 107–108)

Although Husserl clearly talks about words being "embodied" in verbal statements, as we discussed in the chapter on Phenomenology, when we use them in the social context of other *persons*—as opposed to what is occurring intrapsychically in the *individual*—nevertheless for Husserl, as for Bergson, the words of a language are indirectly referential; they are signs of underlying realities that are not "the things themselves," not the reality intended or meant. If this were not the case, then Husserl could never suggest that there are infinite tasks for the phenomenologist. For instance, *Webster's New International Dictionary,* massive and unabridged, is nevertheless not only finite but circular. It's done. What would it be like to conduct infinite phenomenological tasks on the *Dictionary?* Nonsense.

> "Seeing" [i.e., eidetic intuition] does not lend itself to demonstration or deduction. It is patently absurd to try to explain possibilities by drawing logical [linguistic] conclusions [or inferences] from non-intuitive knowledge. Even if it could be wholly certain that there are transcendent [independently existing external] worlds, even if I accept the whole content of the sciences [and the validity of language] of a natural [naively scientific] sort, even then, I cannot borrow from them. I must never fancy that by relying on transcendent presuppositions and scientific [and linguistic] inferences I can arrive where I want to go in the critique of cognition—namely, to assess the possibility of a transcendent objectivity of cogitation. (Husserl, 1964a, p. 31; see also pp. xxi–xxii, 24, 40–41)

According to Husserl, phenomenology is absolutely presuppositionless because it begins with the immediately *given* to consciousness. Words are not only representational but doubly removed from the immediacy of consciousness, first by Locke's perceptual account and then by language.

In this fashion, Husserl seeks to undercut all representational theories of consciousness and cognition along with the correspondence criterion of truth and its effort to "match" ideas to objects. Rather, it is the phenomenological eidetic insights and intuitions produced by the intentionality of consciousness and not the linguistic formulations that should be the focus of our attention when dealing with loneliness; it's not the mere imprecise words of the lonely individual that commands our attention but, more significantly, the inarticulate feelings, intentions, and meanings that permeate the individual's sense of loneliness. Imagine, for instance, a behavioral therapist assessing a patient for the first time who states, "I am lonely" and the clinician responds by asking, "From a scale of one to ten, how would you rate your loneliness?"

Thus, as Husserl concludes, "we can make our speech conform in a pure measure to what is 'seen' in its full clarity" in intuition (ibid., p. 24). But if our speech and words must *conform* to "eidetic insights," it follows once again that meanings are primary and words are derivative. For Husserl, phenomena directly present to consciousness always surpass language and can be "seen" independently of linguistic associations. This is not the ineffability of mysticism. It is not meant to imply that the *experience* of loneliness is *beyond* normal awareness but rather experience is temporally fluid and it is pointless for one to try to pick up its "elements" drop by drop, word by word, as if it were a puddle of water rather than an undulating flow of consciousness.

Beyond this, do we have any other evidence or empirical confirmation that it is possible to think without language or words, and more specifically to experience loneliness without rendering it into words? I believe we do. It derives from Admiral Richard Byrd's polar expedition in 1934. After several months of living utterly alone in the arctic, the explorer recorded the following in his diary entry of May 11:

I find . . . that the absence of conversation makes it harder for me to think in words. Sometimes while walking, I talk to myself and listen to the words, but they sound hollow and unfamiliar. Today, for instance, I was thinking of the extraordinary effect of the lack of diversions upon my existence; but describing it is beyond my power. I could feel the difference between this life and a normal life; I could see the difference in my mind's eye, but I couldn't satisfactorily express the subtleties in words. That may be because I have already come to live more deeply within myself; what I feel needs no further definition, since the senses are intuitive and exact. (Byrd, 1938, pp. 95–96; Mijuskovic, 1978b)

Just as significantly, the author admits that he was unable to put pen to paper and compose the autobiography of his polar adventure until a full four years after the incidents described in his chronicle were behind him. It was only then that he could attempt to describe the intense loneliness he had experienced in the wake of his solitary expedition. But the point is that he *first* felt and experienced the loneliness *independently* of putting it into words and language, and only later was he able to verbally describe it.

But the mere word "loneliness" can never capture its *quality.* Loneliness, even in terms of intensity, has nothing to do with quantities any more than a loving mother is able to quantify her love for her children. Was I more or less lonely when I was seven years old, ten, thirteen, sixteen? I don't know. I can't remember. How would I measure it? Does the question even make sense?

Correspondingly, Christopher Burney writes that, after surviving eighteen months of solitary confinement in a German prison, he had to delay writing about his experiences until he was sufficiently able to relearn the practical use of his language skills by social use. Only *then* could he describe the events that had transpired during his internment period, although quite clearly he had been self-conscious of his loneliness, his situation, his condition, and what had happened to him while he suffered in confinement during the entire length of time that he was held captive (Burney, 1951). I would conclude, therefore, that language and consciousness can be viewed independently of each other and that we may be perfectly conscious of what is happening to us without reverting to either words or language. In sum, we can self-consciously experience, feel, think about, and intuit loneliness without having to express it in words either to ourselves or to others.

Although therapy may consist in the *use* of language, it is the feelings, meanings, and relations that *precede* the words that are the reality, the targets of our phenomenological descriptions and insights. And this relation of precedence, the priority of consciousness before language, cannot be reversed.

Now the question is not whether we need language to communicate and conduct therapy—clearly we do—after all it's a practical enterprise—but rather what is the *target* of our communication when we are engaged in contending with loneliness; is it the feelings, meanings, the reflexions that are the source and focus of treatment; or is it the words the subject utters and invokes? For behaviorists, it is the simple lifeless words, and therefore verbal contracts are regarded as highly sacrosanct; they are thought to serve as objective, quasiscientific, measurable criteria of psychiatric progress or failure. Indeed, at my mental health clinic, all fifty psychiatrists, nurses, and clinicians meet weekly to conduct peer and quality assurance reviews to ensure that all the charts conform to cognitive-behavioral standards or we run the risk of having our funding disallowed by the insurance carriers. Talk about pragmatic, that is, financial concerns!

By contrast, insight treatment seeks to explore and concentrate on the issues of the past, the emotional complexities, and the synthetic *a priori* relations we have been outlining throughout this study.

But there is something else as well. Behavioral and cognitive therapists, because of their confinement to the temporal present, do not take into sufficient account human *development,* the peculiar and singular journey, the unique odyssey that each of us travels in order to arrive at our present destination and situation. And yet it is to be expected that the past has left indelible marks on our present state of mind as well as our attained developmental stage of separate lonelinesses. This is important. For as each of us struggles against loneliness, the autobiographies of our defeats, successes, and accommodations are all essential features of our present condition and future expectations. Even the defeats are replete in meanings waiting to be exploited fruitfully as "lessons learned" and hopefully recruited for positive insights.

The following passage from John Gibson's commentary on Locke is offered from the perspective of a historian of philosophy, but I believe it has a direct application to our discussion because it exposes the roots of the problem while cognitive and behavioral methods only neglect psychological development.

For thinkers of the seventeenth century [and beyond], to whom all ideas of development were entirely foreign, the place which is now filled by the conception of evolution [and development] was occupied by the idea of composition, with the implied distinction between the simple and the complex. A complex whole being regarded as the mere sum of its constituent parts, these latter were not thought to undergo any modification as the result of their combination; similarly, the whole was supposed to be directly resolvable into its parts without remainder. The whole temporal process containing nothing but different compositions of the same simples, out of which nothing genuinely new could emerge, the historical point of view from which we could trace development in time, and seek to comprehend the new determinations which arise in its course, was without significance. To comprehend a complex whole, all that was required was a process of direct analysis by which the simples contained in it were distinguished. Then starting with the simples, thought could retrace with perfect adequacy the process by which the whole had originally been constituted. (Gibson, 1969, pp. 47–48)

Consciousness is a lifelong developmental enterprise. Behaviorism and cognitive therapy, by their emphasis on the present, reject the significance of the temporal process that threads through the journey of one's life. But this continuous temporal accumulation of lonely, solitary meditations constitutes our past and anticipates our future. Without penetration into these loose threads, the entangled fibers of memory, and their exploration loneliness will remain hidden, dangerous, and powerful.

Against the behavioral, "analytic" paradigm of cognition and motivation, one can readily see the dramatic difference, for example, by comparing it against Erikson's eight developmental stages of human life (Erikson, 1963). As we have seen above in Gibson's criticism of classical empiricism, the same objection applies to behaviorism, which essentially denies development as it freezes the present and denies the past.

Beyond that, it's difficult, if not impossible, to understand a *qualitative* psychological development if one is restricted to singular, unconnected, empirical "sense data" or "qualia" and behaviors alone. The *DSM* and cognitive-behavioral therapy essentially fail to appreciate the progressive journey, the processes, the developmental, and the contributory factors in our psychic lives because of their strong tendency to reduce everything to simple sensory and mechanical terms and the present. Indeed, the *DSM* explicitly dismisses etiological considerations as speculative, while at the same time it regards hundreds of diagnoses as completely unproblematic. The precision of mathematics, statistics, quantitative analyses, and measurements is not only artificial but irrelevant to an individual in the throes of loneliness. There is a qualitative complexity to the uncanny, unnerving sense of isolation as emotions, meanings, and intentionalities become enmeshed through the intricate, overlapping, and crisscrossing of mental activities and structures operating within the individual's sense of loneliness. These psychic elements and forces are often in conflict with each other, and only by following the Ariadne thread of our guiding loneliness backwards, in reverse, can we hope to survive the labyrinthine chambers of the Minotaur.

Although cognitive therapy addresses a form of insight, its disadvantage lies in its restriction to the present, to the patient's presumably "incorrect" present belief system, its reduction to the obvious and concrete, and the rejection of the unconscious. Currently, cognitive-behavioral therapy along with the prevailing use of psychiatric medications dominate in the United States because they are cheaper and quicker. In California, the large state institutions—such as Fairview, Sonoma, Lanterman, Metropolitan, Agnews, and Camarillo—that housed thousands and thousands of souls have become ghost villages, while their charges have been moved to group homes, board and care residences, or the community at large. Veterans from our wars in Viet Nam, Iraq, and Afghanistan wander around aimlessly collecting aluminum cans and sleeping under bridges. Both disenfranchised groups are expected to regularly check in to outpatient clinics for their psychiatric medications. Many, many do not. Many resist because of the side effects of the medication. Others are too paranoid. Yet others believe they are not ill, and quite likely many are not unless you believe loneliness is an illness.

The individual struggle against loneliness obviously has a great deal to do with one's motivation, with one's strength or hope for a favorable outcome. In far too many cases, afflicted individuals have given up. I am reminded in this context of a short story by the French novelist, Alphonse Daudet. In "The Man with the Golden Brain," he responds to an admirer who asks him to write a story just for herself alone. In his narrative, he describes how his hero cavalierly goes throughout life spending freely until one day he falls in love with an attractive woman. Unfortunately, she pesters him constantly to spend his gold on the luxurious things she desires. One day, she sees a pair of expensive shoes in a shop window, and she implores him mercilessly to purchase the pair for her until finally he relents and with the payment there is a clot of blood on the gold nugget he proffers and he dies. I assume Daudet wished to demonstrate to his admirer that creative energy comes at a price and it is not an inexhaustible resource. Psychic energy is like that as well. Each of us has a limited amount of this precious resource to expend. If our efforts are not replenished by intermittent successful forays, we tend to give up. When we have spent a lifetime of spending psychic energy to secure friendship and intimacy and failed to gain our goals and exhausted we have little or nothing left, we will expire, if not physically then certainly psychically and spiritually. The aura of futility is the real danger in our battles against loneliness.

In closing this discussion on the disagreement about whether human experience or language is primary, I would invite my readers to reflexively inspect their own minds and "see" if they always think "in words"? How about dreams? Do we need words in order to dream? Are there "silent" wordless dreams? Is the unconscious dependent on language? Do we experience two languages—one that is conscious and the other unconscious? What would it mean to possess an unconscious language? Would it be shareable?

The only human absolute is loneliness; everything else emanates from that psychological source. In my original article on loneliness, I claimed that the opposite of loneliness is a sense of belonging, that human beings have an inordinate need to belong to something, family, friends, a special group, a special religion, a region, a country, humanity at large, whatever—perhaps something "greater" and beyond themselves. The overpowering desire to communicate by whatever means and in whatever fashion underscores our ubiquitous need to have our existence acknowledged by others—often even if it's only indiscriminately. The need to belong and to be recognized as a unique individual is frequently so prevalent that it assumes various forms of sterile communication: cell phones, Instagrams, Twitter, LinkedIn, texting, graffiti, so on and so forth.

Indeed, the entire spectacle of the human drama may reverberate between only two poles: loneliness and belonging.

REFERENCES

Ayer, A. J. (1936). *Language, Truth and Logic.* New York: Dover.

Burney, C. (1951). *Solitary Confinement.* New York: Macmillan.

Byrd, R. (1938). *Alone.* New York: Ace Books.

Erikson, E. (1963). Chapter 7: Eight stages of man. In *Childhood and Society,* New York: W. W. Norton.

Gibson, J. (1969). Locke's *Theory of Knowledge and Its Historical Relations.* Cambridge: Cambridge University Press.

Heidegger, M. (1959). *An Introduction to Metaphysics.* New Haven, CT: Yale University Press.

Hume, D. (1973). *A Treatise of Human Nature.* Oxford, UK: Clarendon Press.

Husserl, E. (1964a). Introduction: In *The Idea of Phenomenology.* Alston, W., & Naknikhian, G. (Eds.). The Hague: Martinus Nijhoff.

Husserl, E. (1964b). Introduction: In *The Paris Lectures.* Koestenbaum, P. (Ed.). The Hague: Martinus Nijhoff.

Mijuskovic, B. (1976). The simplicity argument in Wittgenstein and Russell, *Critica,* VIII:22.

Mijuskovic, B. (1977). The simplicity argument in Schopenhauer and Bergson, *Schopenhauer Jahrbuch,* Number 58.

Mijuskovic, B. (1978). Loneliness and the possibility of a "private language." *Journal of Thought,* 13:1.

Proust, M. (1956). *Swann's Way.* New York: Modern Library.

Ryle, G. (1949). *The Concept of Mind.* New York: Barnes & Noble.

Wittgenstein, L. (1965). *Philosophical Investigations.* New York: Macmillan, Sections 243–265.

Chapter 7

The Unconscious and the Subconscious

Can a person be lonely and not be aware of it? Is there such a thing as unconscious loneliness? Can people be self-deceived and believe they are not lonely when they actually are?

In his classic fine book, *Loneliness,* Clark Moustakas begins with a very personal declaration in his first paragraph:

I have experienced loneliness many times in my life but until recently I lived my loneliness without being aware of it. In the past, I tried to overcome my sense of isolation by plunging into projects and entering into social activities. By keeping busy and by committing myself to interesting challenging work, I never had to face, in any direct or open way, the nature of my own existence as an isolated and lonely individual. (Moustakas, 1961, p. 1)

Just as all human beings need air in order to live but seldom think about it, just so each of us lives in an atmosphere of loneliness without always being aware of it.

I first became aware of the following novel from Frieda-Fromm-Reichmann's article on "Loneliness." One of the more sustained and subtly frightening portrayals of loneliness of which I am aware is to be found in the Welsh novelist Arthur Machen's *The Hill of Dreams.* In the following, we shall see how a mind can be forced to retreat inwardly toward the farthest regions and the deepest recesses of the soul, into a tunnel of darkness, like a small burrowing creature, which is terrified of the forest full of danger and pain, the world of man, and be completely oblivious of its

descent. In the Introduction to the book, the author unambiguously provides the reader with both the theme and his literary purpose in no uncertain voice:

I asked my self why I should not write a "Robinson Crusoe" of the soul. . . . I
would take the theme of solitude, loneliness, separation from mankind, but, in
place of a desert island and a bodily separation, my hero should be isolated in
London and find his chief loneliness in the midst of myriads of men. His should
be a solitude of the spirit, and the ocean surrounding him and disassociating him
from his kind should be a spiritual deep. (Machen, 1923, p. viii)

The novel chronicles the experiences of an exceptionally sensitive and
lonely young boy, Julian Taylor; his maturation toward adolescence and
adulthood; and his driving ambition to become a novelist. The story begins
when he is twelve and living in the Welsh countryside. From the beginning, it is clear that he is very different from the other children his age.
As a consequence, he becomes especially vulnerable to their dislike and
bullying and a common object of ridicule among the rural girls as well.
Furthermore, there are a number of incidents in which Julian observes
the cruelty of the neighborhood boys toward defenseless animals. Thus, he
sets himself apart from his social and even his filial surroundings. As the
novel progresses, the reader begins to realize early on, whereas Julian does
not, that he is developing a frame of orientation toward the world and
others that is becoming increasingly self-enclosed, monadic, insular,
hermitic, and eventually it will be unsustainable. It is a perspective that
will leave him vulnerable in terms of his psychological survival. Nevertheless, as a consolation against a world he perceives as vain and selfish, he
increasingly begins to slip more and more into extensive periods of fantasy, of daydreams, imagined retreats, and reveries of escapism, while, at
the same time the reader is seductively enlisted in trying to anticipate how
all this will be resolved. Julian's deepening preoccupation progressively
centers on the imaginary fabrication of an ancient village peopled by all
sorts of mythical personages and seductive women, which is suggested by
the physical remnants of Roman ruins still existing throughout the local
Welsh countryside of his time, all contributing reminders of a past Latin
world long gone. Although he is emotionally close to his father, a poor
parson, there is an unbridgeable psychic distance between father and son
despite their hesitant caring overtures toward each other. When he is
fifteen, Julian purchases a copy of De Quincey's *Confessions of an English
Opium Eater,* and we learn no more about it for quite a while. At the age
of twenty, he has a single encounter with a country maid, Annie, and falls

precipitously in love and passionately expresses his deepest devotion to her, while the reader continues to speculate about a positive future outcome to their very brief but intense relationship. As Julian develops into early manhood, he continues to be repelled by the vanity and triteness of his surrounding social milieu. Seeking solitude and avoiding companionship, Julian increasingly wanders alone throughout the ancient Roman hillsides once populated by long forgotten men, events, and deeds, all of which offer him a protection from loneliness by his engagement in fantastic but consoling reveries. As he matures as a writer, he submits a manuscript to a publishing firm and impatiently awaits the decision of the editors. Meanwhile, he continues to be keenly aware and resentful of the disproportionate success and fame of other writers in comparison with his own unsuccessful efforts. His injured dignity constantly rebels at the undeserved good fortune of his competitors in contrast to his own futile efforts, and he increasingly rationalizes his failures in order to overcome the darker elements of his thoughts. After several months, he receives a form letter of rejection from the publishers, only to discover later that his work had been plagiarized to the benefit of another author and to the other's favorable and even laudatory reception and reviews of his purloined work. When he reports the situation to his father and shows him his version of the manuscript, his parent is outraged at the injustice and urges him to take up arms against this miscarriage of moral principles. Puzzlingly enough, Julian elects to do nothing about the affair and seemingly dismisses it from his mind as if he were totally unaffected by it. Later he encounters Annie again, and he is once more sensuously attracted to her physical presence and pours out all his desires, which she wholeheartedly acknowledges and encourages. Again, the reader feels a sense of faint hope in his behalf, but shortly thereafter Annie is summoned away to visit a distant cousin and he is left with only the promise of her return. Once more, instead of missing her consciously, he retreats into his soothing fantasies and imaginatively endows her with the symbolic presence of ideal womanhood in his daydreams. Months later he learns she has married a farmer. He receives the news with apparent equanimity, and to all outward appearances he seems stoically resigned to her loss. Again, as readers, we continue to become progressively uneasy as we realize Julian's internalization of his losses, his alienation from his social environment, his stolen novel, Annie's abandonment and casual betrayal, and even his hesitant distancing from his father are all playing against the background of his repressed ambitions of becoming a successful author and achieving his literary goals. As readers, we also sense the consequent transformation of these losses into imagined psychological compensations as they become dangerously estranging. His response to the world and his avoidance concerning practical matters of survival are obviously becoming more and more unrealistic as they are replaced outwardly by neither sorrow nor anger nor even a determination to pursue his interests and goals in another, more positive direction toward a more concrete purpose, but instead are internalized and immaterialized within a realm of fiction. The disconnection between what he secretly and unconsciously wishes for and the reality of what he is able to achieve is quite transparent to the captivated reader but not to Julian himself. As Julian continues to be completely absorbed in his own created fantasies and writings, he becomes deluded into believing that he has achieved a positive state of being.

As the chemist in his experiments is sometimes astonished to find unknown, unexpected elements in the crucible of the receiver, as the world of material things is considered by some a thin veil of the immaterial universe, so he who reads wonderful prose or verse is conscious of suggestions that cannot be put in words, which do not arise from the logical sense, which are parallel to rather than connected with sensuous delight. The world so disclosed is rather the world of dreams, rather the world in which children sometimes live, instantly vanishing away, a world beyond all expression or analysis, neither of the intellect nor of the senses. (p. 126)

A recurrent phrase in the novel is to "Look for the jar marked *Faunus*; you will be glad," an allusion to the Roman god of primitive drives and forbidden sensuality. Toward the end of the book, we discover that this bottle refers to a vial of opium or laudanum. As Julian continues to withdraw from social relations and economic realities, he retreats further into a deepening nether world of mythical forests and glens, heroic and demonic creatures, and tantalizing women. With the departure of Annie and devoid of securing her in this world, he has immaterialized her in a fictitious realm as he rationalizes her abandonment. At this point in the novel, he unexpectedly comes into an inheritance by way of a distant cousin, which gives him the opportunity to move to London and pursue his dream of being an author and he rents a small garret. But the loneliness has already taken a firm hold, and he struggles to complete his novel. At night, he wanders the solitary streets of London alone and lost. Detached from his fellow man and yet able to economically survive without gainful employment, he begins to fear madness setting in as he "is led farther and deeper into the dark labyrinth of his mind."

He was led back to the old conclusion; he had lost the sense of humanity, he was wretched because he was alien and a stranger amongst citizens. (p. 247)

Crushed by loneliness and the solitude of his life, he avails himself of the "little bottle on the mantelpiece, a bottle of dark blue glass," the Jar marked *Faunus*. And yet . . .

He saw now that from the first he had allowed his imagination to bewilder him, to create a fantastic world in which he suffered, molding innocent forms into terror and dismay. Unhappy above all and forever lost [Julian] sat within the dismal room. Every window was black, without a glimmer of hope, and he who was shut up in thick darkness heard the wind and the rain, and the noise of the elm tree moaning and beating and weeping on the walls. (p. 254)

Thus, enclosed in a monadic blackness of consciousness and completely withdrawn into his self, Julian ceases to write and the story ends with his landlady finding him dead alone in his room. Next to him is his manuscript, and she remarks to her attending companion: "It was all covered with illegible hopeless scribblings; only here and there was it possible to recognize a word."

I was fascinated by rereading this novel as I had done four decades ago. But this time it was from identifying myself as the therapist and Julian as the client. And I realized today how often I feel helpless and inadequate in helping those immersed in the depths of loneliness. I work with individuals who are defined by the mental health system as "chronically, persistently mentally ill" (a bit redundant), and in so many, many cases the roots of loneliness have taken such a firm hold that my successes are few and far between. Currently, our new mandate is brief cognitive-behavioral therapy, six sessions, and if there is no progress, the clients are referred to our medical health care system for psychiatric medications.

Having labored for thirty years in numerous public social welfare agencies, psychiatric hospitals, state institutions, and mental health clinics with clients diagnosed with psychosis, major depression, bipolar disorders, Posttraumatic Stress Disorders (PTSD), anxiety, panic, intermittent explosive disorders, and so on, I believe that more than anything else it is the monadic entrapment of the mind within its self more than any other danger that we must circumvent, overcome, and transcend lest we drown in our own imprisoning well of utter solitude. How dangerous the retreat into the self can be I believe is vividly shown in Julian's tale, which focuses on the destructive forces of the unconscious, in his self-deception, in his retreat toward the dark and enclosed self. In discussing Machen's book, it is my intention to stress the significant role the unconscious takes in our attempts to understand loneliness. We have already indicated that the mind exhibits dual active powers: internally and externally directed forces. In self-consciousness the power of insight rules and prevails. But also so do danger and self-destructive isolation. Meanwhile, if its other force, intentionality, is placed in abeyance and extended suspension, the self will eventually disintegrate as it retreats farther and farther inwardly until it eventually succumbs. Transcendence normally struggles to free itself outwardly, to escape lethargy, to propel itself toward idealized and real projects that are essential to its survival. This alternating dual "bipolar" activity of trying to escape internally within (depression) and rushing externally without (mania) are common features of loneliness. During episodes of extreme loneliness, the self needs to do all it can to conduct a search for a balanced emotional state between destructive narcissism and restorative intimacy. But unless the formulated interior goals meet with external success and are returned enriched within the self, the psyche will increasingly withdraw more deeply into its own isolative world of compensatory daydreams, brooding fantasies, and narcissistic reveries as Julian's tale demonstrates.

Husserl's phenomenological method, of course, denies the possibility of the unconscious, but as we have already seen, the great idealists and rationalists of the seventeenth to the nineteenth centuries affirm it in no uncertain voice, and so we shall part company here with Husserl and explore the role of the unconscious in the dynamics of loneliness and especially with its involvement in its hidden and darker aspects, threads that go back to the first ages of life, of evolution, of prehuman, and human development.

I have suggested that there is a very strong current of subjective idealism in German philosophy, which is rich in fruitful speculation that emphasizes the unconscious and the role it plays within the human mind (Mijuskovic, 2008, pp. 53–83). As we have seen, against Locke's thesis (and it applies later to Hume as well) that in deep sleep and swoons, the soul completely ceases to be active, to think, Leibniz instead holds that the mind *continually* thinks; its essence is to be active; that is the definition of mind, something that thinks; and consequently, it displays a spectrum of activities at various levels as it self-expresses through different forms of awareness from the sensory, appetitive, affective, desiderative, and perceptive; from the unconscious to the self-conscious. According to Leibniz, there is a chain of continuous consciousness within the mind from the very lowest to the very highest.

We recall that the combined views of materialism, empiricism, and behaviorism are unable to account for personal identity and continuity, apart from possibly grounding it in the individual's unique DNA, since all bodily and brain cells are systematically exchanged within a relatively short period of time. But if Leibniz is correct and the self *continually, uninterruptedly* thinks, at least unconsciously, then it follows that the deep self is ultimately constituted by its intimate and unique unconscious elements and activities. For Leibniz, the unconscious essentially represents forgotten memories that are not qualitatively different from their consciously remembered counterparts. In effect, it's something like saying, "Oh, now I remember." For Freud, the recall consists of remembering repressed events of traumatic distress embedded in internal conflicts. But now it is time to extend and deepen our theory of the unconscious and part company with this relatively restrictive view, which confines itself to memory and the current dynamics of the unconscious as promulgated in the Freudian psychoanalytic tradition insofar as it is committed to the "retrievability principle," namely, that unconscious traumatic experiences are always potentially recoverable. Certainly, Freud's depiction of the mind as consisting of all the cities of Rome simultaneously existing within the ego suggests such a possibility, as he proposes in *Civilization and Its Discontents* (Freud, 1961b, pp. 16–18).

But going beyond Leibniz and psychoanalytic theory, Kant opens the possibility that there are *unstructured, nonconscious, subconscious activities,* which are not to be equated with the unconscious and in effect lie below it. These are underlying mental activities and functions that originate— indeed *create*—the very possibility of the unconscious, the conscious, and the self-conscious, but they are *not* themselves retrievable *in principle.* They are of a subterranean origin and constitute the innermost *primeval* source and the first layer of human awareness, and yet these activities themselves are *inaccessible.* They consist of essential *non*accessible activities that are irretrievable by consciousness. Nevertheless, they exert an indirect but powerful force on the self through the medium of fantasy as they persist throughout our lives in the dark and tremulous light of the imagination. They are the deepest submerged roots that are never seen, although they are ultimately responsible for the visible trunk, branches, and leaves of the tree of consciousness. To try to access them is by definition to distort and disperse them. Generally speaking, the conception of the unconscious from Plotinus and on into Freud is a shadowy copy of what is accessible to awareness, a fuzzy repetition of past experiences.

What I am now referring to is something very different not only cognitively but more importantly affectively. This is a deeper, impenetrable subconscious significantly different from the unconscious we have been engaged in discussing so far. It opens the possibility of an abode for the darker, hidden side of our individual affective "nature." These protoplasmic mental forces are beyond "viewing." To attempt to "see" them is akin to turning on a light to see what darkness looks like. Their formative powers are absolutely unknowable; they are the primitive sources of affective— as opposed to cognitive—"spontaneity," which in turn create and thus contribute in generating the emergence of explicit consciousness. In terms of cognition, Kant alludes to the speculative nature of these reflections as "subjective," "hypothetical," and concludes, "I would appear to be taking the liberty simply of expressing an *opinion*, in which case the reader would be free to express a different opinion" (Kant, 1958). His reference to the power of "spontaneity" (A 51–B 75) is a foreshadowing of his subsequent discussion of the productive and reproductive imaginations (A 118). Elsewhere, in the section on Schematism, he alludes to the *imagination* as "an art concealed in the depths of the human soul, whose real modes of activity nature is hardly likely ever to allow us to discover, and to have open to our gaze" (A 141–B 181). Obviously, Kant intends the freedom or spontaneity of the imagination to serve as a bridge between the immediate passive sensuous contents, on the one hand, and the mediate conceptual categories of the understanding, on the other hand. One of the key distinctions in Kant is between the productive imagination, which is spontaneous, creative, and generative, and the *re*-productive imagination that involves empirical factors as in the second moment of immanent time-consciousness (A 99). But although Kant is there concerned with cognitive syntheses, there is nothing in principle that prevents us from endowing the imagination with an *affective* power consisting of darker feelings, possibly of a very primitive, even reptilian origination. Clearly, this is not Kant's direction—but it nevertheless leaves the speculative door quite wide open. Should this interpretation prevail, then loneliness in each of us would be radically individualistic and isolative in the extreme. Its productions would be singularly unreachable and obviously unshareable. It would follow that there are significant barriers to accessing the mind of others as well as our own. Indeed, Kant goes on to declare, "Synthesis . . . is the mere result of the power of the imagination, a blind but indispensible [active] function of the soul. Without which we would have no knowledge whatsoever, but of which we are scarcely ever conscious" (A 78–B 104). Kant attributes this power to the creative *productive* imagination. Accordingly, Kemp Smith draws a critical distinction between the subconscious and the Freudian unconscious.

Now that [Kant] has shown that the consciousness of self and the consciousness of objects mutually condition one another, and that until both are attained neither is possible, he can no longer regard the mind as even possibly conscious of the activities whereby experience is brought about. The activities generative of consciousness have to be recognized as themselves falling outside [or beneath] it. Not even in its penumbra, through some sort of vague form of apprehension can they be detected. Only the finished products of such activities, not the activities themselves, can be presented to consciousness; and only by general reasoning, inferential of agencies that lie outside the conscious field can we hope to determine them. (Kemp Smith, 1962, pp. 263–264, 273)

Leibniz's commitment to the presence of the unconscious is dependent on seeking to establish two conclusions: (a) the continuity of the self; and (b) its continuous *ethical* responsibility with not only God's knowledge of the person's moral acts but also that of the agent as well who ultimately needs to be aware of what they have done. Leibniz wanted moral persons to remain potentially self-conscious regarding the quality of their deeds, since punishment intrinsically requires that the individual knows *what* he is being punished for. Responsibility requires self-knowledge. By contrast, the theory of the subconscious I wish to introduce rises from a more sinister and deeper narcissistic strain, and it is also intended to serve two purposes: (1) to point to a more individual dynamic not accessible to uniform causal laws of repression, as in Freud; but also (2) to recognize the absolute singularity of human motivation—Leibniz's "Principle of Individuation," which asserts that no two substances can be perfectly identical. It follows that each of us contains elements that are absolutely inaccessible to the other person no matter how close we may be to them. This dark hidden soul ultimately may be the only conceivable "explanation" for man's ageless violence toward his fellows that persists to this day. Not even loneliness can ever excuse the level of aggression and cruelty from wars and holocausts and genocides and malicious evil in general. To repeat: This deeper level of consciousness prophesizes a sub-Freudian dynamic.

Leibniz, it is true, taught the existence of subconscious [actually unconscious] perceptions, and so far may seem to have anticipated Kant's recognition of nonconscious processes; but as formulated by Leibniz that doctrine has the defect which frequently vitiates its [Freudian] modern counterpart, namely that it represents the subconscious as analogous in nature to the conscious, and as differing from it only in the accidental features of intensity and clearness or through temporary lack of control over the machinery of reproductive [empirical] association. The subconscious [i.e., unconscious], as thus represented, merely enlarges the private content of the individual mind: it in no respect transcends it. (ibid., p. 273)

These distinctions are critical. Not only is Kemp Smith suggesting that the Freudian unconscious representing itself in the guise of scientific determinism is a weakened version of memory (albeit admittedly often one with an incredibly destructive affective force), but in addition he is saying that there is a vast difference in nature and function between the appointed agencies of the subconscious and that of the unconscious (although above he uses the terms interchangeably).

Kant distinguishes two worlds: (1) an empirical, phenomenal realm transcendentally "arising" from the pure intuitions of space and time as well as the structural categories of the understanding that we all share as rational beings; and (2) a noumenal unknown and unknowable sphere of "things in themselves." This opens the door at both ends of the spectrum of human consciousness. It allows for the conceivability of a purely rational, moral freedom *beyond* our shared phenomenal world, his ethical categorical imperative: "Always act so that the subjective maxim (i.e., the will) of your action can become a universal law legislating for all rational being in any conceivable universe." This ethical command is itself a synthetic *a priori* dictum: The subject wills the universal moral law. *But* the noumenal world also opens a wide entrance that allows for the possibility of an unregulated chaos of untethered destructive urges, for the dominating presence of a Jungian "shadow self" operating *below* consciousness. Thus, in the context of idealist theories of consciousness, "spontaneity," "transcendence," or "freedom" grounds both ends of a prism of awareness; both ethically "beyond" or "above" psychological determinism (the categorical imperative) as well as subconsciously below awareness descending toward a realm of dark, sinister impulses. In the latter case, each of us would experience a complex and tenebrous hidden self (Jung). The result is that there are ineluctable limits to self-knowledge (Mijuskovic, 1979, pp. 11–20). Kant, of course, does not dwell on this darker aspect, and instead he subscribes and defends psychological (and physical) determinism in the empirical, scientific world. Kant, like Freud, is a psychological determinist. But the term "spontaneity," which is conceptually the very opposite of determinism, occurs no less than a dozen times throughout the *Critique*, and so theoretically, in principle, the influential power of this primordial force could exert itself on the subconscious and seep upward into consciousness.

Fichte deepens the focus on the subconscious immeasurably by concentrating solely on the ego's primitive positing force through a purely volitional act that makes self-consciousness itself actual, that radically creates and produces, from a *non*cognitive source, experience itself. Whereas Kant *begins* from empirical self-consciousness and excavates its transcendental presuppositions, Fichte instead starts *before* experience, with the Ego or "I" positing itself unreflectively, then following through by thetically positing the "not-I," which in turn creates a domain of other selves in order for the Ego to engage in ethical activity. The Fichtean Ego spontaneously creates a world of other selves in which the self can operate morally with free will. According to Fichte, in the *Science of Knowledge,* the Ego first exists but simply in a state of undifferentiated consciousness unaware of its self. Its first *act*—one of pure spontaneous, creative *intentionality*—

is to posit the other-than-itself, the non-Ego or the not-I *as an other* in contradistinction to its self, thus producing a field in which to operate ethically and then to dialectically return to its self reflexively. This is highly unusual for an idealist. *It means that the initial act of consciousness is spontaneous and intentional rather than reflexive.* In short, the ego *sui generis* creatively produces the world virtually *ex nihilo* as a sphere for its moral activity. Thus, Fichte, according to Jon Mills, is the first philosopher to consider the actual *a priori* conditions or grounds that make self-consciousness possible without taking consciousness itself as its starting point or presupposition. But, once again, as in Kant, this ultimate *spontaneous* source remains cognitively irretrievable; it represents a completely novel feature, not even thinkable as a remote possibility for behaviorism and empiricism to consider (Mills, 2002). But, again, this arbitrary positing of a will animated as a surge of uncontrolled passions may, for all we know, lie in wait in the dark heart of man. Accordingly, Fichte's thesis suggests that there are purely volitional acts, virtually arbitrary and obviously irrational by definition, since they are prior to reason, which invite the possibility that dark passions ultimately rule the universe of solitary human beings. In any event, there is no assurance that Fichte's "primal act" of the will has only ethical possibilities. After all, by Fichte's own self-imposed declaration concerning first principles, each of us has the option of choosing *any* first principle, since at bottom he attributes their origin to purely personal "inclinations and interests." In Fichte, intentionality clearly trumps reflexion!

According to Lancelot Whyte:

Fichte opens a sequence of German philosophers: Schelling, Hegel, Schopenhauer, and Nietzsche, who developed their conception of the unconscious as a dynamic principle underlying conscious reason. For Fichte the light of consciousness emerges out of the dark of the unconscious. The unconscious processes of the mind had previously been considered by professional philosophers to be mainly concerned with memory and perception; now they became unmistakably the seat of instinct and will. (Whyte, 1978, p. 120)

In Hegel, the subconscious explicitly begins to assume the much darker form of "a night-like abyss," "a night-like mine or pit in which is stored a world of infinitely many images and representations, yet without being in consciousness" (Hegel, 1985, p. 204).

In another work, Hegel declares that,

the soul is in tension: On the one hand, it is a subjective center for itself and, on the other hand, it remains tied to a vast subconscious substantial life. I am a simple bottomless pit sunk into an infinite abundance of possible or virtual experiences. The individual never knows how many experiences have been experienced and absorbed by him [Jung's collective unconscious?] or how many he has forgotten. In abnormal states memories of things forgotten are sometimes brought back. As a unique subjective center of its functions, the soul is a monad which mirrors itself. (Hegel, 1959) 203–204

Hegel even alludes to a prenatal influence:

The natural [primeval *feeling* of] subconscious life may prevail in the soul, as the mother prevails in the embryo. Dreams, prophecies, presentiments, telepathy, clairvoyance, somnambulism, hypnosis, subconscious suggestions, immediately felt—all these occult forces are evidence for the soul in non-spatial [immaterial] purely functional relationships with natural life. The danger of those archaic functions is that they may erupt in physical disturbance or mental sickness in a conscious cultured person. (Section 320, 204)

The conscious soul may lose control over its irrational, subconscious dream-life; the latter intruding into waking life. This loss of unity or split of the soul, and the perversion of its order, is *insanity,* of all kinds and degrees. (Section 321, 204)

Before its cognitive powers develop, the natural soul is a primitive *feel-ing* soul. We gain yet another perspective on Hegel's view of loneliness through his comments on madness, which can be reconstructed by con-sulting Sections 402–408 of his *Philosophy of Mind,* where he announces that it is first necessary to address "why insanity must be discussed before the healthy individual consciousness" (Section 408). It's important to indicate that he is committed, as Leibniz before him, to a series of con-scious levels from the prenatal, the subconscious, and then to the uncon-scious; and he even refers to the fetus's active relation within "the mothers womb" in terms of its "monadic [drive for] individualism" (Sec-tion 405 and Note 2 and Section 406, Note 3). The initial moment of self-consciousness is essentially animated by a *desire* for unity grounded in an even more primordial stage of "Freudian narcissism," as Daniel Berthold-Bond informs us.

What this means is that at the level of soul, the I or self has not yet developed into full conscious awareness of its self and its surrounding world. Indeed, much like Freud's interpretation of "primary narcissism," the soul for Hegel does not distin-guish between inner and outer at all; the soul is a "differenceless unity" prior to the opposition between interior and exterior realities (Section 308, Note). The soul is the subconscious state of the mind, "the dull stirring, the inarticulate breathing of the spirit through its subconscious and unintelligent individuality." (Berthold-Bond, 1995, p. 26, cf. pp. 43, 46, 77)

This primitive stage with its animating and telelogical *desire* for unity is grounded in a unity of immediate feeling—not cognition—and it acts, it functions independently of an as yet merely potential other self. Indeed, Hegel briefly considers melancholy or loneliness (one of the four humors of Hippocrates) as connected to suicide, and then the essential definition of madness follows as consisting of a "state in which the mind is shut up in itself, has sunk into itself, whose peculiarity . . . consists in no longer being in immediate contact with actuality but in having positively separated itself from it" (Section 408, Note; Berthold-Bond, pp. 19–20). (Originally and semantically, the term "melancholy" meant loneliness, as in Robert Burton's 1621 treatise, *The Anatomy of Melancholy.*) It is because of the individual's unbridled, unchecked freedom that "Man alone has the capacity of grasping himself in this complete abstraction of the 'I.' This is why he has, so to speak, the privilege of folly and madness" (Section 408, Note). In short, the lonely, tormented soul retreats inwardly, seeking solace solely within, and thus loses its ability to relate and share in the common world of the other. Hence, according to Hegel, madness occurs when the individual mind withdraws from intercourse with the shared world of others and regresses into its innermost recesses, into "the dark infernal powers" of the subconscious and dreams (Section 408, Note). In this restricted condition of "communing merely with its interior states, the opposition between itself and that which is for it—the world of reality—remains shut up within itself" (Berthold-Bond, p. 26). One of the basic assumptions of this study is that in order to overcome, to transcend loneliness, it always depends on our ability to share emotions and meanings with others. If that is the case, I am contending that there are very definite limits to sharing that precludes and limits human attachments.

Well prior to mankind's current condition of social evolution, we have inherited and absorbed certain primeval dispositions that have unknowingly accompanied us through time and thus continue to be the warp and woof of our nature. These underlying powers have not been shed or left behind. We have not lost our affective archaic gills born timelessly within the deepest and darkest waters of the oceans. One only needs to consider the current American "action" movies and video games reeling with themes of horror, destruction, violence, aggression, and death in order to realize how many of us evaluate "entertainment."

For Schopenhauer, the Will *is* the subconscious, "the thing in itself," a monolithic, universal, malignant, purposeless but *impersonal* force manifesting itself through our individual irrational drives as each of us fashions self-deceptive rationalizations excusing our true hidden motives. It consists of a blind, powerful, insatiable, and destructive surge, whose manifestations serve to form and to structure an insincere tissue of motives that have no likeness to their ultimate dark source. Man is not only at war with others but also in conflict with himself. This internal ferment is fueled by instinctual impulses, sexual urges, and irrational motives. All these are in turn grounded in the subconscious. The Will serves as a permeating dark power, arbitrary, and insistent within all human existence. For Schopenhauer, the Will *is* Kant's noumenal "thing-in-itself." We are not only strangers to others but even strangers to ourselves (Hesse, *Steppenwolf*).

Schopenhauer called the phenomena representations and the thing in itself will, equating will with the unconscious as conceived by some of the Romantics. Schopenhauer's will had the dynamic character of blind driving forces, which not only reigned over the universe, but also conducted man. Thus, man is an irrational being guided by internal forces, which are unknown to him and of which he is scarcely aware. Schopenhauer compared consciousness to the surface of the earth, the inside is unknown to us. The irrational forces consist of two instincts: the instinct of conservation and the sexual instinct, the latter by far the more important of the two. He compares the sexual instinct to the innermost features of a tree of which the individual is but a leaf. (Ellenberger, 1970, pp. 208, 273).

Finally, in Nietzsche, the principle of the Will to Power is manifestly present in all of nature but especially in man where it seduces us into disguised self-deceptions and rationalizations about our actual motives by tailoring them when we socially need to do so in order to assert ourselves more forcefully over others aesthetically, ethically, politically, or otherwise, while at the same time we ruthlessly pursue our unbridled lusts accompanied by a secrete desire for mastery over others and indirectly over ourselves. Our sublimated desires are but masks to hide the true visage of our souls. We shamelessly hide from ourselves through elaborate substitutions and sublimations our real and primitive desires for psychological dominance. If we possessed absolute power to do as we please, we might find that our limitless lusts and demands would astonish even ourselves (Gide, *The Immoralist*). As William Barrett suggests, Nietzsche's model of the Will to Power principle is originally derived from the uncompromising respect the ancient Greeks accorded to the primitive, titanic, instinctual forces of self-assertion ascribed to the god Dionysius: "He who would make the descent into the lower regions runs the risk of succumbing to what the primitives call 'the perils of the soul'—the unknown Titans that lie within, below the surface of our selves" (Barrett, 1962, pp. 178–180).

Nietzsche was led to consider the human mind as a series of drives and eventually the emotions as a "complex of unconscious representations and states of the will". . . . It was Nietzsche's concern to unveil how man is a self-deceiving being, who also is constantly deceiving his fellow men. . . . Since man lies to himself even more than to others, the psychologist should draw conclusions from what people really mean, rather than from what people say and do. (ibid., p. 273)

And yet, along with Kierkegaard, Nietzsche is the other great master of the nineteenth-century existential movement grounded in the deepest expressions of human loneliness. Without the hope of an accepting God and human love, and yet a sense of isolation as extreme as Carazan's, he declares a fading plea for his own salvation through love.

No one talks to me other than myself, and my voice comes to me as the voice of a dying man. With you, beloved voice, with you, the last vaporous remembrance of all human happiness, let me have an hour longer. With your help I shall deceive myself about my loneliness. I shall lie my way back into society and love. For my heart refuses to believe love is dead, cannot bear the terror of the loneliest loneliness. It compels me to talk as if I were two. (unpublished text)

This poignant, heartfelt declaration is but a step way from insanity.

In sum, according to the above quintet of philosophers, the individual subconscious will forever remain latent and submerged but active, unrecognized and powerful, while its manifest surface appearances will be familiar, all-too familiar in nightmares and madness. It is a realm of consciousness where feelings of fear and anger rage deep within the self. Sometimes its soft ripples disturb the surface of the waters of consciousness, but this is only a deceptive manifestation of its deeper underlying currents. Often, it is in our daily news and through our public media that we are forced to become aware of the uglier current that runs deep and cold, hot and destructive, in the actions of men. In this Kingdom of Feelings, Reason is an invited guest who never attends.

We may also recall that Freud quite pessimistically declares that the goal of life is death.

[I]t is possible to specify this final goal of all organic striving. It would be a contradiction to the conservative nature of the instincts if the goal of life were a state of things which had never yet been attained. On the contrary, it must have been an *old* state of things from which the living entity has at one time departed and to which it is striving to return by the circuitous path along which its development leads. If we are to take it as a truth that knows no exception that everything living dies for *internal* [subconscious?] reasons—becomes inorganic once again—then we shall be compelled to say that '*the aim of all life is death*' and, looking backwards, that '*inanimate things existed before living ones.*' . . . In this way the first instinct came into being: the instinct to return to the inanimate state. (Freud, 1961a, p. 32)

This death drive, later christened by Neo-Freudians as the principle of Thanatos, became connected in Freud with narcissism, destruction, and aggression. The self, trapped between the impulses of the Id and the conscience of the Superego, "Helpless in both directions, the ego defends itself vainly, alike against the instigations of the murderous id and against the reproaches of the punishing conscience" (Freud, 1960, p. 43). During my therapy sessions focusing on loneliness with innumerable individuals over many years, I frequently heard them express the wish that they had never been born. Thoughts of death are very often connected with a final retreat. One of the great novelists of loneliness, Thomas Hardy, concludes two of his classics, *Tess of the d'Ubervilles* and *The Mayor of Casterbridge*, with the wishes of the two protagonists to be buried in an unmarked grave signifying that they wished they had never been born.

And how often are suicides, murders, serial killings, and mass murders in the media described as the work of "loners." And yet we persist in failing to make the connection between loneliness and death.

My point in the foregoing is that the self can never be understood along the metaphor or paradigm of a behavioral "brain-machine" and a *tabula rasa* precisely because, among many other considerations, there are powerful unconscious but even more indeterminate subconscious forces at work. Whatever the subconscious *does,* it is not a thing or even an identifiable *cause.* It is a surging, insidious force, an indeterminate unknowable activity. How else to account for wars and holocausts, man's inhumanity to man, serial killers, mass murderers, homicides, suicides, acts of unbridled aggression, and malicious torture? If Freud is on the right track, with his theory of sexual impulses and energy, coupled with the principle of Thanatos, then cruelty and death are no more than a catastrophic amplification of Lekh's thwarted sexual passion, lust, and malicious evil, evil done simply for its own sake.

We can now see that the power of the subconscious travels in a completely different direction than Freud's (and Kant's) determinist account, which offers a rather straightforward causal sequence presenting psychological traumas as causes while the neurotic symptoms function as their consequent effects. In this sense and to this extent, Freud, in many ways, clearly remains entrenched in the scientific camp of determinism. But when he enlists the mythical forms of the Titans swallowing their children, the sons castrating their father, the myth of Aristophanes in the *Symposium,* Narcissus, Eros, the god of death, Thanatos, Oedipus, and beyond clearly he has in mind the entire tragic House of Atreus along with Agamemnon, Clytemnestra, Orestes, Iphigenia, Electra, and other mythical forces, he has most assuredly left science behind for a dark humanism.

All of the preceding, of course, is well beyond anything even conceivable by the narrowness of "scientific" cognitive-behavioral theory. But let us invent what it would be like to imaginatively implement the forces, the powers of the subconscious—admittedly an obviously self-defeating task by definition—still, what *might* it be like? Perhaps if we speculate and consider seriously what sorts of feelings, instincts, impulses, lusts, drives, and especially fears of loneliness would find expression, where could we turn for insight? How deeply and darkly does the source of our true "personal identity" lie? In what abyss of timelessness does the nucleus of our innermost narcissistic self descend?

Joseph Conrad's *Heart of Darkness* traces the immanent voyage of the soul as it turns within itself, through the dark penumbral recesses of consciousness, what the Conradian critic, Albert Guerard, has described as a Jungian descent into the depths of the individual soul, a study of dark introspection, a perilous night journey into the center of the ego, and a visit within "the black inward abyss of the self," the Jungian shadow self. Conrad was heavily influenced by both Schopenhauer and Nietzsche, and these strains become readily apparent in the work as the novel compels us to voyeuristically peer into "the deeper regions of the mind," through those "great dark meditations" of reflexive thought, which, if sufficiently prolonged and intensified, will eventually discover within each self "what no other man can know" (Guerard, 1958, pp. 35–48). The novel depicts Kurtz's (and Marlow's vicarious) internal journey externally symbolized by the Belgian Congo; it is a dark subjective search for meaning, for self-knowledge, for the truth hidden within the depths of consciousness and a deceptive heart. "The mind of man is capable of anything—because everything is in it, all the past as well as the future. What was there after all . . . but truth—truth stripped of its cloak of time" (Conrad, 1971, p. 44). By its very nature, the inquiry into truth assumes the aspect of a dream—a Nietzschean, Dionysian fantasy—as the reflexive turn of consciousness probes deeper toward the primitive subconscious, toward the darker impulses lurking within the domain of the psyche. As Conrad expresses it:

I am trying to tell you a dream—making a vain attempt, because no relation of a dream can convey the dream sensation. . . . No, it is impossible; it is impossible to convey. It is impossible to convey the life sensation of any given epoch of one's existence—that which makes its truth, its meaning—its subtle and penetrating essence. It is impossible. We live as we dream—alone. (p. 44)

Granted that we are incapable of translating the subtle truth-value of a dream into the hard, brittle precision of an objective, public, analytic language, but still is there not something we may succeed in expressing in regard to the solitary existence of man? There is, and the truth, simply stated, is that man is terribly alone and that this loneliness generates disturbing thoughts and dark self-explorations. This is the reality that Kurtz realized within himself. Of course, the symbol of darkness in the novel represents moral evil, but it stands much more for loneliness, for reflexive self-enforced isolation. For Kurtz is desperately alone and lonely: "Is Kurtz alone there [in the jungle]?" "Yes" (p. 52). "Kurtz wandered far in the depths of the forest" (p. 94); "how can you imagine what particular region of the first ages of man's untrammeled feet may take him into by way of solitude—utter solitude" (p. 82); "there was nothing either above or below him. . . . He had kicked himself loose of the earth [i.e., his fellow man]. . . . He was alone" (p. 112). Kurtz's existence transpires not only within the emptiness of a moral vacuum, symbolized by the primitive jungle, but in the midst of a psychological void as well. And what he discovers is the utter horror of absolute loneliness: "his soul was mad. Being alone in the wilderness it had looked within itself, and, by heavens it had gone mad" (p. 113). His own self-sentence on his inner vision is to pronounce upon it as "The horror. The horror" (p. 113). And the horror is that each of us, separately, lives throughout our life alone and lonely. But rather than recognize, actually re-cognize this Orphic truth, we mask from ourselves our true condition by extravagantly exploiting false ideals of enlightenment and religion, attributing to ourselves what are in reality egoistic delusions of grandeur—idols of the Tribe, Cave, Marketplace, and Theater in the Baconian sense—anything lest we encounter the dark visage of our own desperate isolation, lest we confront the heart of darkness which gnaws within, a blackness that is more than a match for the jungle darkness without. This is where Carazan's metaphysical nocturnal dream intersects with Kurtz's psychological horror.

In an earlier work, Conrad referred to

[t]he tremendous fact of our isolation, of the loneliness impenetrable and transparent, elusive and everlasting; of the indestructible loneliness that surrounds, envelopes, clothes every human soul from the cradle to the grave, and, perhaps beyond. (Conrad, 1962, p. 225)

This striking declaration is the author's most direct statement of the universal principle that loneliness constitutes the most terrifying evil which dwells in the mind of man. And it is so because it consists of an inextinguishable terror within, like being buried alive forever (Antigone's original sentence avoided by her suicide, Sophocles), a destiny that persists as long as consciousness operates. It is a fear that devours the heart of self-conscious being but rejuvenates itself only to be devoured again.

The themes of invading loneliness, the collapse of personal identity, and both coupled with the opacity of the subconscious, are powerfully interwoven in William Golding's *Pincher Martin: The Two Deaths of Christopher Martin* (1956). The work masterfully exploits the "stream of consciousness" style of narrative as it guides the reader in a destructive descent toward the nether regions of the soul. It is dedicated to the Crusoean motif of disintegrative isolation, and it is, as its famous forerunner, the story of a shipwrecked sailor, who, after his British destroyer is torpedoed by a German U-boat, awakens in complete darkness in the water and kicks off his sea boots in order to facilitate swimming and hopefully his survival. Fortunately, he is able to reach a rocky crag, a small islet upon which he secures himself. As time passes, he experiences incredible physical discomfort and pain as well as a matching loneliness. He desperately clings to his sense of identity in order to preserve his sanity. He remembers that in the past he had adversaries, enemies, and betrayed lovers to assure him of his being, his uniqueness, his identity. Now there is nothing stable to hang on to. At times, he fears he is hallucinating. He perceives his arms as lobster pinchers striving to grasp whatever is available to him for physical and emotional survival; at other times, he is preoccupied with reminiscences of his former life, all the while reminding him of his prior existence when he thought only about himself and never avoided taking greedy advantage of others, of women as well as his closest friends. His mind becomes voraciously preoccupied with his present existence while indulging in an obsessional brooding on the selfish, narcissistic things he had done to others with little or no remorse. He recalls having identity cards and photographs and mirrors to assure him of who he was. But on this rock, he asks himself

How can I have complete identity without a mirror? That is what has changed me. Once I was a man with twenty photographs of myself. . . . I could spy myself and assess the impact of Christopher Hadley Martin on the world. I could find solidity in the bodies of other people by warmth and caresses and triumphant flesh. I could be a character in a body. But now I am this thing [i.e., consciousness] in here, a great many aches of bruised flesh, a bundle of rags, and those lobsters [i.e., his arms] on the rock. The three lights [his two eyes and mind] of my window are not enough to identify me however sufficient they were in the world. But there were other people to describe me to myself—they fell in love with me, they applauded me, they caressed this body, they defined it for me. Here I have nothing to quarrel with. I am in danger of losing my identity. (p. 132)

Now he desperately struggles to physically survive and to psychologically postpone his growing fear of madness by giving names to things:

I am netting down this rock with names and taming it. Some people would be incapable of understanding the importance of that. What is given a name is given a seal, a chain. If this rock tries to adapt me to its ways, I will adapt it to mine [by naming it].

As if words alone could control reality. This passage is reminiscent of Roquentin's encounter with the roots of the chestnut tree in Sartre's *Nausea*. They both consist in the illusionary power of language over things when the reality is that language distorts our vision of the world and men. Language is inherently myopic. Vainly attempting to use words—empty, all too empty words—to enlist language as a device, a tool in order to objectify his mastery over things, to ground his efforts for survival by controlling external objects through words, he seeks to avoid his internal thoughts of loneliness by focusing on the external. But it is a futile and losing battle against the advancing assault of isolation. And yet despite his strongest and most determined intentions—his intentionality—to push beyond and outside his interior self and thus avoid the insistent internal surge of subconscious feelings, the tentacles of his loneliness propel him farther and farther inwardly, deeper and deeper within that inner self, into the farthest recesses of the mind. Assailed by dark thoughts and ravaged by the effects of extreme isolation, Christopher Hadley Martin's singular existence is systematically reduced to a reflexive "black centre" of consciousness.

The centre cried out. "I'm so alone! Christ! I'm so alone. . . . The centre was thinking—I'm so alone, so alone. . . . The centre felt the gulping of its throat, sent eyesight on ahead to cling desperately to the next light and then the next— anything to fasten the attention of consciousness away from the interior blackness." (p. 181)

Notice how both reflexivity and intentionality enter into the quotation, into his desperate plea for survival.

A central motif in the novel is captured through the rather grotesque parable of The Chinese Box, which depicts the self as a nucleus of orgiastic activities and unbridled narcissism. The fundamental principle of narcissism is either to devour others or be devoured yourself. Long ago Thomas Hobbes, in the *Leviathan*, succinctly described the nature of "man's life as solitary, poor, nasty, brutish and short" and consisting of a "war of all against all."

You see when the Chinese want to prepare a very rare dish they bury a fish in a tin box. Presently all the lit'l maggots peep out and start to eat. Presently no fish. Only maggots. . . . Well, when they've finished the fish, they start on each other. . . . The little ones eat the tiny ones. The middle sized ones eat the little ones. The big ones eat the middle sized ones. Then the big ones eat each other. Then there are two and then one and where there was a fish there is now one huge successful maggot. Rare dish. (Hollinger, 2001)

One interpretation is, of course, that Christopher Martin, who spent a lifetime engaged in a narcissistic exploitation of others, is now being consumed by his own greed for existence. But another reading is that having reached the black center of loneliness and the terminus of self-consciousness, there is nothing left but the activity of the self devouring its self (Hollinger, 2001, pp. 76–79). Loneliness is like that; it feeds on itself until there is nothing left, just the rare dish of loneliness to be consumed absolutely alone.

The novel ends when a warship arrives and some seamen discover Martin's body and one of them remarks, "Poor devil, he never had a chance to kick his sea boots off." It's at this point that the reader realizes Pincher Martin died only moments after he recovered consciousness in the sea and very shortly after he had been thrown from the ship and into the waters. In effect, the plot reminds one of a popular expression just before one thinks he is going to die and says, "I saw my entire life flash before my eyes." But in truth, our whole existence is always there before and inside us, "before our eyes," subconsciously, in front of as well as beneath our soul. Few if any of us wish to see it. Possibly, those who have suffered from deep psychotic episodes and destroyed their minds with illicit drugs experience all this in spite of their strenuous efforts to maintain their sanity. The subconscious permeates our deepest sense of identity, but mercifully we are generally shielded from it by the fragile cloak of sanity. But through its profound depth, the subconscious contributes to our sense of irrevocable loneliness. It is constantly present as a background swell that permeates and invades our senses, feelings, and thoughts and only suggests its opaque presence during intense and prolonged assaults of loneliness as it weaves through the catacombs of our being, as it infects us unawares. It's the insidious "black centre" alluded to by Pincher Martin of a compelling and distorting awareness that consumes us when we suffer intensely from loneliness. When we are desperately lonely, we are assailed by all sorts of negative thoughts and feelings. It's loneliness which is the trigger that detonates the black fireworks. We never escape the deeper sources of our existence, our existential being. But these subconscious nightmares are unique to the individual; they are in the last analysis completely unshareable just as two people cannot share the same nightmare and therefore their burden can only be carried alone.

During the course of our lives, we frequently have recourse to soothing daydreams and fantasies. But when we are confronted by the deepest loneliness, by abandonment and betrayal issues, that is when the uglier dynamic of the subconscious invasively manifests and asserts itself, and we are like children in the dark frightened by every object and memory we bump into.

In the past four and a half decades that I have publicly expressed my thoughts in writing, I have managed to keep my personal reflexions out of the "mix," but having survived psychologically in Europe and North Africa from 1937 to 1945 as a child, I must confess I don't share the optimism about the human race that I peripherally belong to. I believe that some human beings are saints, that there is an inextinguishable goodness in them. I believe that most of us are morally lukewarm like my self. But I fear those who are evil; they have the power to destroy us all. As I was composing this study, I couldn't help notice a change in my feelings and attitude as I went on to discuss Thomas Wolfe, Zilboorg, Fromm-Reichmann, Fromm, Conrad, Golding, and especially Kosinski. The only consolation that I could muster for myself was that I observe and marvel at many couples and friends who are completely dedicated to each other, that their loneliness is so greatly minimized by their intimacy and genuine feelings for each other that they can enjoy life and tend to their gardens like the Epicureans of old and Voltaire's Candide.

REFERENCES

Barrett, W. (1962). *Irrational Man: A Study in Existential Philosophy*. New York: Doubleday.

Berthold-Bond, D. (1995). *Hegel's Theory of Insanity*. Albany: State of New York Press.

Conrad, J. (1962). *An Outcaste of the Islands*. New York: Dell.

Conrad, J. (1971). *Heart of Darkness*. New York: Doubleday.

Ellenberger, H. (1970). *The Discovery of the Unconscious: The History and Evolution of Dynamic Psychology*. New York: Dover.

Freud, S. (1960). *The Ego and the Id*. New York: W. W. Norton.

Freud, S. (1961a). *Beyond the Pleasure Principle*. New York: W. W. Norton.

Freud, S. (1961b). *Civilization and Its Discontents*. New York: W. W. Norton.

Golding, W. (1956). *Pincher Martin or the Two Deaths of Christopher Martin*. New York: Capricorn Books.

Guerard, A. (1958). *Conrad the Novelist*. Cambridge, MA: Harvard University Press.

Hegel, G. W. F. (1959). *Hegel's Encyclopedia of Philosophy*. New York: Philosophical Library.

Hegel G. W. F. (1985). *Hegel's Philosophy of Mind.* Oxford, UK: Clarendon Press.

Hollinger, A. (2001). Pincher Martin's losing struggle for identity, *Dialogos: Analyse de Texte,* quoted by Hollinger, 773.

Hume, D. (1973). *A Treatise of Human Nature.* Oxford, UK: Clarendon Press.

Kant, I. (1958). *Immanuel Kant's* Critique of Pure Reason. New York: Humanities Press, xvii.

Kemp Smith, N. (1962). *A Commentary to Kant's* Critique of Pure Reason. New York: Humanities Press.

Machen, A. (1923). *The Hill of Dreams.* New York: Knopf.

Mijuskovic, B. (1979). Loneliness and personal identity. *Psychology: A Quarterly Journal of Human Behavior,* 16:3.

Mijuskovic, B. (2008). Kant's reflections on the unity of consciousness, time-consciousness, and the unconscious, *Philosophy and Theology,* 20:1–2.

Mills, J. (2002). *The Unconscious Abyss: Hegel's Anticipation of Psychoanalysis.* Albany: State of New York Press, 35 ff.

Moustakas, C. (1961). *Loneliness.* New York: Prentice Hall.

Whyte, L. (1978). *The Unconscious Before Freud.* New York: St. Martin's Press.

Chapter 8

Therapeutic Measures

At the start of the study, I proposed suggesting various therapeutic strategies, some possible temporary measures to aid us in our struggle against loneliness. They fall roughly into two categories, which, not unexpectedly, mimic our dual emphasis on cognitive and motivational capacities. First, insight, the reflexive ability to realize both our universal and our personal limitations in terms of loneliness; intentionality in the formation of transcendent goals and the ability to commit to positive values; choice, the wisdom to make intelligent decisions and learn from our mistakes; strategies in short- and long-term planning; religion with its sense of salvation, redemption, consolation, and communion; and finally fantasy and daydreaming. Second, it stresses the motivational features of trusting others; being trustworthy ourselves; enhancing empathy; and forging secure bonds through friendship and intimacy.

Although, of course, it's not possible to clearly separate cognitive from motivational therapeutic strategies from each other, nevertheless there is considerable theoretical value to be gained in making the effort for the sake of clarity and the enhancement of the ability to concentrate on the measures. Obviously, human beings are organic wholes, and therefore they display intellectual capabilities and tendencies as well as affective elements, which readily bleed and seep back and forth into each other. Roughly, the two therapeutic categories unfold as means (*theoria*) to ends (*praxis*). Intelligent insight is the beginning and intimacy is the end.

In the Introduction, I also suggested that there were ethical dimensions surrounding the condition of loneliness and its ramifications, and we will address these as we proceed. But a convenient place to start is with Aristotle, who distinguishes intrinsic values as good in themselves from extrinsic or instrumental values that are helpful for something other than themselves. For example, having healthy teeth is good in itself, while going to the dentist is instrumentally good but unpleasant in itself; therefore, the latter is a means to an end. For Aristotle the power of sight is both intrinsically and extrinsically good. I would say the same about friendship and intimacy. All things being equal, I would submit that loneliness is intrinsically unpleasant and intimacy is intrinsically pleasant. All things being equal, I would propose that when one succeeds or even simply *intends* (the principle of intentionality) to help another human being or creature to feel less lonely, he or she has done something virtuous and ethical (Kant). By contrast, when one *intends* to make another human being or creature feel more lonely and isolated, then they have done the reverse. And I would further contend that having a friend and being a friend is both intrinsically and instrumentally good (ethics). I discuss Aristotle's ethical theory based on his conception of human nature in a recent paper (Mijuskovic, 2007, pp. 133–141) and Kant's ethical principle, specifically his second formulation of the categorical imperative, in an earlier article (Mijuskovic, 2005a, pp. 67–88).

I would hierarchically classify the following measures as predominantly cognitive.

Insight. The most liberating source of relief from a *personal* sense of isolation primarily comes from insight and understanding—not feeling. According to Irvin Yalom, echoing Paul Tillich (1979, pp. 47–48), the four existential "ultimate concerns" of the human condition are (a) loneliness; (b) meaninglessness, since each of us is solely responsible for our decisions in creating values in our lives; (c) anxiety, which is engendered by our radical freedom of choosing our values independently of any assurances from the commands of a theistic God; the universal concept of a stable human nature; or the dictates of our particular society—hence existential *angst*, which is to be distinguished from Freudian anxiety, the latter based on intrapsychic conflicts; and (d) the solitariness of dying alone (Yalom, 1980).

Loneliness is as foreordained as death. Just as each of us dies alone (Tolstoy, "The Death of Ivan Ilych"), each of us lives alone within the realm of our own mind, nestled inside our cocoons and revolving spheres of consoling fantasies and crippling anxieties. Thus, the most important insight is to realize that life consists of an endless struggle over our sense of loneliness, which only releases its grip over us in death. To seek for a permanent victory over loneliness is as futile as it is impossible, just as it would be pointless if we spent all our energies seeking to avoid death and desiring to live forever and be immortal. The best we can hope for are respites of varying duration and intensity from the distress of loneliness.

Of all existing things some are in our power and others are not in our power. In our power are thoughts, impulse, will to obtain and will to avoid, and in a word, everything which is our own doing. Things not in our power include the body, property, reputation, office, and in a word, everything which is not our own doing. (Epictetus, *Manual of Epictetus*)

The *attitude* each of us assumes when confronted with our loneliness is one of the most important things in our power.

In existential writings, as mentioned above, the individuality of death is a main theme. I often compare the human sentence of eventual mortality with the condition of loneliness, since both are inevitable. But there are liberating aspects to loneliness. First, it helps us to realize that we are not alone in our loneliness but that it is rather the universal destiny of each of us together. Like death, loneliness has to be accepted and dealt with circumspectly as something we all have to deal with. We share a common destiny. In that respect and to that extent, we are not alone.

Accustom thy self to believe that death is nothing to us, for good and evil imply death is the privation of sentience, and therefore a right understanding that death is nothing to us makes the mortality of life enjoyable, not by adding to life an illimitable time but by taking away the yearning after immortality. (Epicurus, *Letter to Menoeceus*)

What is true of death is true of loneliness. It is something to face with common sense, dignity, courage, or at least Stoical resignation because we cannot escape it. This is the message of the myth of Sisyphus.

We all recognize loneliness from the outside. We readily see it in the affect, expression, and behavior of others. The difficulty is when we are forced to plunge inside, within ourselves and confront our own loneliness. And, unfortunately, we have a strong tendency to blame others for our uncomfortable and painful sense of isolation. We must assume more responsibility for it and constantly keep in mind that it is an essential trade-off for our transient existence. Again, much depends on the attitude one takes.

Loneliness is deep-seated. By that I mean it is grounded in inaccessible sources that defy ultimate penetration. Insight therapy can reach just so far. Insight teaches us that there are limits to self-knowledge and therefore intrinsic barriers to *permanently* overcoming isolation, alienation, and estrangement. Knowing one's limitations is the beginning of wisdom. But behavioral and cognitive therapies are in a much more disadvantageous position, since they reject both (a) the unconscious and (b) the past, and thus they stand self-barred from exploring the deeper recesses of the mind that *are* accessible and do help in understanding loneliness. By being ignorant of the limitations, cognitive and behavioral therapies only result in increasing anxiety because the patient is led to believe that there is something more or something different that he should be doing; perhaps taking the "right" medication; that he is in some sense failing to do something or missing out on what so many others are enjoying so fully that he envies those who he views as more fortunate (E. A. Robinson, "Richard Cory").

Insight and intelligence also depend on correcting past mistakes and thus maximizing our chances for the intimacy we seek during life's journey, with its various genuine promises of extended periods of satisfaction as well as its tantalizing moments of ecstasy. Insight consists in developing beneficial and fulfilling habits, consuming hobbies and interests, positive acquaintanceships, and deeper intimate relationships. The basic strategy is to "get out of your self." Loneliness is narcissistic and isolative. This naturally brings us to intentionality.

Intentionality, Transcendence, Freedom, and Commitment. A guiding principle in all metaphysical idealism derives from the mind's spontaneous activity, its inherent power to transcend, to go beyond the confines of its monadic existence, in a word, its *freedom.* The difference between freedom in idealism as opposed to freedom in existentialism is that in the former it is rationally *structured* and recognized as such when it is philosophically attained (Hegel); or ethically put into play, since moral freedom operates when you self-consciously, rationally give the moral law to your self and obey your own law, for then you are both subject and sovereign (Rousseau, Kant). It consists in doing as you *should.* By contrast, existential freedom is radically *unstructured* and arbitrary; consequently, we can never be sure if we have chosen "correctly." Its distinguishing characteristic leans toward doing as you *please.* Hence, the feeling of anxiety prevails (Sartre). Both have their advantages and disadvantages, but they are very different. However, the escape from the one-sided, self-absorbed narcissism of self-consciousness depends on successfully breaking "outside, "beyond," "transcending" ourselves and yet returning with the other self within our sphere of immediacy in a mutually fulfilling relationship. The mind has the freedom to create values for its self alone. It has the power to escape the confines of self-consciousness, to commit to projects beyond its self and external to its self; to escape boredom and loneliness by an *engagement,* a commitment to a vision. If the commitment one forges with the other self is *mutually* attained, then one has created and found intimacy. I recall James Howard, author of *The Flesh-Colored Cage,* once telling me the simple but absorbing story of "The Button." It is about a prisoner confined alone in a completely dark cell, and his only way to keep his sanity is to toss a button inside the black enclosure and then search for it in the pitch darkness. Then one day—or night—he is unable to locate it no matter how long and feverishly he seeks it until eventually at some undetermined moment in time his jailers open the cell door and find him dead. And in a corner of the cell's ceiling is a button caught in a spider's web. Just so, the self first inwardly fantasizes and focuses on a goal formulating it reflexively—perhaps even arbitrarily. But then the goal or value must be objectively, intentionally achieved in projects and actions. Only then can the mind return to its self to be reformulated and reinvigorated in order to continue planning for the next project or event before venturing out once more. Sartre points out that we intentionally project, pro-ject ourselves outwardly in the plans and goals we choose; we externalize our goals; we test their success and failure in the world; we create and re-create ourselves by the decisions, the choices we make; only then can we resume and enrich the internal reflexive dialogue with ourselves and prepare to battle forth once more. It is the ego's constant self-duty to re-create and re-confirm its goals or to choose other values. Often the pursuit can be as meaningful as its attainment. In any case, once achieved, the new purpose and commitment must be undertaken. Human beings are teleologically structured. The persistent danger is to retreat and to remain within ourselves. As we are all abundantly aware as therapists, an essential feature of loneliness *qua* depression is deadly isolation, physical immobility, and intellectual stagnation because at the bottom of the well of loneliness there is only darkness, emptiness, and meaninglessness (Golding). How often haven't we heard people complain they feel "empty," "meaningless," "purposeless" when they express their loneliness? Loneliness, emptiness, meaninglessness, and purposelessness are synonyms. And they are all related to Sartre's declaration that existential man is forlorn because he is lonely; anxious because he is condemned to freedom; and in despair because the universe in itself is meaningless. Sartre is right; but it's up to each of us individually to change those existential situations or conditions. Sartre's theme that "existence precedes essence" signifies that first we exist, and only then do we create meanings and values for ourselves alone. Obviously, since the most desired achievement is (generally) human intimacy, then like Howard's button, we must not only find it but continue to seek it and grasp it tenaciously once we have it secured. We must strenuously avoid blaming the other person in moments of loneliness. There are no true introverts, only discouraged extroverts. But two (or more) individuals can, however, forge a solid, permanent dually narcissistic relation with each other just like Plato's primitive race of humans.

Unlike Freudian anxiety, then, which is centered in unconscious internal conflicts, existential freedom is terrifying because individuals create "ethical" meanings and values for only themselves and for which each is alone responsible. There is no one else to blame or hold accountable but ourselves. Indeed, we are free precisely *because* each of us is alone; that is a direct consequence of each person's absolute loneliness—freedom. It follows that each individual has a perfect ability to *intentionally* create meanings, purposes, and values within themselves. Some animals, though self-conscious and highly prone to loneliness, obviously do not create meaningful values. Human beings, however, are quite capable of forging meanings, intentions, and commitments to various other-directed values, to a theistic deity (Kierkegaard), a political cause (Marx), or simply to other individuals as in genuine friendships (Plato, Aristotle, Epicurus, Montaigne, Hume). Intimacy and commitment are *a priori* related. It's inconceivable to establish a relationship of intimacy without the expectation of mutual trust and commitment. Thus, in order to avoid loneliness and engage and succeed in intimacy, one must make a commitment so that the other person(s) in the relationship can assume a sense of trust in you. Intimacy thus presupposes mutual trust; mutual (age-appropriate) respect; and mutual affection. Above all, it is constituted by a *sharing* of feelings, meanings, and values. It also presupposes physically sharing a common time and space with the other self. Telephones, cell phones, emails, and texting won't do it. As Aristotle indicates, the essence of friendship is living together. Along with commitment comes a vision of who one wants to be; what sort of "existential authenticity" one wishes to pursue and establish as the central meaning or value in life. This commitment is as open to the average person as it is to one suffering from psychotic symptoms. In the autobiographical novel, *I Never Promised You a Rose Garden,* the following exchange between a sixteen-year-old psychotic patient, Joanne Greenberg (actually, the author of the book) and Frieda Fromm-Reichmann (Dr. Fried in the novel) takes place:

"The symptoms and the sickness and the secrets have many reasons for being. The parts and facets sustain one another, locking and strengthening one another. If it were not so, we could give you a nice shot of this or that drug or a quick hypnosis and say "Craziness be gone!" And it would be an easy job. But the symptoms are built of needs and serve many purposes, and that is why getting them away makes so much suffering."

"Now that I have realness will I have to give up Yr . . . *all* of it . . . right away?"

"Never *pretend* to give it up. I think you will want to give it up whenever you have the real world to replace it with, but there is no pact with me. I do not ask you to give up your gods for mine. When you are ready, you will choose." (Greenberg, 2004, p. 209)

Interestingly enough, Fromm-Reichmann, a psychoanalyst, proposes an existential answer. This is one of the major solutions. Each of us is intentionally, transcendently, existentially free to *choose* our first principles, meanings, and values; to decide between narcissism or empathy; isolation or intimacy; emptiness or fullness; meaninglessness or meaningfulness. To be condemned to freedom may be a curse, as Sartre intimates, but it is also our salvation.

Strategies. I was a student at the University of Chicago (1956–1963) and had the pleasure of taking Social Science 1 with Reuel Denney, one of the co-authors, along with David Riesman and Nathan Glazer, of *The Lonely Crowd.* In their sociological tract, they discuss three forms of social and cultural organization and their respective values: (1) tradition-oriented (e.g., India with its rigid caste system) as opposed to both (2) inner- and (3) outer-directed societies, their point being that the United States in the 1950s was entering into a transitional change in value selection, a paradigm shift from stressing (2) internalized, authoritative, and individualized inner-directed values (as instantiated by Max Weber's classic tract, *The Protestant Ethic and the Spirit of Capitalism*) and (3) instead turning to other-directed values based on "signals" from peers and the fashionable standards of "popularity" (Mijuskovic, 1992, pp. 147–164). I think that's interesting because it suggests that each of us has a pronounced tendency to address and soothe our loneliness either by trying to please ourselves or attempting to please others, either by internally or externally directed predispositions. Both, of course, are reactions to the problem of loneliness. These differences in methods and goals command some consideration. When I face my loneliness, do I try to coax, persuade, or force others to conform to my preferences and values; or do I try adjusting and complying with those of the others? My point is that the two tendencies confirm our distinctions of reflexivity and intentionality. In terms of individual strategies, it reminds me once more of my colleague, James Howard's study of loneliness (Howard, 1975). As Howard views it, there are two basic personality types, and therefore two very dissimilar strategies used by individuals in trying to avoid loneliness: (a) "Incorporators," who seek relief by convincing, seducing, forcing, or trapping the other within their sphere of influence (reflexivity); and (b) "Decapsulators," who seek relief by turning themselves inside out in order to please and join those without (intentionality). We take in or we give out in our struggles to reach the other self and connect. Howard goes on to emphasize that as strategies they can be altered or adjusted, depending on circumstances and experience. But from an operational and strategic standpoint, it's important to realize that the option is ours. When I had a summer job on the Chicago truck docks, it was clearly to my advantage to decapsulate, to blend in, to conform to the blue-collar standards of my fellow dock workers, to please others or risk alienating my companions at work. Staying aloof would have been a disaster. Back at the University in the fall quarter, it was much more comfortable and natural strategically to try to incorporate others within my field of interest and values, to please myself, to bring others inside my preferences and values. Obviously, the above distinctions have a conceptual familiarity with Jung's dichotomy of extroverts and introverts as personality types. But as strategies, there is always a choice on how best to approach loneliness depending on various external, environmental, or social situations and circumstances. Finally, one of the most important strategies is to seek companions who share your values. Although it may or may not be true that "you cannot run away from your self," it's utterly foolish to stay around people who exemplify a value system antagonistic to your own.

Choice. We have already alluded to choice in our discussion of Insight, but now we should expand on it. On a more practical and mundane level, it's worth summoning Aristotle's ethical and forensic concept of choice and its connection to human responsibility in dealing with loneliness. Intelligence, common sense, and insight precede successful choices. Choice itself results in an action; it is the outcome of conscious planning. It is voluntary as opposed to compelled or as the outcome of ignorance concerning the relevant circumstances surrounding a proposed action. When executed well, it shows as the successful result of a rational deliberation between alternative courses of action. It is grounded in a fusion of reason and desire, ratiocinative desire or desiderative reason. It is obviously a combination of both cognitive and motivational factors. As Aristotle (1941, pp. 35–37) states, "Intellect itself, however, moves nothing but only the intellect which aims at an end and is practical" (*Nicomachean Ethics,* VI, 2, 35–37). In this regard, choice exhibits both cognitive elements as well as affective features, both self-consciousness and intentionality, or both *theoria* and *praxis*. Further, we only deliberate about matters in our power. No one deliberates about whether the sun will rise tomorrow or whether they will die or be lonely. Those decisions are out of our control. We may deliberate on how to confront our impending demise or prevailing loneliness but not on whether we shall die or whether we will be lonely. Loneliness exists in the human heart as a permanent condition of our existence as surely as death exists in the human body.

Choice, then, deals with the variable, with calculated risks, with matters and situations that can be otherwise than they are. And yet, it is based on insight, past experiences, moderation, and the formation of good habits forged in the crucible of the past. As The Philosopher further points out, we do not hold children responsible until they reach maturity because they have not attained the age of deliberation and insight and therefore choice. But we do blame the adult alcoholic for his negligence because at one time he had the ability to refrain from becoming an alcoholic. Choices are always made in regard to the *means* we take in order to avoid loneliness; but the *end* is always the same and invariable, a diminution and relief from loneliness. For a long time, behavioral and cognitive psychotherapists have been trained to "focus on feelings," to ask open-ended questions—"And how did that make you feel?" Perhaps the question should be, "What do you think about it?" and "What can you do about it?" Be especially aware that a great many people relieve their sense of loneliness by caring and helping others, by making others less lonely. The strategy to focus on feelings is overrated. The problem is *why* this has happened to you and *what* are you going to do about it.

Fantasy and Daydreams. These are voluntary creations of the imagination, which we freely indulge in because they are pleasant or compensatory. By contrast, for instance, nightmares are involuntary. Fantasy as a defensive preventive to isolation is obviously universally prevalent and unquestionably implemented more than any other method of delaying or subverting loneliness. It is, however, at best, only a temporary remedy. In extreme cases, of course, it can lead to psychosis. Nevertheless, all human beings resort to fantasy whenever they are confronted with loneliness and boredom. Boredom is merely a minor form of loneliness. Who knows what portion of our waking state is allotted to pleasant, satisfying reveries of fame as well as retaliatory imaginings of revenge and self-righteousness. Fantasy is a singularly important inheritance from our deepest primitive state of feelings and thoughts generated during our brief but highly significant stage of Freud's "oceanic feeling" and James's affective "assailment" within infant consciousness. It both thrives and festers within the domain of the human mind from birth to death. And so it is that its ubiquitous prevalence and ease of access enables fantasy to be valued, retained, and applied throughout our lives, as in Julian's case. Daydreams can be extremely helpful in warding off boredom, entertaining grand schemes of success, and harmless imagined pleasures. They can motivate us toward great accomplishments. And they can consist of powerful and successful defense mechanisms for those of us who are forced to exist under intolerable conditions; or even merely unpleasant ones for prolonged periods of time, as, for example, during tedious or stressful employment. But they can also disorient us from realities in life that have to be realized and addressed.

As far as daydreams and fantasies are concerned, I have little original to contribute beyond recognizing their influence and importance in our lives, and I expect each of us will formulate our own criterion of health or overdependence in regard to these indulgences. But I do believe it is worth cautioning against their dangerous and seductive powers if they are used as the sole or even main antidotes to loneliness. Again, as in so many human situations, it's worth heeding Aristotle's formula, "Everything in moderation."

Medication. In 1909, Freud and Jung were invited to give a series of lectures at Clark University in Worcester, Massachusetts. The talks were well received by the American Psychological Association, and for the next fifty years or so psychoanalysis was the dominant force in the psychiatric world in the United States and "talk therapy" ruled. Around the 1960s, during the Kennedy administration, however, the American Psychiatric Association persuaded the federal government that all mental disorders are actually caused by chemical imbalances in the brain. Indeed, the 1990s were heralded as the "Decade of the Brain" and the deinstitutionalization of untold thousands and thousands of mental patients from state hospitals throughout the United States commenced. During the same period, psychiatrists and mental health clinics increasingly turned to the use of psychiatric medications as a means of curing mental "diseases." The shift in treatment practices was predicated on a major change in conception. According to the behavioral paradigm, the brain, human behavior, and psychiatric medications are all three grounded in the same substance: Matter. In a *Newsweek* magazine article, dated February 7, 1994, titled "Beyond Prozac: How Science Will Let You Change Your Personality with a Pill," the essay promised to cure shyness, anxiety, fearfulness, and obsessions. Operating only with three concepts, namely, neurons as cellular units; synapses as the junction point between two neurons; and serotonin as neurotransmitters and mood regulators, the model offered a causal explanation of how electrochemical impulses result in thoughts, emotions, memories, will, feeling, and action. No mention was made in regard to the role or even the existence of sensations and whether they are mental, physical, or both.

By contrast, I would submit that this explanation is woefully inadequate as an account of meanings, relations, creativity, self-consciousness, and intentionality. The problem is that this behavioral paradigm glides "imperceptibly" from physical neurons to human thoughts and consciousness. Neurons (1) "*communicate* through chemicals" and "excite" other neurons, thus "producing" or causing "thoughts, emotions, memories, and will." (2) Electrical impulses "hear sounds." And (3) neurons "culminate" in "a thought, feeling, or action." The difficulty is that not only are (mental?) sensations and their transitional conduits disregarded from any mention, but it appears that neurons and electrical impulses *directly* cause consciousness. It's like saying when I turn my table lamp on, "I have awakened the light bulb into thinking." Communication is a mental term; neurons don't communicate any more than they enjoy going to the movies. When I play a game of billiards, I would never think of the billiard balls as "communicating" among each other. Neurons don't experience "emotions" and "memories" and "will" any more than they abuse drugs. And electrical impulses don't hear sounds. Humans, however, do.

Loneliness is not a disease. It's not a sickness. It's the human condition. It's as natural to feel lonely as it is to think. If the theory of loneliness I have offered is persuasive and consistent with the dynamic model of a reflexive and intentional consciousness I have proposed, then medication may not be the only or the best or the safest therapeutic intervention available. Indeed, after serving for three decades in psychiatric hospitals and institutions, outpatient mental health clinics, and social service agencies, my personal clinical judgment leans heavily toward "talk therapy" and the human bonding that takes place between caring and responding human beings. In addition, I believe that psychiatric medications in the United States can be overdone and are often damaging (Ridgeway, 2011). But for most Americans treated in the public sector, who have an unquestioning faith in science and technology, medication is the "drug of choice." In many other instances, however, it's the choice of the family, the school system, or the penal system rather than that of the individual.

Incidentally, there is also a very strong countermovement against medication in Europe and Britain, a movement called "philosophical counseling" and "philosophical psychotherapy," which may prove to serve as an antidote to the overuse and overdependence on psychiatric medications (Mijuskovic, 1995, pp. 85–100, 1997, pp. 23–25, 2005b, pp. 1–18). There is a possibility that for many subjects their crises are intellectual rather than psychological. For example, I treated a priest who had lost his faith and wished to leave the Church. This wasn't a psychological issue but rather what used to be called an "intellectual crisis." He had lost his faith, not his mind.

The following hierarchy seeks to offer predominantly motivational and emotional measures involved in reducing loneliness. To be sure, again, they cannot exist in a "pure" state independently of their intellectual counterparts.

Trust. I place this first under the category of affective considerations because as I have previously argued, very young children under the age of one year can die from loneliness and neglect if not sufficiently nurtured.

As early as 1955, when I was a first-year student in college, I registered for a course in Psychology. Our textbook was *Psychology and Life,* 4th edition. A particular section sparked my interest. In the text, the condition was known as *marasmus.* It pertained to the thousands of infants who were institutionalized because of their mothers' participation in factories in support of the war effort in England during World War I. It was described as a psychosomatic disorder, "as a wasting away with no apparent or determinable organic basis." The book went on to say, "Marasmus is rare today, but at the close of the First World War, it was held accountable for half the deaths of babies under a year old." The work of Margaret Ribble in 1943 and 1944 was prominently discussed at some length, and I have never forgotten the impact it made on me in those early years of my studies (Ruch, 1953, pp. 134–136). Thirty-five years later, I wrote the article "Loneliness and Intimacy," which I cited at the beginning of this study (Mijuskovic, 1990, 1991).

Essentially, loneliness is narcissistic. That's not a moral judgment (although it can be, depending on the context). It simply means that when, under the stress of chronic loneliness and anxiety and anger, each of us, as an individual, strongly tends to withdraw within ourselves, to isolate, to self-protectively retreat back toward the security of the womb; to recapture a period before there was either self or a rejecting other. We *always* need the other self as a "sounding board," as a means of reverberating our feelings and thoughts. We cannot survive psychologically, emotionally, or intellectually without the external, reciprocating "other" human or sentient agent. We need the other self as much as it needs us. And we need not only to be cared for but also, even more, we need to care for others. Indeed, loneliness researchers have discovered that the improvement rate for hospital discharges is considerably shortened when a pet is waiting for them at home. And this is where trust comes in. Obviously, trust can only occur in the context of a relationship between two (or possibly more) human beings; often if too many individuals are involved, it frequently leads to "conflicts of interest." How often we observe, in a triad, two people ganging up on the third. We need to reach out to another self-conscious being, divine, human, or animal. In its mature and ideal *constitutive* formation, it involves Kant's second formulation of the categorical imperative: "Always treat the other self as if they were an end in themselves having infinite worth and value and never as a means to your own selfish or utilitarian ends." If the other person in the relationship feels and thinks the same way you do, then mutual trust and genuine intimacy have been achieved. Trust is sustained by good intentions (Kant). It is first and foremost the basis, as Erikson emphasizes, for healthy human relationships. On its successful implementation, everything else positively follows.

Empathy Leading to Intimacy. The motivational importance of empathy and its role in loneliness will require some elaboration because it involves our final defense and response to the charge of solipsism that is leveled against Husserl in particular, but it also applies in general to any subjective idealist standpoint, including my own. In any case, in dealing with the issue, it will be helpful to bring Husserl back in for the ensuing discussion.

Husserl wants the phenomenological method to produce objective, intersubjective, and truly scientific results. Thus, in Meditation Five of the *Cartesian Meditations,* he seeks to avoid the criticism of solipsism and subjective idealism, and he thinks he is able to do so by invoking the concepts of (a) *"appresentation and analogical apperception,"* and (b) *empathy* within an essentially *cognitive* context.

The *Cartesian Meditations* consists of five Meditations. The fifth alone is virtually as lengthy as the first four. The opening section of the Fifth Meditation is significantly and ponderously enough titled, "Uncovering the Sphere of Transcendental Being as Monadological Intersubjectivity: Section 42: *Exposition of the problem of experiencing someone else, in rejoinder to the objection that phenomenology entails solipsism."* The entire Fifth Meditation is, not surprisingly, heavily influenced by Leibnizian and Kantian considerations and metaphors. In it, Husserl tries to argue on cognitive, epistemological principles that the ego is connected to others intersubjectively on the basis of the ego's *indirect* "appresentation." Thus, Section 50 is titled "*The mediate intentionality of experiencing someone else, as 'appresentation' (analogical apperception").* What is troubling Husserl is, as he confesses, the following:

When I, the meditating [self-conscious] I, reduce myself to my absolute transcendental ego by phenomenological epoche [reduction, bracketing] do I not become *solus ipse;* and do I not remain that, as long as I carry on a consistent self-explication [without resorting to intentionality] under the name phenomenology? Should not a phenomenology that proposed to solve the problems of Objective [real transcendent, external] being . . . be branded therefore as transcendental solipsism? But what about other egos, who surely are not a mere intending *in me,* merely synthetic unities of possible verification *in me,* but, according to their meaning, precisely *others*? Have we not therefore done transcendental realism an injustice? The doctrine may lack a phenomenological foundation; but essentially it is right in the end since it looks for a path from the immanency of the ego to the transcendency of the other [self]. (Husserl, 1964, pp. 89, 94)

The precise problem is how to travel from the immanency of *my* ego to the transcendency of the *other* ego and to constitute the other as immanent within me. After all, the other is not *actually* in me but only consciously *intended* by me, constituted by me as a meaning *separate* from myself.

The second ego, however, is not simply there and strictly presented; rather is he constituted [meant, intended] as "alter ego". . . . The "Other," according to his own constituted sense, points to me myself; the other is a "mirroring" of my own self and yet not a mirroring proper, an analogue of my own self and yet not an analogue in the usual sense. (ibid., p. 94; Smith, 2013, pp. 219–221)

First, this won't work because as Spiegelberg indicates and Husserl confesses, "appresentation is the *indirect* perceptual presentation of an object as mediated through the direct presentation of another . . . or of other minds through their bodies" (Spiegelberg, 1965, pp. 158–159, 712). When Husserl brackets the existence of the external world, he at the same time excludes other bodily selves and, of course, any hope of gaining direct access to their minds as well. Second, according to Husserl, the whole point of the bracketing procedure is that meanings are constituted *immediately in my consciousness* and hence are *directly* open to phenomenological, eidetic insight, to intuition. But *ap*-presenation is and the *an*-alogical are both *indirect, mediate,* and hence inferential. This is no better than Descartes's discussion of the automatons and men in Meditation II. And lastly, mirroring is an especially poor metaphor for consciousness of the other self. Mirrors only provide two-dimensional images; they offer at best only a flat surface. But if I am to capture the innermost significance of the other, his feelings and thoughts, to be able to eidetically or intuitively "grasp"—*versus* comprehend—the other's loneliness, his innermost feelings and thoughts, I must somehow penetrate or enter immediately *into* his multiple dimensionalities of feelings, meanings, unconscious, and conscious thought processes—an obviously hopeless task if we are restricted to mirroring metaphors, *ap*-presentations, and *an*-alogical inferences once removed from consciousness.

Interestingly, this may be where art may provide us with some insight. Rather than invoking the metaphor of a mirror, let us instead enlist the metaphor of a window. In terms of representing consciousness, a window is precisely a "medium" through which and into which one can both look outside as well as inside. Two great master artists of loneliness are Edward Hopper and Andrew Wyeth, who seem to successfully depict human loneliness in a very special way. In several paintings, "Evening Wind" (1921), "Eleven AM" (1926), "Evening in a City" (1944), "Cape Cod Morning"(1950), and "Morning Sun" (1955), Hopper draws a woman looking out of a room toward some unspecified scene outside. Since windows exhibit a twofold perspective, namely, of looking out as well as peering within, this is symbolized in "Evening Wind" by showing a strong breeze blowing the curtains *into* the interior of the room. Many of Hopper's paintings display houses without any human beings present, although, of course, houses are fabrications made for human use and consumption. The sense of pervasive loneliness is so eerie that one thinks of the houses as lonely and empty of human meaning and presence. Similarly, Wyeth's painting, "Wind from the Sea" (1947), pictures a room, devoid of a human subject, focusing on an open window with the curtains blowing in again. The second painting, "The Chambered Nautilus" (1956), shows a woman alone sitting upright in a bed and gazing *out* the window obviously lost in thought while on a table inside the room is a conspicuous seashell, a nautilus, symbolizing the loneliness of the room and the isolation of its single inhabitant.

Well, what about empathy? Will that help us? This may be more hopeful at least initially. Husserl was familiar with the works of Theodor Lipps. Originally, empathy (*einfuhlung*), which literally means "feeling into," was a term used by Lipps as an *aesthetic* concept. One projects—pro-jects and enters into—intentionally goes beyond, transcends one's feelings by inserting, in-fusing them into an aesthetic object, and thus the self is absorbed by the objects' *qualitative* expressions. Clearly, this implies an act of *intentionality*. In the context of aesthetics, according to Lipps, value is not an objective or scientific fact but rather the result of a free creation of the imagination, of fantasy, and thus it belongs to the world of subjective appearances. It is inseparable from *ex*pression, ex-pression, out-wardness, since its "spiritual aesthetic" source is derived from the realm of the subjective mind and posited "outside" the self, but at the same moment it is posited *inside* the object. An *aesthetic* account of empathy follows, based on a model of aesthetic *contemplation*. (Think Schopenhauer.)

Attention is not aware of itself [not self-conscious]; it is directed outward [perception *versus* apperception; consciousness *versus* self-consciousness; projection *versus* introjection, intentionality *versus* reflexion] to the object and absorbed therein. Nevertheless, what provides aesthetic meaning to the object and what constitutes the ground of its enjoyment, is the very act of contemplation. The mind unconsciously enlivens the outward form by fusing into it the modes of its own activity—its striving and willing, its sense of freedom and power. The moods thus transported into the object do not spring from the real or moral ego, but only from the ego in so far as contemplative. It may be analyzed into two factors: first, there is the inner activity, the emotion of pride, the feeling of freedom, etc.; second there is the external sensuous content as bare physical content. The aesthetic object springs into existence as a result of the fusion of these two factors. The ego unconsciously supposes itself at one with the object and there is no longer any duality. Empathy simply means the disappearance of the twofold conscious-ness of self and object and the enrichment of experience that arises from this interpenetration. (Rader, 1960, p. 369)

In the above passage, we certainly notice one very active element of consciousness—intentionality. The question is whether there is also an active element of reflexivity. The assumption in this case is that contem-plation is not self-conscious.

In the Fifth Meditation, Husserl's version of empathy is compromised because he tries to transform empathy into a *cognitive* structure and likens it to an immediate, direct, intuitive *appresentation,* an apperception through the other's consciousness.(Smith, 2013, 219–221). However, it is through the presentation of an external, other self—in this case the *body* of the other self. But this will never do. It still falls woefully short of intuitive access to the *mind* of the *other* self. If loneliness was relieved by human bodies, I would hang out with crowds of strangers. Generally, idealist philoso-phers, like Berkeley, similarly to Husserl, argue on analogical grounds—and therefore via inferential proofs—for the assurance of the existence of other selves. For instance, I see you writhing and screaming on the floor, and I infer that you are in pain because that's exactly how I behave when I am in pain. But it still remains a guess and not an intuition. There can be no eidetic insights on a *cognitive* level into the mind of the other self, through either the other's mind or body.

In Lipps, the empathy is concentrated in the *aesthetic* contemplation, which is grounded in the self's projection of freedom into objects (paint-ings, statues) or persons (actors, dancers). The problem with Lipps's view is that it is an *asymmetrical* relation; the aesthetic object is incapable of reciprocating contemplatively. Similarly, in Husserl, although his motive for establishing empathy derives from a *cognitive* relation of "pairing" of self and other in the interest of phenomenological "intersubjectivity," there is no guarantee that the other self shares the *same* value of rational objectiv-ity. However, when we transfer empathy into the *ethical* sphere of caring and concern, we have reached a *quality* whose very essence is inseparable from primary, direct, immediate contact with a separate but conjoined other self. One cannot be ethical alone nor empathic alone; one cannot be moral if she or he is the only person in the universe. That would be a contradiction in terms. Contra Kant, one does not have moral duties to one's self.

But if we discard both (1) Lipps's aesthetic paradigm as contemplative; and (2) Husserl's model as cognitive; but instead (3) transform empathy into a motivational and ethical relation, then we may have achieved a truly *immediate* fusion with the other self. After all, the *feeling* of empathy *a priori* requires a mutually constitutive synthetic relation between self–other–self in terms of: (a) a dual identity and (b) an affective unity. This is not possible on either Lipps's aesthetic account or Husserl's cognitive approach. And although Hegel comes to mind here because he holds that the self and the other self mutually presuppose each other in the Lordship and Bondage section of the *Phenomenology*, his is a decidedly conflicted relational synthesis ill-designed to solve loneliness or offer any promise of intimacy. As we have seen previously, analogous to Marx's conception of the battle between capitalists and proletariats; or Sartre's struggle between two egos fighting for dominance at the expense the other, victory signals the conquest of one's self over the other with the loss of freedom for the vanquished, hardly a relation fostering mutual empathy. But empathy, unlike sympathy, has to be mutual. If I'm reading about a sad incident in the morning newspaper, I can't be empathic if the object of my concern is physically absent or I don't even know the person. I can pity the person and feel sympathy, but I cannot be empathic. A transcendental condition for empathy is that both of the involved parties are mutually engaged in the same emotion and each self is aware of the other's feelings; it is a shared union constituted by the *same* feelings, understanding, and insight into the emotions of care and concern experienced by both. If this is correct, then it follows that both intentionality and reflexivity are constituted within empathy. So if we view ethical empathy as constituted by an *a priori* relation of care and concern for a special or significant other self *and* at the same time the other is experiencing the *same, identical* feelings and meanings, then perhaps it will work. Again, assuming one cannot be empathic to one's own self, it follows that empathy must be a *symmetrical* synthetic *a priori* relation. By relating/connecting/unifying/binding one's self to the other in a synthetic *a priori* fashion through and within the *meaning* of the affective/motivational unity of care and concern, we will have successfully entered *directly, immediately* into a dual relation of intimacy with the other self. We will have moved into a psychological, motivational, and emotional relation rather than an aesthetic or cognitive one. This direct transition is effected by an intention, a projection *of caring, of concern* and therefore it is an *ethical* rather than a contemplative or cognitive relation. But it is at the same time a reflexive relation because each self is aware of the other's concern for its self. We then realize that our salvation from loneliness consists in something quite common and natural to each of us—to wit, inserting our self—our feelings and meanings and values—into the sphere of the other and the other's realization and acceptance that we have done so and an appreciation of the kindness or concern we have bestowed upon her or him, which is reciprocal if the intent of empathy is to be fulfilled by both consciousnesses. The ethical, the moral "object" *qua* subject springs into existence; the transcendent is transformed into the immanent, resulting in the synthetic fusion of two poles—the ego and other ego coupled through intentional and reflexive acts of consciousness in which there is no longer any difference between two selves but instead a supportive, interlocked, relation results. Empathy *means* the disappearance of an un-reconciled twofold consciousness of self and a separate, distinct other being; it is an unbreachable unity of two selves as one. Empathy occurs when a caring mother empathizes with her crying child and the child accepts her concern without a feeling of separation; when a loving couple grieves for their dead infant without any sense of being distinct from each other; when a mother shares the bonding exhilaration with her daughter giving birth; when an athlete rejoices in the success of his teammate; when two soldiers empathize and share a fear of imminent death with each other. Each of us has the capacity to intentionally project our feelings, thoughts, and values into the other as reflexively our own in a sharing manner. Each of us has the saving spiritual grace of emotional ethical empathy. Accordingly, empathy is a caring relation of concern and affection for another self *as* our own self, a reaching out with and through my self *into* the other self *as* my self. When it is mutual—and it *must* be mutual—it results in intimacy through empathy. Maslow, for instance, includes sexual, orgasmic "peak experiences" (hopefully, mutually enjoyed) as examples of such an immersive union of emotions during which both the distinction and fusion of two partners melt into one. This particular sexual enjoyment tends to be rather brief. But there are other empathic experiences that may not be as intense but nevertheless are of lengthier and more permanent duration and thus more desirable. Often, when a devoted couple has lived together intensely for a long time and death separates the union, it is not unusual for the survivor to follow within six months. This is a sign that their relation had been deeply and ethically empathic. They shared, albeit intermittently, during their joint existence an empathic feeling and concern for each other throughout their lives. In this connection, I recall an O. Henry short story, "The Gift." It involves a young couple, poor, but very much in love. His pride consists in owning a gold watch. Her pride consists of her beautiful long hair. At Christmas time neither of them has any money to buy the other a gift. Nevertheless, when the special day arrives, she gives him a gold chain for his watch, which she purchased by selling her hair, and he gives her an expensive tortoise shell comb, which he bought by pawning his gold watch. Often Kant's categorical imperative is compared to the Golden Rule, "Do unto others as you would wish them to do unto you." But it's much more than that. It means

"Place the other person *before* your self." It's sacrificial in intent. That's the transcendental condition making empathy possible. Imagine two souls placing the happiness of the other before their own interests. Then you've got something going.

But in the culturally oriented *Crisis of the European Sciences and Transcendental Phenomenology,* Husserl invokes empathy throughout the text as if it were an unproblematic concept, never mentioning solipsism as a serious difficulty requiring special attention (see especially Part III, A, Sections 54b and Section 59). So quite dramatically and suddenly the entire intersubjective communal life-world is *directly* open to all! We are already "embedded" in it!

Friendship. From Plato's frequent reference to the Friends of the Forms to Aristotle's Books Eight and Nine of the *Nicomachean Ethics* devoted to the intrinsic values of friendship to the Epicureans' praise of the joy of small groups of men living together and sharing intellectual pleasures, the principle of close friendship dominated the ethical lives of the early Greek philosophers. Indeed, in Greek thought, the bond of friendship represents the highest value attainable during our earthly sphere of mortal existence, our temporary visit in the world. But again it is Aristotle who explores, formulates, and endorses the most persuasive criteria for its establishment. Aristotle thus announces, "For without friends, no one would choose to live, though he had all other goods" (*Nicomachean Ethics,* VIII, 1, 5–6). Friendship, like the gift of vision, has both intrinsic and extrinsic qualities; it is both good in itself and useful, final and self-sufficient. It requires nothing beyond itself when it is attained. It is also implanted in us by nature through the realization that the solitary self is insufficient in fulfilling the cognitive and affective requirements for a satisfying human existence, for happiness, for well-being.

Perfect friendship is the friendship of men who are good, and alike in virtue; for these wish well alike to each other *qua* good, and they are good in themselves. Now those who wish well to their friends for *their* sake are most truly friends; for they do this by reason of their own nature and not incidentally; therefore their friendship lasts as long as they are good—and goodness is an enduring thing. (*Nicomachean Ethics,* VIIII, 3, 1156b, 7–12)

According to Diogenes Laertius, Aristotle also describes friendship as consisting of "two bodies dwelling within one soul." But perhaps the best expression of this empathic intimacy of true friendship is carried forward by Montaigne in the following passage.

In the friendship I speak of, our souls mingle and blend with each other so completely that they efface the seam that joined them, but cannot find it again. If you press me to tell you why I loved him, I find that this cannot be expressed except by answering: Because it was he, because it was I. (Montaigne, 1968, p. 139)

This description of intimacy is from Emily Bronte's *Wuthering Heights:*

But surely you and everybody have a notion that there is, or should be an existence of yours beyond you. What were the use of my creation if I were entirely contained here? If all else perished, and he remained I should still continue to be, and if all else remained and he were annihilated, the universe would turn to a mighty stranger. I should not seem a part of it. . . . I am Heathcliff—he's always, always in my mind—not as a pleasure, any more than I am always a pleasure to myself—but as my own being—so don't talk of our separation again—it is impracticable [i.e., inconceivable]. (Bronte, 2003, p. IX, 77)

Religion. Faith as a motivator within religion provides relief from loneliness in the form of a promise of eternal salvation. Theism especially offers a caring, personal—albeit transcendent—Deity through the promise and assurance of eternal companionship serving as an antidote to the poisonous effects of loneliness. Faith in a higher Being or Power in the universe can be incredibly consoling and satisfying as an answer to loneliness. Judaism offers a sense of belonging and security not only within a spiritual context but a social one as well. Similarly, Catholicism offers a hierarchical structure of belonging from popes to cardinals to bishops to priests to believers. As Aquinas comments, everything in its place and a place for everything, human creatures especially included. Protestants elect to dispense with the mediation of the priesthood and seek for a direct communion with their Christian God. Hinduism, with its concepts of karma, purification through a knowledge of many different lives, and reincarnation advocates for eventual salvation through a system that proposes we are punished by our sins rather than for our sins but eventually we will get there. Buddhism offers salvation through enlightenment and holds that all life is suffering; all suffering is grounded in desire; all desire is grounded in the atman, the ego, the soul, the self; eliminate the atman and you will have extinguished all desire, even the desire not to desire. The five *skandhas,* as dispositional attributes, are intended to replace the soul as a substance. All of the above offer responses and solutions to loneliness by seeking to assure us that we exist but not alone.

Exercise. Finally, the *easiest* motivational activity recruited and frequently employed in avoiding loneliness and boredom is physical exercise. That is why we so often observe joggers with their knees bandaged painfully running in the wind and rain and bicyclists in their outlandish harlequin costumes pedaling madly through dangerous traffic conditions. Exercise helps because the participant's motivational energy is concentrated on a single centering external goal of getting healthier, stronger, younger, handsomer, more beautiful, and thus more desirable for that special other ego. The exercise enterprise transforms the intentionality principle of consciousness into a physical goal.

REFERENCES

Aristotle. (1941). *The Basic Works of Aristotle.* McKeon, R. P. (Ed.). New York: Random House. *Nicomachean Ethics*, VI, 2.

Bronte, E. (2003). *Wuthering Heights.* New York: Dell.

Descartes, R. (1955). *Philosophical Works of Descartes.* New York: Dover.

Greenberg, J. (2004). *I Never Promised You a Rose Garden.* New York: New America Library.

Howard, J. (1975). *The Flesh-Colored Cage.* New York: Hawthorn.

Hume, D. (1973). *A Treatise of Human Nature.* Oxford, UK: Clarendon Press.

Husserl, E. (1964). *Cartesian Meditations.* The Hague: Martinus Nijhoff.

Mijuskovic, B. (1990). Intimacy and Loneliness. *Journal of Couples Therapy*, I:3/4, 39–48; reprinted in (1991) *Intimate Autonomy: Autonomous Intimacy*, Brothers, B. J. (Ed.). London: Haworth Press, 38–48.

Mijuskovic, B. (1992). Organic communities, atomistic societies and loneliness. *Journal of Sociology and Social Welfare*, XIX:2.

Mijuskovic, B. (1995). Some reflections on philosophical counseling. In *Essays in Philosophical Counseling*. Cohen, E. & Tillmanns, M. (Eds.). Lanham, MD: University Press of America.

Mijuskovic, B. (1997). Some further reflections on philosophical counseling. *Zeitschrift fuer Philosophische Praxis*, 2/96.

Mijuskovic, B. (2005a). Ethical principles, criteria, and the meaning of life. *The Journal of Thought*, 40:4.

Mijuskovic, B. (2005b). Theories of consciousness, therapy, and loneliness. *International Journal of Applied Philosophy*, 3:1; reprinted in (2013). *Counseling, Philosophy, and Psychotherapy*, Cohen, E. & Zinaich S. (Eds.).

Mijuskovic, B. (2007). Virtue ethics. *Philosophy and Literature*, 31:1.

Montaigne. (1968). *The Complete Essays of Montaigne.* Frame, D. (Trans.) Stanford, CA: Stanford University Press.

Rader, A. (1960). *A Modern Book of Aesthetics.* New York: Holt, Rinehart & Winston.

Ridgeway, J. (2011). Mass psychosis in the US: How big pharma got Americans hooked on anti-psychotics. www.aljazeera.com.

Ruch, F. (1953). *Psychology and Life*. Chicago: Scott, Foresman and Company.

Smith, D. W. (2013). *Husserl*. New York: Routledge.

Spiegelberg, H. (1965). *The Phenomenological Movement: A Historical Introduction*. The Hague: Martinus Nijhoff.

Tillich, P. (1979). *The Courage to Be*. New Haven, CT: Yale University Press.

Yalom, I. (1980). *Existential Psychotherapy*. New York: Basic Books.

Afterword

The present book is closely related to and dependent upon my prior historical study of consciousness, *The Achilles of Rationalist Arguments* (1974); a substantive treatment of consciousness in *Contingent Immaterialism* (1984); and an interdisciplinary work, which argues for the primacy of loneliness in human consciousness, *Loneliness in Philosophy, Psychology, and Literature* (2012). In effect, the philosophical ground of my interpretation of loneliness rests on a position best described as qualified dualism, or, as I have elsewhere defined it, as "contingent immaterialism," which holds that both matter and minds exist, though in a problematic relationship. Further, I also contend that Aristotle's *Metaphysics* (1075a) and *Nicomachean Ethics* (Book X) in the ancient age (Aristotle, 1941), Hume's *A Treatise of Human Nature* in the modern period (Cummins, 1995, XXI:1, 47–56.), and Sartre's *Being and Nothingness* in contemporary times (Sartre, 1966, pp. 760–761) present similar variants on "dualism," which, though different from each other, avoid the classic mind–body problem.

The depth and continuity of the issues involved in the foregoing studies may be appreciated if one considers that in 2008, following my lead, an anthology appeared dedicated to Kant's treatment of the unity of consciousness in *The Achilles of Rationalist Psychology*, edited by Thomas Lennon and Robert Stainton (2008) and, along with Neo-Phrenologists Patricia Churchland (1986), John Cacioppo (2002), and John McGraw's *Intimacy and Isolation*, which present opposing views to my theory of loneliness (McGraw, 2010, I, pp. 18–19), all these works amply testify to the ongoing relevance of issues relating theories of consciousness to human loneliness.

REFERENCES

Aristotle. (1941). *The Basic Works of Aristotle*. R. P. McKeon (Ed.). New York: Random House: *Metaphysics; Nicomachean Ethics*.

Cacioppo, J. (2002). *Foundations in Social Neuroscience*. Cambridge: MIT Press.

Churchland, P. (1986). *Neurophysiology: Toward a Unified Science of the Mind and Brain*, Cambridge: MIT Press.

Cummins, P. (1995). Hume as dualist and anti-dualist, *Hume Studies*, 21:1, 41–55.

Lennon, T., & Stainton, R. (2008). (Eds.). *The Achilles of Rationalist Psychology*. New York: Springer.

McGraw, J. (2010). *Intimacy and Isolation*. New York: Rodopi.

Mijuskovic, B. (1974). *The Achilles of Rationalist Arguments: The Simplicity, Unity, and Identity of Thought and Soul from the Cambridge Platonists to Kant: A Study in the History of an Argument*. The Hague: Martinus Nijhoff.

Mijuskovic, B. (1984). *Contingent Immaterialism: Meaning, Freedom, Time and Mind*. Amsterdam: Gruner.

Mijuskovic, B. (2012). *Loneliness in Philosophy, Psychology, and Literature*, 3rd edition. Bloomington, IN: iUniverse.

Sartre, J-P. (1966). *Being and Nothingness: An Essay on Phenomenological Ontology*. New York: Washington Square Press.

Index

About the Author

BEN LAZARE MIJUSKOVIC did his undergraduate work at the University of Chicago and holds a PhD in Philosophy and MA in Literature, both from the University of California at San Diego. He received tenure in the Philosophy Department at Southern Illinois University in Carbondale in 1975, and he has been teaching philosophy and the humanities since then at various universities, including the University of California at San Diego, San Diego State University, the University of San Diego, Long Beach State University, Chapman University, and California State University at Dominguez Hills where he still teaches.

Mijuskovic is also a licensed therapist (LCSW), and he has worked as a social worker in Chicago for the Cook County Department of Public Aid and for the War on Poverty's Headstart program. He later worked in California for over 30 years as an Adult Protective Services and Child Protective Services worker, and as a therapist for the counties of San Diego, Orange, and Los Angeles. He has worked in psychiatric hospitals for children, adolescents, and adults, in medical hospitals; at a state institution; and an institute for mental disease. He has published three studies and more than sixty articles on the subject of consciousness and loneliness.

He was born in Budapest, Hungary, in 1937. Following the German advance into the Sudentland in Czechoslovakia in 1939, his father, a Yugoslavian diplomat, was transferred to Jerusalem, Palestine, and assigned to a British intelligence unit as a cryptographer to decipher Italian Fascist communications. At the time, the Italian forces were occupying Monenegro. In 1940, the small family was dispatched to Cairo, Egypt, and as the war continued in 1941 his father volunteered to fight as a cavalry officer in the British Eighth Army under Field Marshall Montgomery, who was engaged against Field Marshall Rommel's famed Afrika Korps and Panzer Divisions. Toward the close of the war, in late 1944, his father was again reassigned, this time to the embassy in Ankara, Turkey, before being finally dispatched to Washington, D.C.